ONE MAN'S MEAT

BOOKS BY E. B. WHITE

Poems and Sketches of E. B. White

Essays of E. B. White

Letters of E. B. White

The Trumpet of the Swan

The Points of My Compass

The Second Tree from the Corner

Charlotte's Web

Here Is New York

The Wild Flag

Stuart Little

One Man's Meat

The Fox of Peapack

Quo Vadimus?

Farewell to Model T

Every Day Is Saturday

The Lady Is Cold

An E. B. White Reader
    edited by William W. Watt and Robert W. Bradford

The Elements of Style
    William Strunk, Jr. (revised and enlarged by E. B. White)

A Subtreasury of American Humor
    co-edited with Katharine S. White

Is Sex Necessary?
    with James Thurber

ONE

MAN'S

MEAT

E. B. White

HARPER COLOPHON BOOKS
Harper & Row, Publishers
New York, Cambridge, Philadelphia, San Francisco
London, Mexico City, São Paulo, Sydney

A hardcover edition of this book is published by Harper & Row, Publishers, Inc.

Editor's note. Three of the pieces in this volume were published first in *The New Yorker.* "The Summer Catarrh" appeared July 30, 1938, under the title "Daniel Webster, the Hay Fever, and Me." "The World of Tomorrow" appeared May 13, 1939, under the title "They Came With Joyous Song." "The Flocks We Watch by Night" appeared November 11, 1939. For the sake of clarity, all the other pieces carry the date when they were written, rather than the date when they appeared in print in *Harper's.*

The following three pieces appear also in *Essays of E. B. White*: "On a Florida Key," "Once More to the Lake," and "The World of Tomorrow."

First HARPER COLOPHON edition published 1983.

Designer: Sidney Feinberg

Library of Congress Cataloging in Publication Data

White, E. B. (Elwyn Brooks), 1899-
  One man's meat.
  I. Title.
PS3545.H518705   1982   818'.5209   82-47763
ISBN 0-06-091081-X (pbk)   AACR2

83 84 85 86 87 10 9 8 7 6 5 4 3 2 1

CONTENTS

INTRODUCTION

One Man's Meat will be forty-one years old come spring. Published first in 1942, it has remained in print in one form or another almost without interruption since it appeared. Never a big seller, it early showed staying power. A book that manages not to fade away after a few years occupies a special place in the heart of its author. I confess to a special feeling for *One Man's Meat.*

The original edition consisted of forty-five pieces assembled from the monthly column I had been writing for *Harper's Magazine* since 1938. After the book came out, I continued to contribute to the magazine, and in 1944 a new and enlarged edition of *One Man's Meat* was published. It contained an additional ten essays—a total of fifty-five. This edition was popular. The United States had entered the war, and the war had entered the book. Soon my casual pieces depicting life on a saltwater farm in New England were finding their way to members of the Armed Forces in a paperback Overseas edition, and letters of thanks were arriving from homesick soldiers in distant lands. This relieved my mind, as I had been uneasy about indulging myself in pastoral pursuits when so many of my countrymen were struggling for their lives, and for mine. The Overseas edition, incidentally, was banned for a while, then reinstated without the matter's being explained. (Some conscientious watchdog must have found it too rich a diet for our fighting men.) I recall a twinge of satisfaction in having a book banned: it suggested that my stuff might be more substantial than it appeared on first glance.

In all, there have been eight editions of *One Man's Meat,* not counting a British edition, two German translations, and one French translation.

When it was twelve years old, my publishers decided that the book was a classic, and they forthwith brought it out (hardbound) in their "Harper's Modern Classics" series. This established me officially as an American Author, no longer to be trifled with. The Classics edition opened with an introduction by Morris Bishop, and this delighted me, because it was Professor Bishop who, years before, when he discovered I was headed for the country, had said, "I trust that you will spare the reading public your little adventures in contentment."

When I look back almost half a century to the events leading up to my move from New York to Maine, events that conspired to produce this book of essays, I am appalled. My decision to pull up stakes was impulsive and irresponsible. Prior to 1938, I had been working happily and gainfully for *The New Yorker,* writing its editorial page "Notes and Comment," contributing stories and articles, and doing odd jobs around the place. My wife, an early career woman, had a job with the magazine that absorbed her and fulfilled her. We were living in the city in a rented house, uptown on the East Side. The depression had left us unscathed, the war was just a rumble in the sky. Everything was going our way.

Yet, sometime in the winter of 1938, or even before that, I became restless. I felt unhappy and cooped up. More and more my thoughts turned to Maine, where we owned a house with a barn attached. I don't recall being disenchanted with New York—I loved New York. I was certainly not disenchanted with *The New Yorker*—I loved the magazine. If I was disenchanted at all, I was probably disenchanted with *me.* For one thing, I suspected that I was not writing quite the way I wanted to write, and sometimes I was oppressed by my weekly deadline. For another, in my job as commentator, I was stuck with the editorial "we," a weasel word suggestive of corporate profundity or institutional consensus. I wanted to write as straight as possible, with no fuzziness.

Quite aside from all this, I had never felt really at home in the house we were renting. The rooms were always too hot and dry; I fell asleep every night after dinner. And the house wasn't downtown in the Village, which had been my stamping ground for years and where I still felt at home whenever I returned. Some sort of drastic action seemed the only answer to my problem—and that is exactly what happened. Without considering what it would do to my wife to be uprooted from *The New Yorker,* or what it would do to my son to be switched from a private school in Manhattan to a two-room schoolhouse in the country, and without a thought of what I would be using for money in my rural incarnation, I led my little family out of the city like a daft piper. My wife was deeply shaken by the exodus, but she never flinched. She was sustained by her weird belief that writers were not ordinary mortals and had to be coddled, like a Queen Bee.

One Man's Meat was not a premeditated book, it was an accident. Two days before I left town for good, Lee Hartman, editor of *Harper's Magazine,* asked me to lunch. Before the meal was over he had invited me to contribute a monthly department. He offered me three hundred dollars a month, and I accepted on the spot. This last-minute, unexpected job as columnist was the genesis of *One Man's Meat.* It turned out to be one of the luckiest things that ever happened to me. I was a man in search of the first person singular, and lo, here it was—handed to me on a platter before I even left town.

Once in everyone's life there is apt to be a period when he is fully awake, instead of half asleep. I think of those five years in Maine as the time when this happened to me. Confronted by new challenges, surrounded by new acquaintances—including the characters in the barnyard, who were later to reappear in *Charlotte's Web*—I was suddenly seeing, feeling, and listening as a child sees, feels, and listens. It was one of those rare interludes that can never be repeated, a time of enchantment. I am fortunate indeed to have had the chance to get some of it down on paper.

The saltwater farm that served as the setting for this most tumultuous episode in my life has seen many changes in forty years. The sheep have disappeared, along with several other accessories. The elms have disappeared. I am still visible, pottering about, overseeing the incubations, occasionally writing a new introduction for an old book. I do the Sunday chores. I stoke the stove. I listen for the runaway toilet. I true up the restless rug. I save the whale. I wind the clock. I talk to myself.

Certain things have not changed. Despite the great blizzard of April, the swallows arrived on schedule and are busy remodelling the mud nests in the barn. The goose sits. Rhubarb is showing. (I used to eat rhubarb because I loved rhubarb. Now I eat it because it retards arthritis.) The Egg has been an enduring theme in my life, and I have allowed my small flock of laying hens to grow old in service. Cosmetically they leave much to be desired, but their ovulation is brisk, and I greet them with the same old gag when I enter the pen: "White here. Cubism is dead."

I keep telling myself that it is time to quit this place, with its eleven rooms and its forty acres, and cut myself down to size. I may still do it. But I can envision what would happen if I did: I would no sooner get comfortably settled in a small house on an acre of land than I would issue instructions to build a small barn and attach it to the house through a woodshed. A bale of hay would appear mysteriously in the barn, and there would soon be a bantam rooster out there, living in the style to which he feels he should be accustomed. I would be right back where I started.

EBW

May 1982

ONE MAN'S MEAT

REMOVAL

Several months ago, finding myself in possession of one hundred and seventeen chairs divided about evenly between a city house and a country house, and desiring to simplify my life, I sold half of my worldly goods, evacuated the city house, gave up my employment, and came to live in New England. The difficulty of getting rid of even one half of one's possessions is considerable, even at removal prices. And after the standard items are disposed of—china, rugs, furniture, books—the surface is merely scratched: you open a closet door and there in the half-dark sit a catcher's mitt and an old biology notebook.

I recall a moment of peculiar desperation over a gold mirror that, in spite of all our attempts to shake it off, hung steadfastly on till within an hour or so of our scheduled departure. This mirror, which was a large but fairly unattractive one, rapidly came to be a sort of symbol of what I was trying to escape from, and its tenacity frightened me. I was quite prepared simply to abandon it (I knew a man once who, tiring of an automobile, walked away from it on the street and never saw it again), but my wife wouldn't consent to abandoning anything. It seems there are rules, even to the sort of catharsis to which we were committed: I could give the mirror away or sell it, but I was not privileged to leave it in the house, which (she said) had to be stripped clean.

So I walked out the door hatless and in my shirtsleeves and went round the corner to a junk shop on Second Avenue—a place which displayed a thoroughly miserable assortment of bruised and castoff miscellany. The proprietor stood in the doorway.

"Do you want . . ." I began. But at that instant an El train joined us and I had to start again and shout.

"Do you want to buy a gold mirror?"

The man shook his head.

"It's *gold!*" I yelled. *"A beautiful thing!"*

Two kibitzers stopped, to attend the deal, and the El train went off down the block, chuckling.

"Nuh," said the proprietor coldly. "Nuh."

"I'm giving it away," I teased.

"I'm nut taking it," said the proprietor, who, for all I know, may have been trying to simplify his own life.

A few minutes later, after a quick trip back to the house, I slipped the mirror guiltily in a doorway, a bastard child with not even a note asking the finder to treat it kindly. I took a last look at myself in it, and I thought I looked tired.

ॐ

Lately I haven't had time to read the papers, as I have been building a mouseproof closet against a rain of mice. But sometimes, kindling a fire with last week's *Gazette,* I glance through the pages and catch up a little with the times. I see that a mother is ready to jump from a plane six miles above the World of Tomorrow, that a sailor has read *Anthony Adverse* standing up, and that Orson Welles (or was it Booth?) sighs for the waning theater.

The news of television, however, is what I particularly go for when I get a chance at the paper, for I believe television is going to be the test of the modern world, and that in this new opportunity to see beyond the range of our vision we shall discover either a new and unbearable disturbance of the general peace or a saving radiance in the sky. We shall stand or fall by television—of that I am quite sure.

It must have been two years ago that I attended a television demonstration at which it was shown beyond reasonable doubt that a person sitting in one room could observe the nonsense taking place in another. I recall being more amused by what was happening in the tangible room where I sat than by what appeared in the peephole of science. The images were plain enough, however, and by paying attention I could see the whites of a pretty woman's eyes. Since then I have followed the television news closely.

Clearly the race today is between loud speaking and soft, between the things that are and the things that seem to be, between the chemist of RCA and the angel of God. Radio has already given sound a wide currency, and sound "effects" are taking the place once enjoyed by sound itself. Television will enormously enlarge the eye's range, and, like radio, will advertise the Elsewhere. Together with the tabs, the mags, and the movies, it will insist that we forget the primary and the near in favor of the secondary and the remote. More hours in every twenty-four will be spent digesting ideas, sounds, images—distant and concocted. In sufficient accumulation, radio sounds and television sights may become more familiar to us than their originals. A door closing, heard over the air; a face contorted, seen in a panel of light—these will emerge as the real and the true; and when we bang the door of our own cell or look into another's face the impression will be of mere artifice. I like to dwell on this quaint time, when the solid world becomes make-believe, McCarthy corporeal and Bergen stuffed, when all is reversed and we shall be like the insane, to whom the antics of the sane seem the crazy twistings of a grig.

When I was a child people simply looked about them and were moderately happy; today they peer beyond the seven seas, bury themselves waist deep in tidings, and by and large what they see and hear makes them unutterably sad.

One odd fact I seem to have picked up in my research is that the performers in telecasting studios will be required to wear a small electric buzzer, or shocker, round their ankle, from which they will get their cues. The director will buzz when it is time for a line, and Actor Smoothjowl will wince slightly at the little pain and appear suddenly to all the people of Melbourne.

ز♥

This life I lead, setting pictures straight, squaring rugs up with the room—it suggests an ultimate symmetry toward which I strive and strain. Yet I doubt that I am any nearer my goal than I was last year, or ten years ago, even granted that this untidy world is ready for any such orderliness. Going rapidly through the hall, on an errand of doubtful import to God and country, I pause suddenly, like an ant in its tracks, and with the toe of my sneaker shift the corner of the little rug two inches in a southerly direction, so that the edge runs parallel with the floor seams. Healed by this simple geometry, I continue my journey. The act, I can only conclude, satisfies something fundamental in me, and if, fifteen minutes later on my way back, I find that the rug is again out of line, I repeat the performance with no surprise and no temper. Long ago I accepted the fact of a rug's delinquency; it has been a pitched battle and the end is not in sight. At least one of my ancestors died lunging out of bed at the enemy, and it is more than likely that I shall fall at last, truing up a mediocre mat.

Intellectually, I am ready to admit that there is no special virtue in an accurate alignment of inanimate objects, that a picture hanging cock-eyed on the wall and a rug askew are conceivably as effective as they would be straight; but in practice I can't go it. If it is my nature to adjust the stance of a watercolor rather than to enjoy its substance, then that's the whole of it, and I'm lucky to get even the dubious enjoyment that I occasionally experience from coming upon it and finding it square.

The other day something or other started me thinking about these rugs and pictures (ordinarily I carry on the war absent-mindedly), and by reconstructing a twelve-hour period, I figured out that I had straightened a certain rug four times, another twice, a picture once—a total of seven adjustments. I believe this to be par for my private course. Seven times three hundred and sixty-five is two thousand five hundred and fifty-five, which I think I can give as a fair estimate of my yearly penance.

ε∾

I got a letter from a lightning rod company this morning trying to put the fear of God in me, but with small success. Lightning seems to have lost its menace. Compared to what is going on on earth today, heaven's firebrands are penny fireworks with wet fuses.

THE SUMMER CATARRH

DANIEL WEBSTER, one of the most eloquent of men, was fifty years old when he first began to suffer from the summer catarrh. I was only six when my first paroxysm came on. Most of Mr. Webster's biographers have ignored the whole subject of hay fever and its effect on the man's career. In my own case, even my close friends possess very slight knowledge of the part pollinosis plays in my life. I suspect that the matter has never been properly explored.

In May, 1937, the *Yale Journal of Biology & Medicine* published a paper by Creighton Barker called "Daniel Webster and the Hay-Fever."* I have just come across it in my files and have reread it with the closest attention. Monday will be the first day of August; at this point in the summer my own fever (which is the early type) is waning. From my study window I can look across to the stubble fields where the hay was cut two weeks ago and can feel the relaxed membrane and general prostration characteristic of the last stages of the disease. Webster, who suffered the autumn type of pollinosis, was in midsummer merely anticipating the approach of trouble. August found him wary, discreet. On August 19, 1851, he wrote to President Fillmore: "I have never had confidence that I should be able to avert entirely the attack of catarrh, but I believe that at least I shall gain so much in general health and strength as to enable me, in some measure, to resist its influence and mitigate its evils. Four days hence is the time for its customary approach."

The four days passed with no ill effects. The fever was late arriving

---

*Presented before the Beaumont Club, March 12, 1937.

that year. On the evening of the 25th, Mr. Webster took a blue pill, and the following morning a Rochelle powder. The weather was clear and quite cool. Not till the 31st do we find in his correspondence any evidence of distress. Then (writing to Mr. Blatchford), "Friday about noon: I thought I felt catarrhal symptoms. There was some tendency of defluxion from the nose, the eyes did not feel right, and what was more important, I felt a degree of general depression which belongs to the disease."

Here, in the fading lines of this apprehensive letter, history suddenly grows vivid, and I experience an acute identity with one of the major characters. Webster had had Presidential ambitions, but by this time it had become apparent to him that anyone whose runny nose bore a predictable relationship to the Gregorian calendar was not Presidential timber. He was well past middle life when this depleting truth was borne in on him. I (as I have said before) was a child of six when it became clear to me that a hypersensitivity to the blown dust of weeds and grasses was more than a mere nasal caprice—it was of a piece with destiny.

In 1905, when my parents first discovered in me a catarrhal tendency, hay fever was still almost as mysterious as it was when Mr. Webster was taking his iodate of iron and hydriodate of potash by direction of his physician—who was thinking hard. The first indication I had that I was different from other boys came when I used to go out driving on Sunday afternoons in the surrey. I noticed that every time I rode behind a horse my nose began to run and my eyes grew unbearably itchy. I told my father that it was the smell of the horse that did this thing to me. Father was skeptical. To support a horse at all was a considerable drain on his finances and it was going a little far to ask him to believe that the animal had a baleful effect on any member of the family. Nevertheless he was impressed—I looked so queer, and I sneezed with such arresting rapidity.

He refused absolutely to admit that his horse smelled different from any other horse, and at first he was disinclined to believe that his son had any peculiarity of the mucosa. But he did call a doctor.

The doctor dismissed the horse and announced that I suffered from "catarrhal trouble." He rocked back and forth in the rocker in my bedroom for about ten minutes in silent thought. Then quickly he arose.

"Douse his head in cold water every morning before breakfast," he said to Mother and departed.

This treatment was carried out, with the aid of a cheap rubber spray, daily for almost two years. I didn't mind it particularly, and except for destroying the natural oil of my hair it did me no harm. The chill, noisy immersion provided a brisk beginning for the day and inoculated me against indolence if not against timothy grass and horse dander.

It was twelve or thirteen years after the Missouri Compromise had temporarily settled the slavery question that Webster had his first attack of the fever. A Whig and an aristocrat, he undoubtedly accepted this sudden defluxion from the nose as a common cold. He was in the prime of life; his youthful ideals had matured; his powers had been demonstrated. He was an ornament to the young republic, when he began to sneeze. Years later, with the ragweed dust of many summers in his veins, he joined Clay in the Compromise of 1850 and heard his own friends vilify him for betraying the cause of humanity and freedom.

How little these critics knew of the true nature of his defection. They said he had his eye on the vote of the South. What could they know of the scourge of an allergic body? Across the long span of the years I feel an extraordinary kinship with this aging statesman, this massive victim of pollinosis whose declining days sanctioned the sort of compromise that is born of local irritation. There is a fraternity of those who have been tried beyond endurance. I am closer to Daniel Webster, almost, than to my own flesh. I am with him in spirit as he journeys up from Washington to Marshfield, in the preposterous hope that the mountain air will fortify and sustain him—to Marshfield, where he will be not just partially but wholly impregnated with ragweed bloom. I am with him as he pours out a pony of whiskey, to ease the nerves. I pour one, too, and together we enjoy the momentary anesthesia of alcohol, an anesthesia we both know from experience is a short-lived blessing, since liquor (particularly grain liquor) finds its way unerringly to the membrane of the nose. I am at his side as he sits down to write another letter to Fillmore. (I understand so well the incomparable itch of eye and nose for which the only relief is to write to the President of the United States.) "I go to Boston today where Mrs. Webster is, and thence immediately to Marshfield. By the process thus far, I have lost flesh, and am not a little reduced. Yesterday and Sunday were exceedingly hot, bright days, and although I did not step out of the house, the heat affected my eyes much after the catarrhal fashion. I resisted the attack, however, by the application of ice."

Ice with a little whiskey poured over it, he neglected to add.

Webster died on October 24, 1852, of liver trouble and dropsy. They did a post-mortem on him and found a well-marked effusion on the arachnoid membrane. It was in the cards that he would never attain to the Presidency; his reaction to flower dust nullified his qualities of leadership. I am sure Webster knew this, in his bones, just as I knew, sneezing in the back seat of the surrey, that I was not destined to achieve my secret goal.

Our lives, Webster's and mine, run curiously parallel. He had an expensive family and expensive tastes—so have I. He liked social life. I do, too. He liked eating and drinking, specially the latter, and was happy on his great farms in Franklin and in Marshfield, whither he turned for sanctuary during the catarrhal season. The fact that he sought the burgeoning countryside in ignorance of what he was doing, while I expose myself wittingly to the aggravation of hay, does not alter the case. Webster lived to align himself on the side of compromise. In time of political strain my own tendency is toward the spineless middle ground. I have the compromising nature of a man who from early childhood has found himself without a pocket handkerchief in a moment of defluxion. Had I lived in slave days, I would have sided with Clay and been reviled by my friends.

It is only half the story. Webster, even though he knew very little about the cause of hay fever, must have found, just as I find, in this strange sensitivity to male dust and earth's fertile attitude a compensatory feeling—a special identification with life's high mystery that in some measure indemnifies us for the violence and humiliation of our comic distress and that makes up for the unfulfillment of our most cherished dream.

INCOMING BASKET

I⊤ seemed to me that I should have to have a desk, even though I had no real need for a desk. I was afraid that if I had no desk in my room my life would seem too haphazard.

The desk looked incomplete when I got it set up, so I found a wire basket and put that on it, and threw a few things in it. This basket, however, gave me a lot of trouble for the first couple of weeks. I had always had *two* baskets in New York. One said IN, the other OUT. At intervals a distribution boy would sneak into the room, deposit something in IN, remove the contents of OUT. Here, with only one basket, my problem was to decide whether it was IN or OUT, a decision a person of some character could have made promptly and reasonably but which I fooled round with for days—tentative, hesitant, trying first one idea then another, first a day when it would be IN, then a day when it would be OUT, then, somewhat desperately, trying to combine the best features of both and using it as a catch-all for migratory papers no matter which way they were headed. This last was disastrous. I found a supposedly out-going letter buried for a week under some broadsides from the local movie house. The basket is now IN. I discovered by test that fully ninety per cent of whatever was on my desk at any given moment were IN things. Only ten per cent were OUT things—almost too few to warrant a special container. This, in general, must be true of other people's lives too. It is the reason lives get so cluttered up—so many things (except money) filtering in, so few things (except strength) draining out. The phenomenon is difficult for me to understand and has not been explained, to my knowledge, by physicists: how it is that, with a continuous interchange of goods or "things" between people, everybody can have more coming in (except money) than going out (except strength).

My inability to make a simple decision concerning a desk basket is an indication of some curious nervous weakness. Psychiatrists know about it, I don't doubt, and have plenty of theories about its cause and cure. Question: Does a psychiatrist have an IN basket?

ॐ

Every year or so one reads about a railroad conductor on a suburban train making his last run and being fêted by the passengers, most of whom know him well. This sort of farewell celebration seems to be peculiar to railroad men. All sorts of other people step out of harness and nobody thinks much about it, but a railroad man finishing his work excites the populace unduly. I think this is probably because commuters see, in conductors and brakemen and engineers, the personification of their own frustrated transit—a man who has ridden far and got nowhere. Journey's end for a conductor on a commuter's run is an occasion of unequalled sadness, a sadness so poignant that it usually must be drowned in gin if there is a club car on the train. Somebody has reached the end of the strange run, from here to there and back again.

SECURITY

.

I T was a fine clear day for the Fair this year, and I went up early to see how the Ferris wheel was doing and to take a ride. It pays to check up on Ferris wheels these days: by noting the volume of business one can get some idea which side is ahead in the world—whether the airborne free-men outnumber the earthbound slaves. It was encouraging to discover that there were still quite a few people at the Fair who preferred a feeling of high, breezy insecurity to one of solid support. My friend Healy surprised me by declining to go aloft; he is an unusually cautious man, however—even his hat was insured.

I like to watch the faces of people who are trying to get up their nerve to take to the air. You see them at the ticket booths in amusement parks, in the waiting room at the airport. Within them two irreconcilables are at war—the desire for safety, the yearning for a dizzy release. My *Britannica* tells nothing about Mr. G. W. G. Ferris, but he belongs with the immortals. From the top of the wheel, seated beside a small boy, windswept and fancy free, I looked down on the Fair and for a moment was alive. Below us the old harness drivers pushed their trotters round the dirt track, old men with their legs still sticking out stiffly round the rumps of horses. And from the cluster of loud speakers atop the judges' stand came the "Indian Love Call," bathing heaven and earth in jumbo tenderness.

This silvery wheel, revolving slowly in the cause of freedom, was only just holding its own, I soon discovered; for farther along in the midway, in a sideshow tent, a tattoo artist was doing a land-office business, not with anchors, flags, and pretty mermaids, but with Social Security Numbers, neatly pricked on your forearm with the electric needle.

He had plenty of customers, mild-mannered pale men asking glumly for the sort of indelible ignominy that was once reserved for prisoners and beef cattle. Drab times these, when the bravado and the exhibitionism are gone from tattooing and it becomes simply a branding operation. I hope the art that produced the bird's eye view of Sydney will not be forever lost in the routine business of putting serial numbers on people who are worried about growing old.

The sight would have depressed me had I not soon won a cane by knocking over three cats with three balls. There is no other moment when a man so surely has the world by the tail as when he strolls down the midway swinging a prize cane.

ৡ

Secretary Wallace thinks the farm income this year will be about seven and a half billion dollars, which is about twice what it was in 1932 but which will hardly pay me for my time even so. Since coming to live on the land I am concerned with all such reports. From a limited experience with farm operation, I should call seven and a half billion dollars scarcely enough to pay off the farmers in a dozen States. I should estimate that the farm income, with or without crop control, would have to be about a hundred times greater than it is to make it worth any man's while to work the land.

For example, let us consider my one remaining turkey. She is all that is left of a brood of six. Three were victims of a liver disorder, two were foully struck down by a weasel. This surviving bird, in order for me to turn her over at a profit, would have to be sold for somewhere in the neighborhood of four hundred and fifty dollars. This is a conservative figure that I shall itemize presently. I have been keeping books on the bird and know what I am talking about. Of course my turkey and I constitute a branch of farming the Secretary of Agriculture does not necessarily take into consideration, either in his national planning or in his cost accounting. Yet we are part of the rural scene these days; our ilk is increasing and must eventually be taken into account. I suppose Mr. Wallace looks upon my sort not as farmers but as middle-aged eccentrics; but here we are. By no means all of America's soil today is tilled by practical people doing things in a sensible way.

Hatched June 19th, the turkey is a Bourbon Red, one of those beautiful, cocoa-colored birds with white tail feathers and a fine sense of catastrophe. This one is rather pindling for her age, for I've been busy this summer and haven't pushed her along. Her account figures up about as follows:

Cost of egg	$ .30
Cost of gas to place where I got egg	1.20
Remodeling chimneys of dwelling house on property, $800.00	
Share chargeable to turkey 1/10th	80.00
Corn for broody hen	.25
Growing mash	1.25
Scratch	1.30
Hired man's time feeding, watering, etc.	20.00
My time, puttering, reading bulletins, vacillating, whipping off dog, spreading oilcloth over pen, rearranging hopper, setting skunk trap, at estimated hour basis of what I might have earned by putting my time to better advantage	168.40
Pair strap hinges	.15
Installing low-pressure steam heat in dwelling house so we can survive in this climate on Thanksgiving Day, $1300.00. Turkey's share 1/10th	130.00
Total	$402.85

Now there is my bird in black and white. The figures of course are open to question, and there would be plenty of people (dreamers like Henry Tetlow, for instance) who might quibble with them. I am attributing one-tenth of my heating and remodeling expenses to this turkey, which is just a guess. It would seem conservative, for the bird certainly had a great deal to do with my settling down here. The item of $168.40 is also part guesswork, as there is nothing harder to estimate than a writer's time, nothing harder to keep track of. There are moments—moments of sustained creation—when his time is fairly valuable; and there are hours and hours when a writer's time isn't worth the paper he is not writing anything on.

This turkey, although a mediocre and backward bird, is of profound interest to me and a highly significant thing in my life. She runs with some young bantams and will presumably develop blackhead before Thanksgiving if the government pamphlets are correct, but she is my bid for security. The world being in an unusually disturbed condition, the desire for security, whether we respect it or despise it, has grown quietly in all of us, even in the young. I read the other day of a meeting of Youth —I forget where—and "security" was a dominant note in the resolutions that were passed. This is a new thing and I fear unpromising. Young people have never bothered much about security, they have traditionally gone after adventure, romance, and derring-do. Now they are holding out their arm for the branding iron, surrendering their free selves to an illusive certainty. I must have been groping toward this disreputable end when I bought a few turkey eggs last May. Somewhere in the back of a man's head there lingers the conventional picture of the harvest home of the early colonists—a Puritan with a gun on his arm, a wild turkey being brought in from the red-and-gold woods for the feast day, the abundant and natural life of our stern and rock-bound coast. No doubt when I carve up this four hundred and fifty dollar fowl I shall enjoy a momentary glow of self-sufficiency and thrift and certainty, as treacherous as the hopes of a daffy old Californian dreaming his dreams of thirty dollars every Thursday.

ड़•

The young girls of this village used to choose nursing for a career, many of them. But one of the teachers in the high school tells me that this year most of her girl graduates aimed to become hostesses for an air line. (Or even for a bus line: some of the large cross-country busses now carry hostesses.) Here again are security and adventure locked in a death grip. To a young girl in a small town the inside of a passenger plane is the glamorous corridor to life, with marriage (safety through danger, strength through joy) at the end of the voyage. Statistics show that virginal hostesses, the ministering angels of the sub-stratosphere, last only a scant few months, then they marry an Eastern branch manager en route to his branch through the sky.

ड़•

While the old wars rage and new ones hang like hawks above the world, we, the unholy innocents, study the bulb catalogue and order one dozen paper-white Grandiflora Narcissus (60 cents) to be grown in a bowl of pebbles. To the list that my wife made out I have added one large root of bleeding heart, to remind us daily of wounded soldiers and tortured Jews.

ड़•

My thirty-six pullets are ready to go into the laying house, and all the pamphlets say I must cull them rigidly. It strikes me the Federal pamphleteers are strangely out of date in their terminology: isn't "purge" the word they are groping for?

Incidentally, this is one farm on which there will be no purge. I'm putting the whole flock into the laying house. Those that like to lay eggs can do that; the others can sit around the groaning board, singing and whoring.

CLEAR DAYS

"You take it after a rain," said Henry . . .

Henry and I were sunning on the steps of the store. I was waiting for my wife to come along in the car and pick me up; Henry, being without attachments, was waiting for the end of time. For a brief spell we were as sensible as two cats, on the warm boards.

"You take it after a rain," said Henry, "a fox hasn't fed all night, because it's been rainin', and he'll be lookin' to feed in the morning. That's the time you got to be there with your gun."

I nodded wisely, wondering what the Meadow Brook Hunt would make of this kind of goings-on.

"I killed five foxes one fall, just half a mile from here, still-huntin'. No dog nor nuthin'. I outwitted 'em. You know where McKee's shop is, well right there, where the woods comes clean to the road in a point. I knew that's where he'd have to cross the road, to git to where the rabbits were thick. I just set there behind the wall and waited. Only you got to be mighty quiet and nice. A fox has awful good eyes."

It was the first chance Henry had ever had to tell me confidentially about himself, and it seemed significant that he had plunged without preliminaries into his triumphant chapter. From his dull galaxy of days he had picked out these five bright mornings. Every man has his memory of achievement. It is something to have known where a fox was going to cross the road.

ဦ

The burning question around here now is what I am going to do about my deer. They always speak of it as "my" deer, and it has come to seem just that. I often think of this not impossible animal, walking statelily through the forest paths and wearing a studded collar with "E. B. White, phone Waterlot 40 Ring 3" engraved on it.

"You goin' to get your deer?" I am asked by every man I meet—and they all wait for an answer. My deer-slaying program is a matter of considerable local concern, much to my surprise. It is plain that I now reside in a friendly community of killers, and that until I open fire myself they cannot call me brother.

The truth is I have never given serious thought to the question of gunning. My exploits have been few. Once I shot a woodchuck my dog had already begun to take apart; and once, in the interests of science, I erased a domestic turkey—crouching silently on a log six feet from the bird's head, as cool as though I were aiming at my own grandmother. But by and large my hunting has been with a .22 rifle and a mechanical duck, with dusk falling in gold and purple splendor in the penny arcades along Sixth Avenue. I imagine I would feel mighty awkward discharging a gun that wasn't fastened to a counter by a small chain.

This business of going after some deer meat is a solemn matter hereabouts. My noncommittal attitude has marked me as a person of doubtful character, who will bear watching. There seems to be some question of masculinity involved: until I slay my dragon I am still in short pants, as far as my fellow-countrymen are concerned. As for my own feelings in the matter, it's not that I fear buck fever, it's more that I can't seem to work up a decent feeling of enmity toward a deer. Toward *my* deer, I mean. I think I'd rather catch it alive and break it to harness.

Besides, I don't really trust myself alone in the woods with a gun. The woods are changing. I see by the papers that our Eastern forests this season are full of artists engaged in making pencil sketches of suitable backgrounds for Walt Disney's proposed picture "Bambi"—which is about a deer. My eyesight isn't anything exceptional; it is quite within the bounds of probability that I would march into the woods after my deer and come home with a free-hand artist draped across my running board, a tiny crimson drop trickling from one nostril.

ॐ

Long before the coming of the cold I was on the barn roof, laying clear cedar shingles, five inches to the weather. My neighbors' roofs all showed signs of activity, so I built some staging and mounted my own beanstalk to see what I could see. It seems a long while ago that I was up there, hanging on by the seat of my pants: those clear days at the edge of frost, with a view of pasture, woods, sea, hills, and my pumpkin patch stretched out below in serene abundance. I stayed on the barn, steadily laying shingles, all during the days when Mr. Chamberlain, M. Daladier, the Duce, and the Führer were arranging their horse trade. It seemed a queer place to be during a world crisis, an odd thing to be doing—there was no particular reason for making my roof tight, as the barn contained nothing but a croquet set, some swallows' nests, and a stuffed moosehead. In my trance-like condition, waiting for the negotiations to end, I added a cupola to the roof, to hold a vane that would show which way the wind blew.

In some respects, though, a barn is the best place anybody could pick for sitting out a dance with a prime minister and a demigod. There is a certain clarity on a high roof, a singleness of design in the orderly work of laying shingles: snapping the chalk line, laying the butts to the line, picking the proper width shingle to give an adequate lap. One's perspective, at that altitude, is unusually good. Who has the longer view of things, anyway, a prime minister in a closet or a man on a barn roof?

I'm down now; the barn is tight, and the peace is preserved. It is the ugliest peace the earth has ever received for a Christmas present. Old England eating swastika for breakfast instead of kipper is a sight I had as lief not lived to see. And though I'm no warrior, I would gladly fight for the things Nazism seeks to destroy. (Living in a sanitary age, we are getting so we place too high a value on human life—which rightfully must always come second to human ideas.)

The sacrifice Mr. Chamberlain made to preserve the Ideal of Peace reminded me of the strange case of Ada Leonard, the strip artist of superb proportion. Miss Leonard, if you remember, took sick of a ruptured appendix; but rather than have it out she risked her life in order to preserve, in unbroken loveliness, the smooth white groin the men of Chicago loved so well. Her suffering was great, and her courage admirable. But there comes a point beyond which you can't push Beauty, on account of the lines it leaves in the face. Peace is the same. The peace we have with us today is as precarious and unsatisfactory as the form of a strip artist with peritonitis.

ϧ❧

It is not likely that a person who changes his pursuits will ever succeed in taking on the character or the appearance of the new man, however much he would like to. I am farming, to a small degree and for my own amusement, but it is a cheap imitation of the real thing. I have fitted myself out with standard equipment, dungarees and a cap; but I would think twice before I dared stand still in a field of new corn. In the minds of my friends and neighbors who really know what they are about and whose clothes really fit them, much of my activity has the quality of a little girl playing house. My routine is that of a husbandman, but my demeanor is that of a high school boy in a soft-drink parlor. This morning, carrying grain to my birds, I noticed that I was unconsciously imitating the young roosters—making a noise in my throat like a cock learning to crow. No farmer has the time or the temperament for vaudeville of this sort. He feeds his flock silently, sometimes attentively, sometimes absentmindedly, but never banteringly. He doesn't go round his place making noises in his throat.

Another time I caught myself carrying a paper napkin in my hand, as I wandered here and there. I have never seen a farmer carrying a paper napkin around his barnyard.

For all its implausibility, however, my farming has the excitement, the calamities, and sometimes the nobility of the real thing. For sheer surprise there is nothing to beat this life. For example, I had read widely on the subject of lice and mites, had treated my flock diligently. The specter of infestation was with me constantly. Yet when trouble finally came to my farm, it was not my hens that developed lice, but my Victrola. The old machine, I discovered the other day, is fairly alive with parasites —in the seams where the old needles lodge, and running in and out of the little cup where old and new needles mingle in democratic equality. I use Black Leaf 40 (nicotine sulphate) for my hens, smearing it on the roosts according to directions on the bottle. But I'm damned if I know how to apply nicotine sulphate to a Victrola, and there is nothing in my agricultural bulletins that covers the subject. I suppose I could rub the stuff on a Benny Goodman record and let him swing it, but it sounds like a mess. It is this sort of thing that makes the land so richly exciting: you never know where the enemy is going to strike.

CHILDREN'S BOOKS

Among the goat feathers that stick to us at this season of the year are some two hundred children's books. They are review copies, sent to my wife by the publishers. They lie dormant in every room, like November flies.

This inundation of juvenile literature is an annual emergency to which I have gradually become accustomed—the way the people of the Connecticut River valley get used to having the river come into their parlor. The books arrive in the mail by tens and twenties; we live with them for a few crowded, fever-laden weeks and then fumigate. Lacking shelf space, we pile them everywhere—on chairs, beds, davenports, ledges, stair landings. Some of them we tuck away in spidery cupboards, among the crocks and fragments of an older civilization. Turn over a birch log on my hearth and you won't find a beetle, you'll find *Bumblebuzz,* the chronicle of a bee. Throw open the door of our kitchen cabinet, out will fall *The Story of Tea.* Pick up a sofa cushion and there, mashed to a pulp, will be a definitive work on drums, tomtoms, and rattles. For the past three weeks I have shared my best armchair with the *Boyhood Adventures of Our Presidents* and a rather heavy book about the valley of the Euphrates. Mine is an uncomfortable, but not uninstructive, existence.

I have naturally come to know something about children's books from living so close to them and gazing hatefully at their jackets. A man can't be dogged from room to room by camels, pandas, and cocker spaniels and not gain some knowledge of their peculiar quality. Besides, although I resent their presence, I am not quite proof against children's books: yesterday I could have been found flat on my stomach studying, with every evidence of complete absorption, an outdoor handicraft book in which I had discovered a chapter on how to build a tree-house. (There may have been, in this particular case, an unconscious urge to escape to green mansions; but anyway, there I was, and I didn't stop till I read that the finishing touch to a boy's 1939 tree-house was to equip it with a small radio.)

A man today should keep abreast of what the children of his country are reading. Juvenile books seem to follow old familiar paths, but in new clothes and with a new sense of destinations. Indians, animals, fairies, these old reliables still occupy the key positions. Indians seem, if any-thing, to be gaining—gaining in stature and in numbers. The child of twenty-five years ago had his Fenimore Cooper Indian, his cigar-store Indian, his lead-soldier Indian, and his Indian suit with a feather head-dress; but he thought of an Indian as an agreeably bloodthirsty but by-gone creature of history, definitely suspect. Today, thanks to progressive education and some appreciative artists and writers in the Southwest, the Indian stands reborn—in a fine clean region of his own, half way between DiMaggio and Christ. He is high class. His pottery, his dance, his legends, his profile are cultural and good. To my own son the American Indian is a living presence, more vivid than Popeye. To my boy next month isn't December—it is the Month of the Long Night Moon.

It's a funny thing about Indians. Everything about their persons and their habits seems to satisfy the imagination of youngsters. The farther the Indians get from the original, as the years roll on, the more dignity and caste they seem to acquire. There is a certain charm in this tardy deification of the American primitive, but it sometimes strikes me as a little far from life: or maybe I don't meet the right Indians. The only live Indians I've come up against in the past few years were a rather pale group I saw in the Grand Central Galleries, sulkily admiring their own paintings, and an extremely brisk master-of-ceremonies at the Sports-man's Show, squealing into a loud speaker like a moose.

Close physical contact with the field of juvenile literature leads me to the conclusion that it must be a lot of fun to write for children—reasonably easy work, perhaps even important work. One side of it that must be exciting is finding a place, a period, or a thing that hasn't already been written about. This season's list indicates that the authors set about their task with a will. One of them, as I said before, hit upon the valley of the Euphrates. Another one shut his eyes, opened an atlas, and let his finger fall on the Louisiana bayous. Another, with enviable prescience, managed to turn out the third book of a trilogy on Czechoslovakia. Munro Leaf, scouring the earth for another *Ferdinand,* wound up in the Scotland of the MacGregors and the Maxine Sullivans. (Such is the staying power of success, you can have this rather flat tale in either the standard or the special de luxe edition.)

The custom of providing an authentic background for books for the young is almost universal. Authors are most specific. This winter, if a child should yearn to read of an American country town, he can have his choice between a country town in the Eighties and a country town in the Seventies. If his fancy turns to the California scene, he can have the Mexican quarter of Los Angeles or a prune ranch in the Santa Clara Valley. If he dotes on the deep South, he can assuage his hunger in the black section of Charleston, the black section of a small town in Florida, or that Louisiana bayou. If depressions are his hobby, he can enjoy the depression of 1817 on the Ohio River or the depression of 1932 on the Potomac. Let his glance rest on the sea, he can amuse himself with the displacement of a battleship, the misadventures of a yawl in a storm, or, tiring of surface matters, he can go right down into the sea in company with nymphs, scuds, and crayfish. If yaks are his passion, he can have a whimsical London yak or a yak of a more practical sort in Tibet. Modern tidewater Virginia vies with Williamsburg before the Revolution. Ecuador competes with Bali. A mongrel of Kips Bay competes with an outlaw dog on a high windswept tract of Exmoor. Hawaii, Bermuda, South Africa, the Gobi Desert, the Ionian Sea—the authors go journeying on.

Not less impressive than its geographical scope is the polyglot character of this literature. A child who romps around in the juvenile field today picks up a smattering of many tongues and dialects. I have just been browsing hit and miss in a deep pile of books, opening them in the middle and reading a page or two. The experience has left me gibbering.

The first book I opened was *Exploring With Andrews*. "Shortly after we left," I began, "torrential downpours swept away half a dozen *yurts* pitched at the bottom of a steep bluff."

Without going back to find out what a *yurt* was, I drifted on into the next book, *Soomoon, Boy of Bali*. It was my luck to alight on page 40, where, from somewhere in the village, "came the deep, hollow tones of a *gamelang*."

Yurts to you, gamelang, I thought to myself, and picked up the next book. It happened to be *Benjie's Hat*.

"Thee is an abomination, Eliphalet!" cried a character in this book.

"Who'all 'bomination?" squeaked Eliphalet.

"Thee is," declared Benjie.

I laid Benjie down and picked up *King of the Tinkers*, which seemed to have an Irish flavor to it.

"Sit down here wid me," piped up a fellow in my new book, "we'll have a long collogue together."

"I won't mind," interrupted a Hawaiian in *Hawaiian Holiday,* "if I can have Moki sit on my *lanai* and tell me stories until I go to sleep."

All right, Moki, I muttered drunkenly, thee can sit on my *lanai* and we'll all have a good old-fashioned collogue. Groggy, I picked up *Olympiad,* a book about ancient Greece, but I found no surcease. In fact I immediately encountered a young athlete who was being scraped with a strigil and taken to the *konisterion.*

Before I finished my browsing, I had learned how to count up to three in Siamese *(satu, dua, tiga),* and I knew that a *coati mundi* is also called a snookum bear, that *bei shung* is Chinese for panda, that *begashi* is Navajo for cows, and that *gu-bu-du gu-bu-du* is Zulu for bumpity bumpity. Right there I rested.

Like toys, books for children reflect surely the temper of the period into which they are born. With science dominating life nowadays, books for young people are largely scientific in their approach to their subject matter, whatever it may be. Even the cute animals of the nonsense school move against impeccable backgrounds of natural history; even a female ant who is sufficiently irregular to be able to talk English lays her eggs at the proper time and in the accepted manner.

In this year of infinite terror, when adults search the sky for trouble and when the desire of everyone is for a safe hole to hide in, it is not surprising to find writers of juveniles glorifying the idea of safety. There are two safety books on my sofa. One is called, somewhat wistfully, *Safety Can Be Fun.* The other, *The Safe-Way Club,* struck me as not far short of hilarious. It tells about a neighborhood organization started "by some fun-loving children to prevent accidents" and it contains the priceless sentence: "The Safe-Way Club had two weeks to get ready for the Parent-Teacher Association Meeting, and what busy weeks they were!"

One laughs in demoniac glee at this sort of wild fantasy, but the laugh has a hollow sound. Books on safety for children by today's grown-up authors somehow lack conviction, and the very want of it is sobering. It is an odd place, this front yard of World Crisis, where adults with blueprints of bombproof shelters sticking from their pants pockets solemnly caution their little ones against running downstairs with lollypops in their mouths.

I have heard it said that rats collect trinkets, that if you expose a rat's nest, you may find bright bits of glass and other small desirable objects. A child's mind is such a repository—full of gems of questionable merit, paste and real, held in storage. What shining jewels shall we contribute this morning, sir, to this amazing collection? Educators and psychologists are full of theory about the young: they profess to know what a child should be taught and how he should be taught it, and they are often quite positive and surly about the matter. Yet the education of our young, in schools and in libraries, is a function of home and state that gives every appearance of having brilliantly failed the world. A Sunday night radio invasion of the little people from Mars is still more credible than a book on the courses of the stars.

Much of our adult morality, in books and out of them, has a stuffiness unworthy of childhood. Our grown-up conclusions often rest on perilously soft bottom. Try to tell a child even the simplest truths about planetary, cosmical, or spiritual things, and you hear strange echoes in your own head. "Can this be me?" a voice keeps asking, "can this be me?" Dozens of times in the course of trying to act like a parent I have caught myself telling my boy things I didn't thoroughly comprehend myself, urging him toward conventional attitudes of mind and spirit I only half believed in and would myself gladly chuck overboard.

Such thoughts trouble you when you delve in children's books. A book like *Johnny Get Your Money's Worth*, for example, a primer for the young skeptic, inducting him into the world of consumers, where he mustn't even buy a pencil without biting it to see if it's made of cedar. Or a sycophantic book like *Favorite Stories of Famous Children* (when interviewed Miss Temple wore white linen with hand embroidered triangles in Alice Blue). Or the group of youth novels, which seem almost like parodies of the novel form, and whose expurgated account of life is an insult to the intelligence of adolescents.

A large amount of the published material is dull, prosy stuff, by writers who mistake oddity for fantasy and whose wildly beating wings never get them an inch off the ground. (Incidentally, one of the few books that struck me as being in the true spirit of nonsense is one called *The 500 Hats of Bartholomew Cubbins*, by Dr. Seuss.) Some of the books are patronizing, some are mushy, some are grand. Almost all are beautifully illustrated. From them you can discover how to build everything from a Chippewa water drum to a pair of undersea goggles. The exciting thing about them is that, whatever else they are, they are free to be read, untainted by anything but the rigors and joys of pure creation. From *Bumblebuzz* to the *Boy Scouts Yearbook of Fun in Fiction*, there's nothing that can be construed as government propaganda.

The gamut of life must seem splendidly wide to children whose books these are. They may begin with *Little Orphan Willie Mouse*, but they must end with *Windows of the World,* whose unsparing author fixes them with his eye and asks:

> And if you are in the trenches, what can you hope for? If you're a man between 18 to 40, that's probably where you'll be. You may be burned to death by flame-throwers, riddled by machine-gun bullets, pulverized by hurtling bombs, chewed by rats in the night, suffocated in leaking gas masks, thrust through your eyes, chest, or belly with triple-bladed bayonets, poisoned with drinking water polluted by unburied bodies.

From such macabre interrogation I had to turn away, being no longer a child. Luckily I found solace in a good wholesome juvenile mystery, that began: "The long, luxurious Rolls Royce, glittering with chromium and enamel, slid over the crest of Cajon Pass and shot down the smooth incline leading into the desert. The hour was sunset."

Sunset in Cajon Pass, and a Rolls Royce under me! This was more like it!

PROGRESS AND CHANGE

MY FRIENDS in the city tell me that the Sixth Avenue El is coming down, but that's a hard thing for anyone to believe who once lived in its fleeting and audible shadow. The El was the most distinguished and outstanding vein on the town's neck, a varicosity tempting to the modern surgeon. One wonders whether New York can survive this sort of beauty operation, performed in the name of civic splendor and rapid transit.

A resident of the city grew accustomed to the heavenly railroad that swung implausibly in air, cutting off his sun by day, wandering in and out of his bedchamber by night. The presence of the structure and the passing of the trains were by all odds the most pervasive of New York's influences. Here was a sound that, if it ever got in the conch of your ear, was ineradicable—forever singing, like the sea. It punctuated the morning with brisk tidings of repetitious adventure, and it accompanied the night with sad but reassuring sounds of life-going-on—the sort of threnody that cricket and katydid render for suburban people sitting on screened porches, the sort of lullaby the whippoorwill sends up to the Kentucky farm wife on a summer evening.

I spent a lot of time once, doing nothing in the vicinity of Sixth Avenue. Naturally I know something of the El's fitful charm. It was, among other things, the sort of railroad you would occasionally ride just for the hell of it, a higher existence into which you would escape unconsciously and without destination. Let's say you had just emerged from the Child's on the west side of Sixth Avenue between 14th and 15th Streets, where you had had a bowl of vegetable soup and a stack of wheat cakes. The syrup still was a cloying taste on your tongue. You intended to go back to the apartment and iron a paragraph or wash a sock. But miraculously, at the corner of 14th, there rose suddenly in front of you a flight of marble stairs all wrapt in celestial light, with treads of shining steel and risers richly carved with the names of the great, and a canopy overhead where danced the dust in the shafts of golden sunshine. As in a trance, you mounted steadily to the pavilion above, where there was an iron stove and a man's hand visible through a mousehole. And the first thing you knew you were in South Ferry, with another of life's inestimable journeys behind you—and before you the dull, throbbing necessity of getting uptown again.

For a number of years I went to work every morning on the uptown trains of the Sixth Avenue El. I had it soft, because my journey wasn't at the rush hour and I often had the platform of the car to myself. It was a good way to get where you wanted to go, looking down on life at just the right speed, and peeking in people's windows, where the sketchy pantomime of potted plant and half-buttoned undershirt and dusty loft provided a curtain raiser to the day. The railroad was tolerant and allowed its passengers to loll outdoors if they wished; and on mornings when the air was heady that was the place to be—with the sudden whiff of the candy factory telling you that your ride was half over, and the quick eastward glance through 24th Street to check your time with the clock in the Metropolitan Tower, visible for the tenth part of a second.

The El always seemed to me to possess exactly the right degree of substantiality: it seemed reasonably strong and able to carry its load, and competent with that easy slovenly competence of an old drudge; yet it was perceptibly a creature of the clouds, the whole structure vibrating ever so slightly following the final grasping success of the applied brake. The El had giddy spells, too—days when a local train would shake off its patient, plodding manner and soar away in a flight of sheer whimsy, skipping stations in a drunken fashion and scaring the pants off everybody. To go roaring past a scheduled stop, hell bent for 53rd Street and the plunge into space, was an experience that befell every El rider more than once. On this line a man didn't have to be a locomotophobe to suffer from visions of a motorman's lifeless form slumped over an open throttle. And if the suspense got too great and you walked nervously to the front of the train the little window in the booth gave only the most tantalizing view of the driver—three inert fingers of a gloved hand, or a *Daily News* wedged in some vital cranny.

One thing I always admired about the El was the way it tormented its inexperienced customers. Veterans like myself, approaching a station stop, knew to a fraction of an inch how close it was advisable to stand to the little iron gates on the open type cars. But visitors to town had no such information. When the train halted and the guard, pulling his two levers, allowed the gates to swing in and take the unwary full in the stomach, there was always a dim pleasure in it for the rest of us. Life has little enough in the way of reward; these small moments of superiority are not to be despised.

The El turned the Avenue into an arcade. That, in a way, was its chief contribution. It made Sixth Avenue as distinct from Fifth as Fifth is from Jones Street. Its pillars, straddling the car tracks in the long channel of the night, provided the late cruising taxicab with the supreme challenge, and afforded the homing pedestrian, his wine too much with him, forest sanctuary and the friendly accommodation of a tree.

Of course I have read about the great days of the El, when it was the railroad of the élite and when financial giants rode elegantly home from Wall Street in its nicely appointed coaches. But I'm just as glad I didn't meet the El until after it had lost its money. Its lazy crescendos, breaking into one's dreams, will always stick in the mind—and the soiled hands of the guards on the bellcords, and the brusque, husky-throated bells that had long ago lost their voices, cuing each other along the whole length of the train. Yes, at this distance it's hard to realize that the Sixth Avenue El is just a problem in demolition. I can't for the life of me imagine what New York will have to offer in its place. It will have to be something a good deal racier, a good deal more open and aboveboard, than a new subway line.

ह•

I suppose a man can't ask railroads to stand still. For twenty or thirty years the railroads of America stood about as still as was consistent with swift transportation. The gas mantles were removed and electric lights installed, but outside of that the cars remained pretty much the same. It's only in the past couple of years that the railroads, fretting over the competition from busses and planes, have set about transforming their interiors into cocktail lounges, ballrooms, and modern apartments.

In my isolated position here in the country, I have plenty of time to study Pullman trends—which are readily accessible in full-page color ads in the popular magazines. I note that the Pullman Company, although emphasizing the high safety factor implicit in Pullman travel, is advertising a new type of accommodation called, somewhat ominously, "S.O.S." This is the Single Occupancy Section. It is for the dollar-wise and the travel-wise, the ads point out. From the illustration, the single occupancy section appears to have a dead body in it, hooded in a sheet, bound and gagged. There is also a live occupant—a girl in a pink dressing gown, apparently in the best of spirits. A more careful examination of the photograph reveals that the dead body is nothing more nor less than the bed itself, which has reared up on its hind end and been lashed to the bulkhead, while the occupant (who is single, of course) stands erect and goes through the motions of dressing in comfort.

I feel that the Pullman Company, in introducing the note of *comfort* into its adventurous calling, is perhaps slipping outside of the particular field in which it has made such an enviable reputation. This being able to stand erect in an ordinary single berth and dress in something like ease —isn't it likely to destroy the special flavor of Pullman travel? I don't take a night journey on a railroad for the sake of duplicating the experiences and conveniences of my own home: when I travel I like to get into some new kind of difficulty, not just the same old trouble I put up with around the house.

Travelers, I will admit, differ temperamentally, differ in their wants and needs; but for me the Pullman Company will never improve on its classic design of upper and lower berth. In my eyes it is a perfect thing, perfect in conception and execution, this small green hole in the dark moving night, this soft warren in a hard world. In it I have always found the peace of spirit that accompanies grotesque bodily situations, peace and a wonderful sense of participation in cosmic rhythms and designs. I have experienced these even on cold nights when I all but died from exposure, under blankets of virgin gossamer.

In a Pullman berth, a man can truly be alone with himself. (The nearest approach to this condition is to be found in a hotel bedroom, but a hotel room can sometimes be depressing, it stands so still.) Now if a modern Pullman proposes to provide headroom for everyone, it will have to answer for whatever modification this may cause in human character. The old act of drawing one's pants on and off while in a horizontal position did much to keep Man in a mood of decent humility. It gave him a picture of himself at a moment of wild comic contortion. To tuck in the tails of a shirt while supine demanded a certain persistence, a certain virtuosity, wholly healthful and character-building.

The new single occupancy section, besides changing all this and permitting a man to stand erect as though he had no ape in his family background, has another rather alarming feature. The bed not only is capable of being cocked up by the occupant, to resemble a cadaver, but it can be hoisted by a separate control from the aisle by the dark, notional hand of the porter as he glides Puckishly through the car. It does not sound conducive to calm.

&

In resenting progress and change, a man lays himself open to censure. I suppose the explanation of anyone's defending anything as rudimentary and cramped as a Pullman berth is that such things are associated with an earlier period in one's life and that this period in retrospect seems a happy one. People who favor progress and improvements are apt to be people who have had a tough enough time without any extra inconvenience. Reactionaries who pout at innovations are apt to be well-heeled sentimentalists who had the breaks. Yet for all that, there is always a subtle danger in life's refinements, a dim degeneracy in progress. I have just been refining the room in which I sit, yet I sometimes doubt that a writer should refine or improve his workroom by so much as a dictionary: one thing leads to another and the first thing you know he has a stuffed chair and is fast asleep in it. Half a man's life is devoted to what he calls improvements, yet the original had some quality that is lost in the process. There was a fine natural spring of water on this place when I bought it. Our drinking water had to be lugged in a pail, from a wet glade of alder and tamarack. I visited the spring often in those first years, and had friends there—a frog, a woodcock, and an eel that had churned its way all the way up through the pasture creek to enjoy the luxury of pure water. In the normal course of development, the spring was rocked up, fitted with a concrete curb, a copper pipe, and an electric pump. I have visited it only once or twice since. This year my only gesture was the purely perfunctory one of sending a sample to the state bureau of health for analysis. I felt cheap, as though I were smelling an old friend's breath.

Another phase of life here that has lost something through refinement is the game of croquet. We used to have an old croquet set whose wooden balls, having been chewed by dogs, were no rounder than eggs. Paint had faded, wickets were askew. The course had been laid out haphazardly and eagerly by a child, and we all used to go out there on summer nights and play good-naturedly, with the dogs romping on the lawn in the beautiful light, and the mosquitoes sniping at us, and everyone in good spirits, racing after balls and making split shots for the sheer love of battle. Last spring we decided the croquet set was beyond use, and invested in a fancy new one with hoops set in small wooden sockets, and mallets with rubber faces. The course is now exactly seventy-two feet long and we lined the wickets up with a string; but the little boy is less fond of it now, for we make him keep still while we are shooting. A dog isn't even allowed to cast his shadow across the line of play. There are frequent quarrels of a minor nature, and it seems to me we return from the field of honor tense and out of sorts.

SALT WATER FARM

A SEACOAST farm, such as this, extends far beyond the boundaries mentioned in the deed. My domain is arable many miles offshore, in the restless fields of protein. Cultivation begins close to the house with a rhubarb patch, but it ends down the bay beyond the outer islands, hand-lining for cod and haddock, with gulls like gnats round your ears, and the threat of fog always in the pit of your stomach.

I think it is the expansiveness of coastal farming that makes it so engrossing: the knowledge that your fence, on one side at least, shuts out no neighbor—you may climb it and keep going if you have a boat and the strength to raise a sail. The presence in the offing of the sea's fickle yield, those self-sown crops given up grudgingly to the patient and the brave, is an attraction few men are proof against. Beyond one blue acre is another, each one a little farther from the house than the last. On a summer's day I may start out down the lane with a pail to pick a few berries for my wife's piemaking, but there is always the likelihood that I will turn up hours later with two small flounders and a look of profound accomplishment. A man who has spent much time and money in dreary restaurants moodily chewing filet of sole on the special luncheon is bound to become unmanageable when he discovers that he can produce the main fish course directly, at the edge of his own pasture, by a bit of trickery on a fine morning.

Below the barn are the asparagus and the potatoes and the potato bugs in season. Beyond is the pasture, where, amid juniper and granite and lambkill, grow the wild strawberries and the tame heifers. Keep walking and you come to the blueberries and cranberries. Take off your shoes, advance, and you are on the clam beds—the only crop on the place that squirts water at you in time of drought. Beyond the clams are the cunners and the flounders, hanging round the dock piles on the incoming tide. Near the ledges, off the point, are the lobsters. Two miles farther, off the red rocks, are the mackerel, flashing in schools, ready for the Sunday afternoon sociable when the whole village turns out for the harvest of fishes. Mackereling is the accepted Sabbath engagement in summertime; there are two or three spots known to be good, and the boats bunch up at these points, a clubby arrangement for man and fish. It is where you meet your friends, and, if the tide serves you, reap the benefit from your friends' toll bait, which drifts down over your hook. Farthest from home are the cod and haddock. You must rise early the day you go to bring them in.

The salt water farms hereabouts give ample evidence that their owners have a great deal on their minds. Rocks and alders are the most conspicuous crops, and if a man can get a job firming the public highway he gives small thought to loosening the soil in his own garden. With the whole sea bottom to rake, he isn't going to spend all his time weeding a bean row. He puts in a vegetable garden in spring, gives it a few vicious pokes with a hoe in June, and devotes the remainder of the year to lustier pursuits—grinding the valves of an old boat-engine, or mending a weir. My neighbor Mr. Dameron, who goes after the lobsters from early spring till late fall, tethers his cow a few paces from his landing, so that he can pick her up handily when he comes in from hauling his traps. The two of them walk up together through the field, he with his empty gas can, she with her full bag of milk.

There is a lively spirit here among us maritime agriculturalists. My neighbors are mostly descendants of sea rovers and are stifled by the confinements of a farm acre. The young men fit easier on an Indian motorcycle than on a disc harrow. And I have noticed that it is the easygoing ones among us who have the best time; in this climate, at the rate a stove eats wood, if a man were to grow too thrifty or forehanded he'd never be able to crawl out from under his own woodpile.

ॐ

Although winter is still in possession of the land, the days are perceptibly longer. Skating on the frog pond under an early rising moon, I am conscious of the promise of pollywogs under my runners, and my thoughts turn to seeds and the germinal prospect. Snow, which came with a bang at Thanksgiving, is an old story to the little boy now; winter's charms fade slowly out like the picture of Charlie McCarthy on the back of his sweatshirt. Sears Roebuck's midwinter catalogue is shelved in favor of seed catalogues. Before another week is gone I shall have to map out a poultry program and decide whether to reduce my egg farming to reasonable family proportions or step it up to a commercial scale.

Last spring I started eighty-four day-old chicks under a coal brooder stove. I assumed that if I began with eighty-four I might, with good luck, wind up with an even dozen. The others I expected to meet a horrible death, since I had read that this is what always happens when a man starts to keep chickens. As things turned out I lost only three birds. One sickened and died, two were spirited away by a killer in the night. The others—eighty-one of them—grew so tall and handsome, and responded so well to loving-kindness and to rich food, and the young cockerels crowed so loudly at daybreak, that they became the talk of the country-side. We ate or sold forty-five broilers and roasters, and ended up with thirty-six pullets, all laying like a house afire. During the month of November I presented my little family with a frightful total of six hundred and seventy-two eggs, several of them double-yolked. In December production fell off slightly, because of the short days and long cold nights, but on the average we've been getting about twenty eggs a day, of which we consume maybe six or eight. The others have to be disposed of by one means or another. I haven't yet recovered from my surprise.

For a few days, after the barrage of eggs started in the laying pen, my game wife tried to keep pace with the preposterous influx. She scheduled egg dishes daily—all sorts of rather soft, disagreeable desserts, the kind convalescents eat doggedly and without joy. We grimly faced a huge platter of scrambled eggs at breakfast, a floating island or a custard at noon, and at night drank eggnogs instead of Martinis. We even gave raw eggs to the dogs; it would improve their coats, we said. And once I saw my wife slip an egg to the pig when she thought nobody was looking. It was no use. For every egg we ate, my pullets laid two. Secretly I was impressed and delighted, although I got darn sick of floating island.

It was perfectly obvious that we now had a first-rate farm surplus problem on our hands (along with a heating problem, an earning-a-living problem, a Christmas gift problem, and six or eight other problems that bloom in the fall). Unless I proposed to set up a target and throw eggs at it each afternoon for diversion, we would have to act and act quickly. Eggs don't keep. I turned instinctively to Sears Roebuck, and after studying the poultry section sent a hurry call for an egg scale and some cardboard egg cartons, the kind that hold one dozen eggs and have a picture of a hen staring fatuously at a nest. Six days later I timidly presented myself at the local store, bearing three dozen strictly fresh twenty-four-ounce fancy brown eggs, neatly packaged, to be credited to my account. I don't know anything that ever embarrassed me more, unless it was the day in St. Luke's Hospital when I misunderstood the nurse's instructions and walked into the X-ray room naked except for my socks and garters.

The steady palming off of surplus eggs on a storekeeper who used to be my friend has done more to unnerve me about the country than anything else, although various people have assured me that I exaggerate the gravity of the situation, and some even say that the store turns right round and resells the eggs at a profit. I don't know. I certainly have never *seen* anybody buy an egg in the stores where I trade. I've often hung around watching. It reminded me of the early days of authorhood, when I used to sneak into Brentano's book store and hang around the counter where my book was kept (one copy of it) hoping that I would some day witness a sale. I never did. I have a suspicion the storekeeper takes my eggs home and eats them himself—or throws them at a target. The eggs simply disappear mysteriously behind the counter and show up as a sixty-cent or a ninety-cent credit on my slip. It has reduced my bills appreciably, but it has damn near destroyed my spirit. I am sure it has left its mark on the storekeeper, whose embarrassment equalled mine and to whom for all I know it has meant the difference between operating my account at a profit and at a loss. Anyway, it has shown me clearly that the personal-contact side of agriculture will never be my forte: I can handle production, but someone else will have to take over the marketing if I am to live through the ordeal.

The truth is I am unfit for barter, being of an apologetic rather than an acquisitive nature. And unless I can raise enough eggs so that I can ship them away impersonally in a standard thirty-dozen crate to the Boston market, I shall have to curtail my activities to a mere subsistence basis.

There are of course more ways than one of dealing with a surplus. One of my favorite people around here (although I have never met him) is an old fellow who has a place on the ridge and who is reputed to be a man of original mind. According to report, as I have it, he wears an overcoat winter and summer—just the same in summer as in winter, his theory being that if an overcoat can keep out the cold then by God it can keep out the heat too. A bachelor, he keeps two cows with whom he dwells contentedly, in peace and in filth. He is a master of surplus. There are days when he gets as much as twenty-four quarts of milk. Somebody once asked him what he did with all that milk.

"Drink what I feel like and throw the rest to hell," he replied testily.

Such strength of character is seldom met with on a farm, though a farm is where it is most urgently needed.

ࢌ

I was sorry to hear the other day that a certain writer, appalled by the cruel events of the world, had pledged himself never to write anything that wasn't constructive and significant and liberty-loving. I have an idea that this, in its own way, is bad news.

All word-mongers, at one time or another, have felt the divine necessity of using their talents, if any, on the side of right—but I didn't realize that they were making any resolutions to that effect, and I don't think they should. When liberty's position is challenged, artists and writers are the ones who first take up the sword. They do so without persuasion, for the battle is peculiarly their own. In the nature of things, a person engaged in the flimsy business of expressing himself on paper is dependent on the large general privilege of being heard. Any intimation that this privilege may be revoked throws a writer into a panic. His is a double allegiance to freedom—an intellectual one springing from the conviction that pure thought has a right to function unimpeded, and a selfish one springing from his need, as a breadwinner, to be allowed to speak his piece. America is now liberty-conscious. In a single generation it has progressed from being toothbrush-conscious, to being air-minded, to being liberty-conscious. The transition has been disturbing, but it has been effected, and the last part has been accomplished largely by the good work of writers and artists, to whom liberty is a blessed condition that must be preserved on earth at all costs.

But to return to my man who has foresworn everything but what is good and significant. He worries me. I hope he isn't serious, but I'm afraid he is. Having resolved to be nothing but significant, he is in a fair way to lose his effectiveness. A writer must believe in something, obviously, but he shouldn't join a club. Letters flourish not when writers amalgamate, but when they are contemptuous of one another. (Poets are the most contemptuous of all the writing breeds, and in the long run the most exalted and influential.) Even in evil times, a writer should cultivate only what naturally absorbs his fancy, whether it be freedom or chinch bugs, and should write in the way that comes easy.

The movement is spreading. I know of one gifted crackpot, who used to be employed gainfully in the fields of humor and satire, who has taken a solemn pledge not to write anything funny or light-hearted or "insignificant" again till things get straightened around in the world. This seems to be distinctly deleterious and a little silly. A literature composed of nothing but liberty-loving thoughts is little better than the propaganda it seeks to defeat.

In a free country it is the duty of writers to pay no attention to duty. Only under a dictatorship is literature expected to exhibit an harmonious design or an inspirational tone. A despot doesn't fear eloquent writers preaching freedom—he fears a drunken poet who may crack a joke that will take hold. His gravest concern is lest gaiety, or truth in sheep's clothing, somewhere gain a foothold, lest joy in some unguarded moment be unconfined. I honestly don't believe that a humorist should take the veil today; he should wear his bells night and day, and squeeze the uttermost jape, even though he may feel that he should be writing a strong letter to the *Herald Tribune.*

SABBATH MORN

IT IS Sunday, mid-morning—Sunday in the living room, Sunday in the kitchen, Sunday in the woodshed, Sunday down the road in the village: I hear the bells, calling me to share God's grace. I enter the living room, a Sunday man, carrying a folder of work—clippings, letters, small ungerminated thoughts in plain wrappers, a writer's reticule. I stand a moment listening to the bells three miles away, the hopeful, chiding bells. Procrastinating, I snap the radio on, and it is Sunday in the radio cabinet, too. *More like the Master is my daily prayer* . . . a hymn singer in the Nazarene Church of South Blur, Maine, into my Sunday living room, spreading a frail soprano along the shelf among the geraniums and the freesia and the hyacinths where stand the authors without their jackets —Henry James, Willa Cather, D. H. Lawrence, A. P. Herbert, Frank T. Bullen, W. H. Hudson, Willard C. Thompson, their heads unbowed, looking straight ahead. *We dedicate this hymn to Miss Nellie Blur, a shut-in of South Blend. Next Sunday we shall take up the first of the beatitudes and until then God bless you* . . .

I sit down, opening the work folder. An organ prelude! The organ makes a curious whine, sentimental, grandiose—half cello, half bagpipes. A prelude, somewhere in a wired church, on this Sunday morning in this year of our . . . (somewhere into the church as into the church three miles away where bells have just grown silent must now be coming the people, the people to the Lord, singly, by twos and threes, and the usher seating them, and the bowing and the handing the printed program). *Praise God from whom all blessings flow* . . . hesitatingly the assembled voices, embarrassed at the sudden sound of their own once-a-week excursion in piety, the too weak, the over strong, *praise Father, Son, and Holy Ghost.*

Ahhhhhhh men.

"Dad?"

My boy enters the living room where Sunday is. He wears corduroy trousers and carries a police whistle.

"What?"

"It sounds as though you had turned the bottom part of this house into a church."

"Yes, it does."

Acts the eleventh chapter . . . Acts, the ee-leventh chapter. The little boy picks up a book, subsides, unlistening, discarding the world of the room, the world of the radio, setting up for himself a tight little world inside the covers of a book. There are many worlds. I see by my folder that in Flushing, the village of tomorrow, the people are building a temple to the Lord at a cost of two hundred and fifty thousand dollars or is it three. The world of tomorrow has so many responsibilities, and on top of everything, religion. *We thank thee that Thou are murr-ciful.*

The police whistle sounds a shrill blast. The prayer ends, and the organ takes up the burden. The people cough, and there is a rustling and re-arranging in the distant pews. I paw around in the folder, uncover the rules for the National Poetry Contest conducted by the Academy of American Poets—to select the official poem of the New York World's Fair, 1939. The choir is singing again, something a little too hard for it this time, struggling bravely, tentatively. A poetry contest! An official ode for the world of tomorrow, a song in the future tense to stir blood that has yet to flow through veins . . . *regular Sunday morning program emanating from the Durr Baptist Church of Runcible, New Hampshire.*

Poems must be typed, double-spaced, on one side of the paper. "No contestant may submit more than three poems" (these inexhaustible poets!). *Bless the Lord O my soul and all that is within . . . who taught us to pray together: Our Father who art in heaven, hallowed be Thy name*

Police!

and the power and the glory forever, amen

This house, this house now held in Sunday's fearful grip, is a hundred and twenty years old. I am wondering what Sabbaths it has known. Here where I sit, grandfather H. used to sit, they tell me—always right here. He would be surprised were he here this morning, to note how the seams in the floor have opened wide from the dry heat of the furnace, revealing the accumulation of a century of dust and crumbs and trouble, and giving quite a good view of the cellar.

My retriever comes in from outdoors, full of greeting on a grand scale. He shakes himself and knocks, with his eager tail, the world of tomorrow from the table at my side.

Isaiah the fifty-second chapter. How beautiful upon the mountains are the feet of him that bringeth good tidings. The little boy has a hammer now, and a metal ball from a pin game. *Psalm 66. We will read there David's exhortation to praise God and after that the male choir . . . does your eye follow down now to the twelfth verse, the twell-fth verse: but thou broughtest us out into a wurring place . . .* (where have I heard this voice before? was it the voice saying good night for Canada Dry, saying hello for Fels Naptha? if mine eye follows down now to the twelfth verse, can I win a Buick by writing twenty-five words?) The boy has returned to his book, is quiet. The book (I can read the title) is "All About Subways," by Grof Conklin. There are *two* dogs in the room now, a dachshund has joined us for the reading of the sixty-sixth psalm. He feints at the retriever, steps back. *Say unto God how terrible art thou in thy works! through the greatness of thy power shall thine enemies . . .* On the child's face now a look of complete absorption, Grof Conklin triumphs over a terrible God, subways over the kingdom on high. All poems should be mailed postpaid to The Academy of American Poets at a wurring place and postmarked not later than the feet of him that bringeth good tidings *. . . from the gospel according to*

"This book is all about New York," says my son, pleased at having discovered familiar ground. He listens a moment to the church service. "Dad?"

"What?"

"That priest just then said they were all going to read together, but I only hear the priest reading."

No matter where we be or what the circumstances we may rest upon His word

He slips back into the subways. In a moment he is at my side, holding up the book for me to look at a photograph of children taking refuge in the Madrid subway from Fascist bombs.

"Is it true?" he asks.

"Sure it's true."

that the blood of Jesus Christ may cleanse us all from sin . . . that by Thy help we shall be different men and women (tomorrow, in the world of tomorrow perhaps?) *and taste the eternal dividend of Jesus Christ our Lord. Be especially with our young folks . . .* The retriever is asleep now. A telegraph key breaks in suddenly, the dit dit darr of the code message, high pitched, peremptory. God is wiring a confirmation. Yes, be especially with our young folks. The boy puts down the book, picks up an old copy of *Life*. There is a picture of a retriever on the cover. The boy shows the picture of the retriever to the retriever, waking him. The dog is unimpressed. A song of comfort, by a male singer. *Trust in Him and He will give thee* ... From the next room, an announcement: one of the dogs has sinned under the piano, and the Dogtex is all gone. A problem in household management, inflicting itself on our Sunday morning. The boy puts *Life* down, blows a quick summons to the police, and settles down thoughtfully with a new book, called *Starcraft*.

   ... so that the kind of lives we live shall remind

"Dad, can we make a telescope?"

"Not today."

The table is being set for dinner, silver against silver clinking, glass being set down, plates being placed around. *God help us so to live* ... and now to get to work! Two letters from my folder, one from the American Committee for Non-Participation in Japanese Aggression ...

"Look, Dad, here's *exactly* what I've been wanting to know—it shows just what Mars looks like." He shows me a picture of Mars. But the letters: Roger S. Greene, of the Non-Participation Committee, calling my attention to the fact that America is providing scrap iron to Japan, bandages to China. (Let not thy right hand know ...) And a letter from the Audubon Society reporting on its sanctuaries, havens for wild birds that are sore oppressed. *For without holiness no man shall ... This is an N.B.C. transcription*

The boy has given up the reflective life among the stars and is playing with an open jackknife on a chain, forming a bridge with his body so that the knife swings back and forth below his belly in a wide arc. Shall I help a wild bird, shall I give comfort to a dying Chinese, shall I ask a little boy to watch out he doesn't cut himself with his knife? *Thy speer-it, thy speer-it ...* I see the wild birds in the green and open forests, beautiful my feet upon the mountains, in the free air up toward levels of abundance, I see the children in the Madrid subway; save the wild birds, save the children, Oh God, save the children—the little boy with the knife, so safe, so safely swinging the knife, with nothing overhead but the wild birds and the planet Mars, wildly swinging.

He hath redeemed me and I am his child. "Telephone! That's our telephone!" It is long distance. Somebody else answers. The boy is using the blade of the knife as a reflector now, throwing the sun around the room, on the ceiling, on the wall, on the retriever's eye. "Pee-ew!" he says. "Something smells!" He goes to find out. A report from the kitchen: French fried potatoes (I wonder how France is this morning).

The folder again. Students at Hunter College will be analyzed at a beauty clinic.

"Dad, why do you have that radio on?"
yes, we'll gather at the river, the beautiful, the beautiful, riv—
"I don't know why."
"I mean, has it anything to do with your work?"
"No. Well maybe it has, in a way." (A parent's manly attempt to give an honest answer.)

Paris: The Duke and Duchess of Windsor returned by train from the Riviera today.

New York: Trichinosis, a disease caused by eating raw or underdone pork, has infested seventeen million persons in this country and resulted . . .

"Lunch is ready."
This is the voice of the radio pulpit in Peaceable, New Hampshire.
"Lunch is ready." *Let us make this world a better place in which to live.*
"Lunch, everybody!"

ॐ

Thus the Sabbath morn. Not a very wholesome report. Having turned the radio on, I simply let it go, as so many people do with radio, allowing it to function as a chatterbox, roiling the air. How far the word of God has tumbled, in families such as this in the world of Today!

In this house we cling to a few relics of religious observance, but there is no heart in it. If we possess faith (and I guess we do) it is of a secret and unconsecrated sort ill at ease in church. Once or twice a year we go to church, as we might visit the Museum of Natural History, on a sudden impulse to see a strange sight, such as a whale suspended in air.

There was a period in the little boy's life when he begged to be taken to church. He had heard about church and was hot to discover its mysteries at first hand. His demands became so insistent that the situation grew embarrassing: we felt mighty cheap, withholding God from our young zealot. At last we made the effort and took him, twice. He never asked to go again.

The church sometimes seems painfully unimaginative in its attempt to perpetuate a faith that has been gutted by so many fires. Whether or not people are essentially less religious than they used to be I don't know, but it is obvious that something has happened. I often think the Christian church suffers from a too ardent monotheism. In my house are many gods. With the boy, Jack Frost is ahead of Jesus, although we have never promoted Jack very hard. I see no harm in Jack and am not sure he shouldn't be taken into the church. He is a gifted spirit with an exciting technique and a gay program. And he is not terrible, like the Lord.

When I feel sick unto death, I cry out in agony to God; when I speak boastingly, I knock on wood. Here is a clear case of divided responsibility, for there appears to be for me a power in wood that God doesn't possess. My boy, likewise, is firm in certain pagan beliefs. One of them is that if you don't say "Rabbit rabbit" on the last night of the old month and "Bunny bunny" on the first morning of the new month, bad luck will attend you. (I can't imagine where he got this fantastic idea, unless it was from me.) He says "Now I lay me down to sleep" each night with a certain sing-song abstraction and an induced piety of demeanor—a far-away sound in his voice. But when he says "Bunny bunny" his mind is on his work.

As parents, we have never worked out a religious program—we just drift. I go to church once in a while and sing the hymns very loud; it clears the blood, and I love the gush of holiness when the old bone-shaking anthems ripple up and down my spine and crackle in my larynx. But for the most part, religion is tucked away in a bottom drawer, among things we love but never use. In two generations there has been a great falling off. When I was a child, I could feel heaven slipping. My father was a God-fearing man, but he never missed a copy of the New York *Times* either. At sixty he began changing back and forth between the Congregational and the Baptist church, grumbling and growling. At seventy he let go altogether, and for the next ten years lived in a miasma of melancholy doubt and died outside the church, groping and forlorn. By the standards of a hundred years ago, my family today is a group of misguided agnostics, seeking after an illusive beauty and fumbling for grace on a frequency of 860 kilocycles.

But the Lord is persistent and lingers in strange places. He enjoys an honorable position among typographers, for He is always upper case. He enjoys a unique legal status, too, in the "Act of God" code, where elemental violence affords exemption from responsibility. Germany thinks she is ousting the Lord, but she fools herself. I am sure that even in Germany holy words are still used in cussing; and though religion may be in abeyance in home or church, one can always find ample assurance, in the God-damning of a nation, that one's Redeemer liveth.

One of the chief pretenders to the throne of God is radio itself, which has acquired a sort of omniscience. I live in a strictly rural community, and people here speak of "The Radio" in the large sense, with an over-meaning. When they say "The Radio" they don't mean a cabinet, an electrical phenomenon, or a man in a studio, they refer to a pervading and somewhat godlike presence which has come into their lives and homes. It is a mighty attractive idol. After all, the church merely holds out the remote promise of salvation: the radio tells you if it's going to rain tomorrow.

EDUCATION

I have an increasing admiration for the teacher in the country school where we have a third-grade scholar in attendance. She not only undertakes to instruct her charges in all the subjects of the first three grades, but she manages to function quietly and effectively as a guardian of their health, their clothes, their habits, their mothers, and their snowball engagements. She has been performing this Augean task for twenty years and is both kind and wise. She cooks for the children on the stove that heats the room, and she can cool their passions or warm their soup with equal competence. She conceives their costumes, cleans up their messes, and shares their confidences. My boy already regards his teacher as his great friend, and I think tells her a great deal more than he tells us.

The shift from city school to country school was something we worried about quietly all last summer. I have always rather favored public school over private school, if only because in public school you meet a greater variety of children. This bias of mine, I suspect, is partly an attempt to justify my own past (I never knew anything but public schools) and partly an involuntary defense against getting kicked in the shins by a young ceramist on his way to the kiln. My wife was unacquainted with public schools, never having been exposed (in her early life) to anything more public than the washroom of Miss Winsor's. Regardless of our backgrounds, we both knew that the change in schools was something that concerned not us but the scholar himself. We hoped it would work out all right. In New York our son went to a medium-priced private institution with semi-progressive ideas of education, and modern plumbing. He learned fast, kept well, and we were satisfied. It was an electric, colorful, regimented existence with moments of pleasurable pause and giddy incident. The day the Christmas angel fainted and had to be carried out by one of the Wise Men was educational in the highest sense of the term. Our scholar gave imitations of it around the house for weeks afterward, and I doubt if it ever goes completely out of his mind.

His days were rich in formal experience. Wearing overalls and an old sweater (the accepted uniform of the private seminary), he sallied forth at morn accompanied by a nurse or a parent and walked (or was pulled) two blocks to a corner where the school bus made a flag stop. This flashy vehicle was as punctual as death: seeing us waiting at the cold curb, it would sweep to a halt, open its mouth, suck the boy in, and spring away with an angry growl. It was a good deal like a train picking up a bag of mail. At school the scholar was worked on for six or seven hours by half a dozen teachers and a nurse and was revived on orange juice in mid-morning. In a cinder court he played games supervised by an athletic instructor, and in a cafeteria he ate lunch worked out by a dietitian. He soon learned to read with gratifying facility and discernment and to make Indian weapons of a semi-deadly nature. Whenever one of his classmates fell low of a fever the news was put on the wires and there were breathless phone calls to physicians, discussing periods of incubation and allied magic.

In the country all one can say is that the situation is different and somehow more casual. Dressed in corduroys, sweatshirt, and short rubber boots, and carrying a tin dinner-pail, our scholar departs at crack of dawn for the village school, two and a half miles down the road, next to the cemetery. When the road is open and the car will start, he makes the journey by motor, courtesy of his old man. When the snow is deep or the motor is dead or both, he makes it on the hoof. In the afternoons he walks or hitches all or part of the way home in fair weather, gets transported in foul. The schoolhouse is a two-room frame building, bungalow type, shingles stained a burnt brown with weather-resistant stain. It has a chemical toilet in the basement and two teachers above stairs. One takes the first three grades, the other the fourth, fifth, and sixth. They have little or no time for individual instruction, and no time at all for the esoteric. They teach what they know themselves, just as fast and as hard as they can manage. The pupils sit still at their desks in class and do their milling around outdoors during recess.

There is no supervised play. They play cops and robbers (only they call it "Jail") and throw things at one another—snowballs in winter, rose hips in fall. It seems to satisfy them. They also construct darts, pinwheels, and "pick-up sticks" (jackstraws), and the school itself does a brisk trade in penny candy, which is for sale right in the classroom and which contains "surprises." The most highly prized surprise is a fake cigarette, made of cardboard, fiendishly lifelike.

The memory of how apprehensive we were at the beginning is still strong. The boy was nervous about the change too. The tension, on that first fair morning in September when we drove him to school, almost blew the windows out of the sedan. And when later we picked him up on the road, wandering along with his little blue lunch-pail, and got his laconic report "All right" in answer to our inquiry about how the day had gone, our relief was vast. Now, after almost a year of it, the only difference we can discover in the two school experiences is that in the country he sleeps better at night—and *that* probably is more the air than the education. When grilled on the subject of school-in-country *vs.* school-in-city, he replied that the chief difference is that the day seems to go so much quicker in the country. "Just like lightning," he reported.

ౙ

It is just a year ago as I write this that I made my spring visit to Peter Henderson in Cortlandt Street, home of Convolvulus Major and the early pea. I bought nineteen dollars' worth of seeds, flower and vegetable. It took the clerk almost an hour, opening and shutting the white drawers, to fish them out; together we studied the list, checked it for errors. Carrying the bundle home in the subway, I was struck with how heavy the seeds were—they weighed as much as a time bomb.

A negro came into the seed store while I was there. He was in clericals and seemed to be quite a fellow. "Give a penny to de Lawd!" he cried, addressing no one in particular. "Give a penny to de Lawd, who makes all dese wonderful seeds to jeminate!" He was a slick one and got a pretty good haul. I put all my money, however, into direct cultivation—the seeds themselves. They did well enough, and we are still eating them out of jars.

Now we're in New York again, for a visit, not just to consult with Peter Henderson but to get back into the good graces of the dentist and to catch up with the theater. I suppose there is no reason for not going to the dentist in the country, but teeth are like sunken reefs: you feel better about them if they are gone over by someone who possesses what the pilot book calls "local knowledge," someone who's been over them before. Also, dentistry is more impressive in town—what the rural man calls cleaning the teeth is called "prophylaxis" in New York.

Quite apart from teeth and dramaturgy and seed buying, it is necessary to come up to the town after a long spell in the country, for a period of privacy and rest. I don't get enough sleep in the country, as the days are too short for my enterprises, with the result that I rise early, go to bed late, and in general prolong the waking hours. And of course there is no privacy in rural surroundings, where a man can't even blow his nose without exciting the community. I thought at first I was going to mind this limelight terribly, this being stared at: the men working on the road, looking up, watching, the men in front of the store, in dooryards, old men coming in through the dusk with an armful of stovewood, stopping in their tracks to watch the car go by, women tending the hens, everywhere the fixed eye. I discovered, however, that the situation was instantly relieved as soon as I acquired the knack of staring back. You've got to stare back. Besides, after you've lived in the country a while you learn that keeping track of the comings and goings of one's friends and neighbors is a very sensible thing indeed, and that it cannot be set down to idle curiosity. Not a car or team passes my door now but I look up, check its speed and direction, identify the driver if possible, and guess the errand. This isn't mere gossip hunting, it is a valuable personal intelligence service. I used to waste hours of time hunting up people who, if I'd used my eyes and ears, I should have known were some place else. It's like war: you've got to have a map with pins. The location of the mail truck, the progress of the snow plow, the whereabouts of the expressman and the fish peddler—such information becomes vastly important. I find that keeping abreast of my neighbors' affairs has increased, not diminished, my human sympathies (if any); and when I get up in the morning and spy one man heading south on foot with a dog and shotgun, and another heading north with a sick child in a blue coupé, the pattern of the day becomes clear and I can conduct my own affairs more wisely and usefully than if I lacked that knowledge. Of course one's horizon tends to close in: in New York I rise and scan Europe in the *Times;* in the country I get up and look at the thermometer—a thoroughly self-contained point of view which, if it could infect everybody everywhere, would I am sure be the most salutary thing that could now happen to the world. My isolation is shortlived, however. An hour later I stop by the store to buy a package of soap chips and I hear the radio telling me the temperature in Providence, Rhode Island. Immediately the shell of my comfortable little world is rudely shattered and I shudder in sympathetic response to Rhode Island's raw mercurial destiny.

There was a time when only God could make a tree, but now John D. Rockefeller, Jr. can do it too. Our visit to New York happens to coincide with the arrival of the great elms along Fifth Avenue, those lovely seventy-foot trees that are springing full grown from the pavement in front of Radio City. I attended the first of the eight miracles and felt like a character in the Old Testament. Nelson Rockefeller was there wearing rubbers (although it was a dry night) and carrying a brief case. The last time I had seen him was at a groundbreaking, when Radio City was still a blueprint. He looked unchanged by the years (I hastily wondered if I did too) but was less camera-shy and more poised, now that the buildings were there, throwing their majestic weight in support of the whole visionary idea. The elm itself, at first horizontal on a truck, lay as though dead, but soon managed, with the help of a winch, to sit bolt upright and look around. Mr. Rockefeller leapt easily to the bole of earth, and the photographers lay down on their backs on the sidewalk for the angle shot that was to distinguish their art. It was the first time I had ever seen a man lie down on Fifth Avenue, although I once saw a fellow down in a fit.

A woman, passing, seeing that somebody was up to the prank of setting out a tree in the shopping district, remarked that she thought it was a mighty silly thing, a tree. "What do they want a tree for?" she said. "It will just be in the way."

I think elm-birth is the prettiest fairy tale in the city's wonderbook, for the big trees are delivered at night, when earth hangs down away from the light and fowls are stirring on their roosts. In all the long swing of time there has never been a fortnight such as this—these midnights when late strolling citizens come suddenly on a giant elm, arriving furtively in the marketplace and sliding into position for early risers to discover on their way to work.

A WEEK IN APRIL

SATURDAY. A full moon tonight, which made the dogs uneasy. First a neighbor's dog, a quarter of a mile away, felt the moon—he began shortly after dark, a persistent complaint, half longing. Then our big dog, whose supper had not sat well, took up the moonsong. I shut him in the barn where his bed is, but he kept up the barking, with an odd howl now and again; and I could hear him roaming round in there, answering the neighbor's dog and stirring up Fred, our dachshund and superintendent, who suddenly, from a deep sleep, roused up and pulled on his executive frown (as a man, waking, might hastily pull on a pair of trousers) and dashed out into the hall as though the moon were a jewel robber. The light lay in watery pools on lawn and drive. The house seemed unable to settle down for the night, and I felt like moaning myself, for there is something about a moon disturbing to man and dog alike.

Once, when I was a child, I waked from a bad dream to find moonlight pouring into the room, falling across my face like the flashlight of a prowler. I was frightened; the moon seemed an intruder in the bedroom. Since that night I have been uncomfortable on moon nights and have seen to it that the shade was drawn. I don't know what it is dogs feel, but it must be something very deep troubling them—perhaps an ancient intimation of good hunting.

Last night my neighbor C. died. He was here at the house in the forenoon, driving his truck. He mentioned that he wasn't feeling just good. Later, in the afternoon, he took a chill. Before midnight he was dead. C.'s death came just a few months after he had got his life fixed up to suit him—a common enough sequel to endeavor. After years of planning it, he built a new workshop last fall, his proper dream. I think the extra effort it took to get his life arranged to his liking was too much for his strength and brought on his death—a coincidence that, in milder form, happens to everyone.

Sunday. Woke to find the wind blowing from the sea, and the sky overcast. Three starlings sat gloomily in the Balm o' Gilead tree, awaiting better times, and in the plowed field some crows held a special meeting and took a vote. In an hour it was snowing.

Dameron, the lobster fisherman, stopped in tonight to return some books. He is the one book borrower I fully trust. He borrows more of my books than anyone ever has before, but he brings back more too, usually wrapped in paper and tied with a string—which is the proper way to transport a book in unsettled weather. Mrs. D. is one of the two people I know who have read *Joseph in Egypt.* I know many who own it, few who have read it.

Dameron stayed a while. He told me that at one time a great deal of clam bait for the Banks fishermen was dug here in this cove. An acre of clams used to be about the best crop any man could cultivate, but nowadays a man can dig a tide in and out and does well to make a dollar. Every tide was good for four to six dollars in the old days. D. says the gulls have ruined clamming: they eat the seed that the clammers leave—that is, the small clams that the rake turns up but that are too small to be harvested. The government protects gulls of course, but D. thinks gulls should be destroyed before they destroy us. Seals too. Seals are death to lobsters. Seals and gulls are the enemies to watch out for, in D.'s opinion, as well as Germany and Italy.

The rumor got round that I was running for the school board. (There was nothing to it.) D. tells me that it was a lucky thing I didn't run. "You would have been murdered." He said he heard a woodcock yesterday and would take me to where I can see its sky dance.

Monday. The cat, David, is lying beside me, a most unsatisfactory arrangement, as he gives me cat fever.

My sensitivity to cats defeats the whole purpose of a cat, which is to introduce a note of peace in a room.

Tuesday. News today from friends who are here in America from Vienna. They are able to stay one year, on a visitor's passport: but they say that one year sounds to them like eternity, after the day-to-day existence of European living. Although they are, in the phrase, Aryans, they are against the Hitler government; hopefully and patiently they await its end. So, they say, do the majority of the citizens of Vienna.

In Vienna the only topic of conversation is genealogy. You go out to visit friends and you spend the evening in the branches of their family tree. The matter of blood is so vital, no one can think of anything else. A writer whose wife's grandmother was a Jew is not permitted to write; a doctor whose father's half-sister lacked the Aryan stamp is not allowed to practice. "These fine people are dying," says my friend.

"But we mustn't talk about it. Spies are everywhere. We dare not speak of Vienna."

Wednesday. Today the warmth struck through for fair and reached the earth, the sun boring into the snow, the ditches alive with overflow and gurgle, the daylight strong and ample along the planks bridging the mud in the yard. Under the spruce boughs that overlay the borders, the first green shoots of snowdrops appeared, the indestructible. When I walked to the mailbox, a song sparrow placed his incomparable seal on the outgoing letters. Spring, however, began officially in the late afternoon when I went into the brooder house, thrust a handful of shavings into the stove and struck a match, starting the fire that must burn steadily and without interruption (dropping 5° a week) for six weeks, warming the two hundred and fifty chicks that are to hatch tomorrow, a hundred miles away, on Maundy Thursday.

Thursday. Today read in the paper about a plan the Catholics have for a sound hookup of schools in the Archdiocese of New York. According to the newspaper account, the plan is contingent on their finding a commercial sponsor. This was the most important item in the news, I thought, far outdistancing the day's aggression in Middle Europe. For although the parochial system is not the pattern for our American public schools, nevertheless, most children's diseases are contagious and I have no doubt this latest one is too. The desire to make one adult voice audible to all children, even though the expenses are best met by a commercial product, is too attractive to be denied for long. Such dissemination is inevitable, just as it was inevitable that one orchestra should serve a hundred hotel dining rooms and that music should be called Muzak. The expenses can be defrayed by the manufacturer of a licorice candy, who then automatically becomes a leading educational force in the nation, holding in his two hands the coveted gift of sound. Probably before these words reach print, the archdiocesan headquarters will be broadcasting direct to the classroom, and one more wall will have crumbled that once made a house. Instruction will be by experts—the invisible experts, speaking with the voice that is not a voice, delivering to the invisible pupil the canned lesson, courtesy of the advertised product.

One of the proponents of the Catholic communications system explained that it would be a most useful device in academic emergencies —as for instance in the case of an examination containing an unfair question being distributed to the schools. "Attention!" he said, pretending that he was already wired to the children. "There is an error in the test paper for 6B in arithmetic. Question 3, part 2, does not belong . . . etc."

There would then presumably be a slight pause for diocese identification, and a two-minute plug for licorice candy.

This emergency of the faulty examination paper and the unfair question is, I should think, just a taste of the greater emergencies that a government-sponsored sound system could cope with. For when the time comes the public educator's voice will be heard in the tiniest schoolhouse on the farthest hill: "Henceforth all children will read only from the Brown book, and will raise the right hand in allegiance to the Third American Realm, saying 'Hail Peabody!' "

I have been trying to think who would be the perfect sponsor for the American educational network, the nationwide hookup that would instruct all children from coast to coast, giving them the Word. I have decided that Wheaties is the perfect company, for Wheaties gives flashlights as premiums—and these lights might help the children find their way out of a room that had grown dark.

Friday. A letter this morning from John McNulty, my most satisfactory correspondent, as he writes infrequently and on matters that concern us both equally. His letter begins: "Dear Andy, Describe in detail the purchase and installation of a Welsbach mantle. In so doing, tell specifically of: (a) The carrying home of the Welsbach mantle and from what kind of store. (b) The kind of box it came in and the method of extraction from the box. (c) The putting of the mantle in place of the old one. (d) Describe the next steps and any attendant spectacle in connection therewith, which may have served to delight the onlookers. P.S. It so happens that on this, the eve of the invasion of Albania, I have spent the afternoon thinking of Welsbach mantles."

MOVIES

T HERE is no movie house in this town so I don't get to many pictures; but I keep in touch with Olympus by reading *Motion Picture* magazine and the daily papers. On the whole this is a higher type of entertainment than seeing the films—although I miss Tarzan and Lamour, and I am not getting ahead very fast with my study of trees in the movies, a work I have been engaged in for some years.

The newspapers of course keep one informed of the marriages, births, deaths, separations, divorces, and salaries of the stars. If Gable weds Lombard, I know about it. When Tone and Crawford reach the end of the road, I am informed. Separations and divorces are scented with the same delicate orange blossoms as marriages and elopements, the same romantic good fellowship. One of the most interesting accomplishments of the film community, it seems to me, is that it has made real for America the exquisite beauty of incompatibility. Divorce among the gods possesses the sweet, holy sadness that has long been associated with marriage among the mortals. There is something infinitely tender about the inability of an actor to get along with an actress.

When it is all over, and the decree is final, the two are even more attentive to each other, are seen oftener together, than ever before. It was a writer in *Motion Picture* who expressed the whole thing most eloquently. He was telling the inside story of the marriage of Hedy Lamarr and Gene Markey, a union that, however felicitous in other respects, was unfortunately not solemnized until after Mr. Markey's union and disunion with Joan Bennett, described as "Hollywood's perfect marriage," and until after the gift (to Miss Lamarr) of a five-thousand-dollar swimming pool by Mr. Reginald Gardiner, described simply as a five-thousand-dollar swimming pool. The writer is explaining how Mr. Markey, after being given his freedom by Miss Bennett, is again seen around Hollywood in the company of glamorous stars, but not really caring for them half as much as he still cared for his ex-wife. "In the finest Hollywood tradition," says the journalist, "they remain affectionate friends."

This tradition of post-marital affection, which is discernible everywhere, is having its effect, I do not doubt, on the culture of our land. Occasionally a divorce-court judge is heard pouting about it, but the girls and boys of America eat it up. Marriage is becoming just a sort of stepping-stone to the idyllic life that lies ahead for the graduates of the course; the wedding march is just a prelude to the larger music of the spirit that accompanies the communion between ex-spouses.

There is something else Hollywood has done and is doing. By its adherence, over so long a period of years, to a standard of living well in excess of anything known in the lives of its audience, it has at last communicated to its audience a feeling of actually living in this dream world and a conviction that the standards of this world are the norm. I noticed this phenomenon recently when I was watching a picture called "Dark Victory."

In this film a wealthy young girl named Judith, played by Miss Bette Davis, on discovering that she has only a few months to live, gives up her swank horsy existence on Long Island and goes to dwell peacefully in Vermont with her newly acquired husband, who is referred to as an "eminent doctor." This Vermont home is certainly a lovely place—nicely located and well kept up. But in one scene, when Judith was talking about how happy the new life was making her, she remarked, in approximately these words: "Why do people clutter up their lives with horses and things? There [in Long Island] I had everything and was miserable. Here I have nothing and am happy."

It is this jibe of hers about having "nothing" that I propose to explore. Remember, she was in a remodeled New England farmhouse. At the moment of making the remark she was standing in a kitchen that had been modernized at considerable expense. It contained a large new electric refrigerator worth somewhere around two hundred and fifty dollars, or maybe three hundred. It also had an enamelled stove and (I think) a Monel metal sink. These things run into money, as anybody knows who has ever tried it. With her in the kitchen were two domestic servants and two English setters. One of the maids was a sort of housekeeper, the other was a cook. I should guess that the housekeeper was pulling down around eighty dollars a month; and she was earning every penny of it, too, for in another scene Judith came plunging in with a tray of nicely prepared food and gave the order to throw it away because she had absent-mindedly taken it into the doctor's laboratory and exposed it to germs. That sort of rough-and-tumble living is tough on housekeepers and they put up with it only if well paid.

All right, we'll say eighty a month for her. The cook was probably getting sixty-five.

Now let's look at the rest of this set-up that Miss Judith tossed off as "nothing." The dwelling was a large Colonial farmhouse that had been restored to make it modern and comfortable. With Vermont the way it is today, full of writers and artists, such houses have quite a market value. I would say that the taxes on the house and land might come to around two or three hundred dollars a year. The insurance would be another two hundred. There would probably be a ninety-dollar annual interest charge on a fifteen-hundred-dollar mortgage that the eminent doctor was carrying either because he had to or because somebody had once told him that a house was more saleable if it had a small mortgage on it.

As for food, heat, light, repairs, etc., I have jotted them down, and on an annual basis they might easily add up to something like this, judging from the glimpses I had of the house, grounds, servants, and general tenor of life there:

Taxes	$ 250.00
Insurance	200.00
Interest	90.00
Heat (15 tons stove and nut mixed @ $16 per ton)	240.00
Light and power (water pump)	184.00
Telephone and telegraph	116.00
Housekeeper	960.00
Cook	780.00
Gardener-chauffeur	1,100.00
Repairs	210.00
Seeds, fertilizer, grain	200.00
Registration on two motor cars, taxes, insurance	120.00
Household furnishings	100.00
Movies, books, medical journals, etc.	200.00
Charity	150.00
Postage, stationery	362.00
Miscellaneous	500.00
Life insurance	350.00
Travel	400.00
Food	1,900.00
Lumber, hardware	60.00
Liquor	150.00
Personal taxes	1,500.00
Veterinary	10.00
Meat, biscuits for 2 setters	45.00

Laundry, dry cleaning	470.00
Gas and oil	346.00
Clothes	700.00
Total	$11,693.00

I have worked out the above budget carefully and believe it to be conservative and in keeping with what I know of New England property and New England standards in households where there are three in help. So it would seem fairly safe to say that this little establishment where Miss Judith was finding such peace in having "nothing" was costing somebody (probably her eminent doctor) somewhere between eleven and twelve thousand dollars a year.

The interesting and really absorbing thing, to my mind, is that to the members of the audience, sitting there with me in the dark, suffering with Judith through her ill health and sharing her joy in her "simple" surroundings—to them the illusion was perfect: this twelve-thousand-dollar country estate for a brief cinematic moment *was* indeed nothing. It represented the ultimate simplicity, the absolute economic rock bottom. It is disturbing to realize that even after we have been reduced to Hollywood's low, we are still rolling in the sort of luxury that eventually destroyed Rome.

A BOSTON TERRIER

I WOULD like to hand down a dissenting opinion in the case of the Camel ad that shows a Boston terrier relaxing. I can string along with cigarette manufacturers to a certain degree, but when it comes to the temperament and habits of terriers, I shall stand my ground.

The ad says: "A dog's nervous system resembles our own." I don't think a dog's nervous system resembles my own in the least. A dog's nervous system is in a class by itself. If it resembles anything at all, it resembles the Consolidated Edison Company's power plant. This is particularly true of Boston terriers, and if the Camel people don't know that, they have never been around dogs.

The ad says: "But when a dog's nerves tire, he obeys his instincts—he relaxes." This, I admit, is true. But I should like to call attention to the fact that it sometimes takes days, even weeks, before a dog's nerves tire. In the case of terriers it can run into months.

I knew a Boston terrier once (he is now dead and, so far as I know, relaxed) whose nerves stayed keyed up from the twenty-fifth of one June to the sixth of the following July, without one minute's peace for anybody in the family. He was an old dog and he was blind in one eye, but his infirmities caused no diminution in his nervous power. During the period of which I speak, the famous period of his greatest excitation, he not only raised a type of general hell that startled even his closest friends and observers, but he gave a mighty clever excuse. He said it was love.

"I'm in love," he would scream. (He could scream just like a hurt child.) "I'm in love, and I'm going *crazy.*"

Day and night it was all the same. I tried everything to soothe him.

I tried darkness, cold water dashed in the face, the lash, long quiet talks, warm milk administered internally, threats, promises, and close confinement in remote locations. At last, after about a week of it, I went down the road and had a chat with the lady who owned the object of our terrier's affection. It was she who finally cleared up the situation.

"Oh," she said, wearily, "if it's that bad, let him out."

I hadn't thought of anything as simple as that myself, but I am a creature of infinite reserve. As a matter of record, it turned out to be not so simple—the terrier got run over by a motor car one night while returning from his amorous adventures, suffering a complete paralysis of the hip but no assuagement of the nervous system, and the little Scotty bitch returned to Washington, D.C., and a Caesarian section.

I am not through with the Camel people yet. Love is not the only thing that can keep a dog's nerves in a state of perpetual jangle. A dog, more than any other creature, it seems to me, gets interested in one subject, theme, or object, in life, and pursues it with a fixity of purpose that would be inspiring to Man if it weren't so troublesome. One dog gets absorbed in one thing, another dog in another. When I was a boy there was a smooth-haired fox terrier (in those days nobody ever heard of a fox terrier that *wasn't* smooth-haired) who became interested, rather late in life, in a certain stone. The stone was about the size of an egg. As far as I could see, it was like a million other stones—but to him it was the Stone Supreme.

He kept it with him day and night, slept with it, ate with it, played with it, analyzed it, took it on little trips (you would often see him three blocks from home, trotting along on some shady errand, his stone safe in his jaws). He used to lie by the hour on the porch of his house, chewing the stone with an expression half tender, half petulant. When he slept he merely enjoyed a muscular suspension: his nerves were still up and around, adjusting the bed clothes, tossing and turning.

He permitted people to throw the stone for him and people would. But if the stone lodged somewhere he couldn't get to he raised such an uproar that it was absolutely necessary that the stone be returned, for the public peace. His absorption was so great it brought wrinkles to his face, and he grew old before his time. I think he used to worry that somebody was going to pitch the stone into a lake or a bog, where it would be irretrievable. He wore off every tooth in his jaw, wore them right down to the gums, and they became mere brown vestigial bumps. His breath was awful (he panted night and day) and his eyes were alight with an unearthly zeal. He died in a fight with another dog. I have always suspected it was because he tried to hold the stone in his mouth all through the battle. The Camel people will just have to take my word for it: that dog was a living denial of the whole theory of relaxation. He was a paragon of nervous tension, from the moment he first laid eyes on his slimy little stone till the hour of his death.

The advertisement speaks of the way humans "prod" themselves to endeavor—so that they keep on and on working long after they should quit. The inference is that a dog never does that. But I have a dog right now that can prod himself harder and drive himself longer than any human I ever saw. This animal is a dachshund, and I shall spare you the long dull inanities of his innumerable obsessions. His particular study (or mania) at the moment is a black-and-white kitten that my wife gave me for Christmas, thinking that what my life needed was something else that could move quickly from one place in the room to another. The dachshund began his research on Christmas eve when the kitten arrived "secretly" in the cellar, and now, five months later, is taking his Ph.D. still working late at night on it, every night. If he could write a book about that cat, it would make *Middletown* look like the work of a backward child.

I'll be glad to have the Camel people study this animal in one of his relaxed moods, but they will have to bring their own seismograph. Even curled up cozily in a chair, dreaming of his cat, he quivers like an aspen.

THE WORLD OF TOMORROW

I wasn't really prepared for the World's Fair last week, and it certainly wasn't prepared for me. Between the two of us there was considerable of a mixup.

The truth is that my ethmoid sinuses broke down on the eve of Fair Day, and this meant I had to visit the Fair carrying a box of Kleenex concealed in a copy of the *Herald Tribune*. When you can't breathe through your nose, Tomorrow seems strangely like the day before yesterday. The Fair, on its part, was having trouble too. It couldn't find its collar button. Our mutual discomfort established a rich bond of friendship between us, and I realize that the World's Fair and myself actually both need the same thing—a nice warm day.

The road to Tomorrow leads through the chimney pots of Queens. It is a long, familiar journey, through Mulsified Shampoo and Mobilgas, through Bliss Street, Kix, Astring-O-Sol, and the Majestic Auto Seat Covers. It winds through Textene, Blue Jay Corn Plasters; through Musterole and the delicate pink blossoms on the fruit trees in the ever-hopeful back yards of a populous borough, past Zemo, Alka-Seltzer, Baby Ruth, past Iodent and the Fidelity National Bank, by trusses, belts, and the clothes that fly bravely on the line under the trees with the new little green leaves in Queens' incomparable springtime. Suddenly you see the first intimation of the future, of man's dream—the white ball and spire—and there is the ramp and the banners flying from the pavilions and the brave hope of a glimpsed destination. Except for the Kleenex, I might have been approaching the lists at Camelot, for I felt that perhaps here would be the tournament all men wait for, the field of honor, the knights and the ladies under these bright banners, beyond these great walls. A closer inspection, however, on the other side of the turnstile, revealed that it was merely Heinz jousting with Beech-Nut—the same old contest on a somewhat larger field, with accommodations for more spectators, and better facilities all round.

The place is honeycombed with streets—broad, gusty streets, with tulips bending to the gale and in the air the sound of distant choirs. There are benches all along for the weary and the halt, but though science's failure to cope with the common cold had embittered my heart and slowed my step, the ball and spire still beckoned me on. It was not particularly surprising, somehow, when at last after so many months of anticipation and after so much of actual travail and suffering, when at last I arrived, paper handkerchiefs in hand, at the very threshold of Tomorrow, when I finally presented myself there at the base of the white phallus, face to face with the girl in the booth behind the little bars behind the glass window with the small round hole, expectant, ready, to see at last what none had ever seen, Tomorrow—it was not, somehow, particularly surprising to see the window close in my face and hear a bald contemporary voice say, "There will be a short wait of a few minutes, please."

That's the way it is with the future. Even after Grover Whalen has touched it with his peculiar magic, there is still a short wait.

The lady behind me was not surprised either, but she seemed apprehensive.

"Anything wrong in there?" she asked testily.

"No, Madam," said the guard. "Just some minor difficulty in the Perisphere."

The lady was not satisfied. "Is there anything in there to scare you?" she asked, looking at the Perisphere rolling motionless in the gray vapors that have hung for centuries above the Flushing Meadows.

"No, Madam," he replied. "The longest escalator in the world moves very slowly."

I clocked the wait. It was twenty minutes. Not bad, for a man who's waited all his life.

Much depends, when you ascend into the interior of the Perisphere, on the moment at which you happen to arrive at the top of the escalator and teeter off in a sidewise direction onto one of the two great moving rings that turn endlessly above the City of Man. If you arrive just as day has faded into night, and without any advance information about being shunted from an upward moving stairway onto a sidewise moving balcony, the experience is something that stays with you. I was lucky. The City of Man, when it first broke on my expectant sight, was as dark as a hall bedroom, and for a second or two I didn't catch on that I myself was in motion—except celestially. If I hadn't recognized Mr. Kaltenborn's electric voice, I would have felt lonelier than perhaps the situation warranted.

"As day fades into night," he said, with the majestic huskiness that science has given speech, "each man seeks home, for here are children, comfort, neighbors, recreation—the good life of the well-planned city."

Trembling in violet light beneath me, there it was—the towers, now to the adjusted eye dimly visible—"a brave new world [such a big voice you have, Grandpa!] built by united hands and hearts. Here brain and brawn, faith and courage, are linked in high endeavor as men march on toward unity and peace. Listen! From office, farm, and factory they come with joyous song."

I don't know how long it takes in there. Ten minutes, maybe. But when I emerged from the great ball, to begin the descent of the Helicline, it had come on to rain.

To be informative about the Fair is a task for someone with a steadier nose than mine. I saw all as in a dream, and I cherish the dream and have put it away in lavender. The great size of the place has been a temporary disadvantage these first few days, when the draftiness, the chill, the disorder, the murky bath of canned reverence in which many of the commercial exhibits are steeped have conspired to give the place the clammy quality of a seaside resort in mid-November. But this same great size, come the first warm, expansive days, will suddenly become the most valuable asset of the Fair. The refurbished ash heap, rising from its own smolder, is by far the biggest show that has ever been assembled on God's earth, and it is going to be a great place to go on a fine summer night, a great place to go on a sunny spring morning. After all, nobody can embrace Culture in a topcoat.

The architecture is amusing enough, the buildings are big enough, to give the visitor that temporary and exalted feeling of being in the presence of something pretty special, something full of aspiration, something that at times is even exciting. And the exhibition is cock-eyed enough to fall, as it naturally does, in line with all carnivals, circuses, and wonderlands. The buildings (there are two hundred of them) have color and a certain dash, here and there a certain beauty. They are of the type that shows up best in strong light. Like any Miami Beach cottage, they look incredibly lovely in sunlight, adorned with a necklace of vine shadow against a clear white skin, incredibly banal and gloom-infested on cloudy days, when every pimple of plaster shows up in all its ugly pretension. The designers of this twentieth-century bazaar have been resourceful and have kept the comfort of the people in mind. Experience has taught them much. The modern technique of sight-seeing is this: you sit in a chair (wired for sound) or stand on a platform (movable, glass-embowered) and while sitting, standing, you are brought mysteriously and reverently into easy view of what you want to see. There is no shoving in the exhibit hall of Tomorrow. There is no loitering and there is usually no smoking. Even in the girl show in the amusement area, the sailor is placed in a rather astringent attitude, behind glass, for the adoration of the female form. It is all rather serious-minded, this World of Tomorrow, and extremely impersonal. A ride on the Futurama of General Motors induces approximately the same emotional response as a trip through the Cathedral of St. John the Divine. The countryside unfolds before you in five-million-dollar micro-loveliness, conceived in motion and executed by Norman Bel Geddes. The voice is a voice of utmost respect, of complete religious faith in the eternal benefaction of faster travel. The highways unroll in ribbons of perfection through the fertile and rejuvenated America of 1960—a vision of the day to come, the unobstructed left turn, the vanished grade crossing, the town that beckons but does not impede, the millennium of passionless motion. When night falls in the General Motors exhibit and you lean back in the cushioned chair (yourself in motion and the world so still) and hear (from the depths of the chair) the soft electric assurance of a better life—the life that rests on wheels alone—there is a strong, sweet poison that infects the blood. I didn't want to wake up. I liked 1960 in purple light, going a hundred miles an hour around impossible turns ever onward toward the certified cities of the flawless future. It wasn't till I passed an apple orchard and saw the trees, each blooming under its own canopy of glass, that I perceived that even the General Motors dream, as dreams so often do, left some questions unanswered about the future. The apple tree of Tomorrow, abloom under its inviolate hood, makes you stop and wonder. How will the little boy climb it? Where will the little bird build its nest?

I made a few notes at the Fair, a few hints of what you may expect of Tomorrow, its appointments, its characteristics.

In Tomorrow, people and objects are lit not from above but from below. Trees are lit from below. Even the cow on the rotolactor appears to be lit from below—the buried flood lamp illuminates the distended udder.

In Tomorrow one voice does for all. But it is a little unsure of itself; it keeps testing itself; it says, "Hello! One, two, three, four. Hello! One, two, three, four."

Rugs do not slip in Tomorrow, and the bassinets of newborn infants are wired against kidnappers.

There is no talking back in Tomorrow. You are expected to take it or leave it alone. There are sailors there (which makes you feel less lonely) and the sound of music.

The living room of Tomorrow contains the following objects: a broadloom carpet, artificial carnations, a television radio victrola incessantly producing an image of someone or something that is somewhere else, a glass bird, a chrome steel lamp, a terracotta zebra, some veneered book cabinets containing no visible books, another cabinet out of which a small newspaper slowly pours in a never-ending ribbon, and a small plush love seat in the shape of a new moon.

In Tomorrow, most sounds are not the sounds themselves but a memory of sounds, or an electrification. In the case of a cow, the moo will come to you not from the cow but from a small aperture above your head.

Tomorrow is a little on the expensive side. I checked this with my cabdriver in Manhattan to make sure. He was full of praise about the Fair but said he hadn't seen it and might, in fact, never see it. "I hack out there, but I got it figured that for me and the wife to go all through and do it right—no cheapskate stuff—it would break the hell out of a five-dollar bill. In my racket, I can't afford it."

Tomorrow does not smell. The World's Fair of 1939 has taken the body odor out of man, among other things. It is all quite impersonal, this dream. The country fair manages better, where you can hang over the rail at the ox-pulling and smell the ox. It's not only that the sailors can't get at the girls through the glass, but even as wholesome an exhibit as Swift's Premium Bacon produces twenty lovesick maidens in a glass pit hermetically sealed from the ultimate consumer.

The voice of Mr. Kaltenborn in the City of Man says, "They come with joyous song," but the truth is there is very little joyous song in the Fair grounds. There is a great deal of electrically transmitted joy, but very little spontaneous joy. Tomorrow's music, I noticed, came mostly from Yesterday's singer. In fact, if Mr. Whalen wants a suggestion from me as to how to improve his show (and I am reasonably confident he doesn't), it would be to snip a few wires, hire a couple of bands, and hand out ticklers. Gaiety is not the keynote in Tomorrow. I finally found it at the tag end of a chilly evening, far along in the Amusement Area, in a tent with some colored folks. There was laughing and shouting there, and a beautiful brown belly-dancer.

Another gay spot, to my surprise, was the American Telephone & Telegraph Exhibit. It took the old Telephone Company to put on the best show of all. To anyone who draws a lucky number, the company grants the privilege of making a long-distance call. This call can be to any point in the United States, and the bystanders have the exquisite privilege of listening in through earphones and of laughing unashamed. To understand the full wonder of this, you must reflect that there are millions of people who have never either made or received a long-distance call, and that when Eddie Pancha, a waiter in a restaurant in El Paso, Texas, hears the magic words "New York is calling . . . Go ahead, please," he is transfixed in holy dread and excitement. I listened for two hours and ten minutes to this show, and I'd be there this minute if I were capable of standing up. I had the good luck to be listening at the earphone when a little boy named David Wagstaff won the toss and put in a call to tell his father in Springfield, Mass., what a good time he was having at the World's Fair. David walked resolutely to the glass booth before the assembled kibitzers and in a tiny, timid voice gave the operator his call, his little new cloth hat set all nicely on his head. But his father wasn't there, and David was suddenly confronted with the necessity of telling his story to a man named Mr. Henry, who happened to answer the phone and who, on hearing little David Wagstaff's voice calling from New York, must surely have thought that David's mother had been run down in the B. M. T. and that David was doing the manly thing.

"Yes, David," he said, tensely.

"Tell my father this," began David, slowly, carefully, determined to go through with the halcyon experience of winning a lucky call at the largest Fair the world had yet produced.

"Yes, David."

"We got on the train, and . . . and . . . had a nice trip, and at New Haven, when they were taking off the car and putting another car on, it was *awfully* funny because the car gave a great—big—BUMP!"

Then followed David's three-minute appreciation of the World of Tomorrow and the Citadel of Light, phrased in the crumbling remnants of speech that little boys are left with when a lot of people are watching and when their thoughts begin to run down and when Perispheres begin to swim mistily in time. Mr. Henry—the invisible and infinitely surprised Mr. Henry—maintained a respectful and indulgent silence. I don't know what he was thinking, but I would swap the Helicline for a copy of his attempted transcription of David's message to his father.

My own memory of the Fair, like David's, has begun to dim. From so much culture, from so much concentrated beauty and progress, one can retain only a fragment. I remember the trees at night, shivering in their burlap undershirts, the eerie shadows clinging to the wrong side of their branches. I remember the fountains playing in the light, I remember the girl who sat so still, so clean, so tangible, producing with the tips of her fingers the synthetic speech—but the words were not the words she wanted to say, they were not the words that were in her mind. I remember the little old Stourbridge Lion, puffing in under its own steam to start the railroads bursting across America. But mostly the Fair has vanished, leaving only the voice of little David Wagstaff and the rambling ecstasy of his first big trip away from home; so many million dollars spent on the idea that our trains and our motorcars should go fast and smoothly, and the child remembering, not the smoothness, but the great—big—BUMP.

So (as the voice says) man dreams on. And the dream is still a contradiction and an enigma—the biologist peeping at bacteria through his microscope, the sailor peeping at the strip queen through binoculars, the eyes so watchful, and the hopes so high. Out in the honky-tonk section, in front of the Amazon show, where the ladies exposed one breast in deference to the fleet, kept one concealed in deference to Mr. Whalen, there was an automaton—a giant man in white tie and tails, with enormous rubber hands. At the start of each show, while the barker was drumming up trade, a couple of the girls would come outside and sit in the robot's lap. The effect was peculiarly lascivious—the extra-size man, exploring with his gigantic rubber hands the breasts of the little girls, the girls with their own small hands (by comparison so small, by comparison so terribly real) restrainingly on his, to check the unthinkable impact of his mechanical passion. Here was the Fair, all fairs, in pantomime; and here the strange mixed dream that made the Fair: the heroic man, bloodless and perfect and enormous, created in his own image, and in his hand (rubber, aseptic) the literal desire, the warm and living breast.

WALDEN

Miss Nims, take a letter to Henry David Thoreau. Dear Henry: I thought of you the other afternoon as I was approaching Concord doing fifty on Route 62. That is a high speed at which to hold a philosopher in one's mind, but in this century we are a nimble bunch.

On one of the lawns in the outskirts of the village a woman was cutting the grass with a motorized lawn mower. What made me think of you was that the machine had rather got away from her, although she was game enough, and in the brief glimpse I had of the scene it appeared to me that the lawn was mowing the lady. She kept a tight grip on the handles, which throbbed violently with every explosion of the one-cylinder motor, and as she sheered around bushes and lurched along at a reluctant trot behind her impetuous servant, she looked like a puppy who had grabbed something that was too much for him. Concord hasn't changed much, Henry; the farm implements and the animals still have the upper hand.

I may as well admit that I was journeying to Concord with the deliberate intention of visiting your woods; for although I have never knelt at the grave of a philosopher nor placed wreaths on moldy poets and have often gone a mile out of my way to avoid some place of historical interest, I have always wanted to see Walden Pond. The account that you left of your sojourn there is, you will be amused to learn, a document of increasing pertinence; each year it seems to gain a little headway, as the world loses ground. We may all be transcendental yet, whether we like it or not. As our common complexities increase, any tale of individual simplicity (and yours is the best written and the cockiest) acquires a new fascination; as our goods accumulate, but not our well-being, your report of an existence without material adornment takes on a certain awkward credibility.

My purpose in going to Walden Pond, like yours, was not to live cheaply or to live dearly there, but to transact some private business with the fewest obstacles. Approaching Concord, doing forty, doing forty-five, doing fifty, the steering wheel held snug in my palms, the highway held grimly in my vision, the crown of the road now serving me (on the right-hand curves), now defeating me (on the left-hand curves), I began to rouse myself from the stupefaction a day's motor journey induces. It was a delicious evening, Henry, when the whole body is one sense and imbibes delight through every pore, if I may coin a phrase. Fields were richly brown where the harrow, drawn by the stripped Ford, had lately sunk its teeth; pastures were green; and overhead the sky had that same everlasting great look that you will find on page 144 of the Oxford pocket edition. I could feel the road entering me, through tire, wheel, spring, and cushion; shall I not have intelligence with earth too? Am I not partly leaves and vegetable mold myself?—a man of infinite horsepower, yet partly leaves.

Stay with me on 62 and it will take you into Concord. As I say, it was a delicious evening. The snake had come forth to die in a bloody S on the highway, the wheel upon its head, its bowels flat now and exposed. The turtle too had come up to cross the road and die in the attempt, its hard shell smashed under the rubber blow, its intestinal yearning (for the other side of the road) forever squashed. There was a sign by the wayside that announced that the road had a "cotton surface." You wouldn't know what that is, but neither, for that matter, did I. There is a cryptic ingredient in many of our modern improvements—we are awed and pleased without knowing quite what we are enjoying. It is something to be traveling on a road with a cotton surface.

The civilization round Concord today is an odd distillation of city, village, farm, and manor. The houses, yards, fields look not quite suburban, not quite rural. Under the bronze beech and the blue spruce of the departed baron grazes the milch goat of the heirs. Under the portecochère stands the reconditioned station wagon; under the grape arbor sit the puppies for sale. (But why do men degenerate ever? What makes families run out?)

It was June and everywhere June was publishing her immemorial stanza; in the lilacs, in the syringa, in the freshly edged paths and the sweetness of moist beloved gardens, and the little wire wickets that preserve the tulips' front. Farmers were already moving the fruits of their toil into their yards, arranging the rhubarb, the asparagus, the strictly fresh eggs on the painted stands under the little shed roofs with the patent shingles. And though it was almost a hundred years since you had taken your ax and started cutting out your home on Walden Pond, I was interested to observe that the philosophical spirit was still alive in Massachusetts: in the center of a vacant lot some boys were assembling the framework of a rude shelter, their whole mind and skill concentrated in the inauspicious helter-skeleton of studs and rafters. They too were escaping from town, to live naturally, in a rich blend of savagery and philosophy.

That evening, after supper at the inn, I strolled out into the twilight to dream my shapeless transcendental dreams and see that the car was locked up for the night (first open the right front door, then reach over, straining, and pull up the handles of the left rear and the left front till you hear the click, then the handle of the right rear, then shut the right front but open it again, remembering that the key is still in the ignition switch, remove the key, shut the right front again with a bang, push the tiny keyhole cover to one side, insert key, turn, and withdraw). It is what we all do, Henry. It is called locking the car. It is said to confuse thieves and keep them from making off with the laprobe. Four doors to lock behind one robe. The driver himself never uses a laprobe, the free movement of his legs being vital to the operation of the vehicle; so that when he locks the car it is a pure and unselfish act. I have in my life gained very little essential heat from laprobes, yet I have ever been at pains to lock them up.

The evening was full of sounds, some of which would have stirred your memory. The robins still love the elms of New England villages at sundown. There is enough of the thrush in them to make song inevitable at the end of day, and enough of the tramp to make them hang round the dwellings of men. A robin, like many another American, dearly loves a white house with green blinds. Concord is still full of them.

Your fellow-townsmen were stirring abroad—not many afoot, most of them in their cars; and the sound they made in Concord at evening was a rustling and a whispering. The sound lacks steadfastness and is wholly unlike that of a train. A train, as you know who lived so near the Fitchburg line, whistles once or twice sadly and is gone, trailing a memory in smoke, soothing to ear and mind. Automobiles, skirting a village green, are like flies that have gained the inner ear—they buzz, cease, pause, start, shift, stop, halt, brake, and the whole effect is a nervous polytone curiously disturbing.

As I wandered along, the toc toc of ping pong balls drifted from an attic window. In front of the Reuben Brown house a Buick was drawn up. At the wheel, motionless, his hat upon his head, a man sat, listening to

Amos and Andy on the radio (it is a drama of many scenes and without an end). The deep voice of Andrew Brown, emerging from the car, although it originated more than two hundred miles away, was unstrained by distance. When you used to sit on the shore of your pond on Sunday morning, listening to the church bells of Acton and Concord, you were aware of the excellent filter of the intervening atmosphere. Science has attended to that, and sound now maintains its intensity without regard for distance. Properly sponsored, it goes on forever.

A fire engine, out for a trial spin, roared past Emerson's house, hot with readiness for public duty. Over the barn roofs the martins dipped and chittered. A swarthy daughter of an asparagus grower, in culottes, shirt, and bandanna, pedalled past on her bicycle. It was indeed a delicious evening, and I returned to the inn (I believe it was your house once) to rock with the old ladies on the concrete veranda.

Next morning early I started afoot for Walden, out Main Street and down Thoreau, past the depot and the Minuteman Chevrolet Company. The morning was fresh, and in a bean field along the way I flushed an agriculturalist, quietly studying his beans. Thoreau Street soon joined Number 126, an artery of the State. We number our highways nowadays, our speed being so great we can remember little of their quality or character and are lucky to remember their number. (Men have an indistinct notion that if they keep up this activity long enough all will at length ride somewhere, in next to no time.) Your pond is on 126.

I knew I must be nearing your woodland retreat when the Golden Pheasant lunchroom came into view—Sealtest ice cream, toasted sandwiches, hot frankfurters, waffles, tonics, and lunches. Were I the proprietor, I should add rice, Indian meal, and molasses—just for old time's sake. The Pheasant, incidentally, is for sale: a chance for some nature lover who wishes to set himself up beside a pond in the Concord atmosphere and live deliberately, fronting only the essential facts of life on Number 126. Beyond the Pheasant was a place called Walden Breezes, an oasis whose porch pillars were made of old green shutters sawed into lengths. On the porch was a distorting mirror, to give the traveler a comical image of himself, who had miraculously learned to gaze in an ordinary glass without smiling. Behind the Breezes, in a sun-parched clearing, dwelt your philosophical descendants in their trailers, each trailer the size of your hut, but all grouped together for the sake of congeniality. Trailer people leave the city, as you did, to discover solitude and in any weather, at any hour of the day or night, to improve the nick of time; but they soon collect in villages and get bogged deeper in the mud than ever. The camp behind Walden Breezes was just rousing itself to the morning. The ground was packed hard under the heel, and the sun came through the clearing to bake the soil and enlarge the wry smell of cramped housekeeping. Cushman's bakery truck had stopped to deliver an early basket of rolls. A camp dog, seeing me in the road, barked petulantly. A man emerged from one of the trailers and set forth with a bucket to draw water from some forest tap.

Leaving the highway I turned off into the woods toward the pond, which was apparent through the foliage. The floor of the forest was strewn with dried old oak leaves and *Transcripts*. From beneath the flattened popcorn wrapper (*granum explosum*) peeped the frail violet. I followed a footpath and descended to the water's edge. The pond lay clear and blue in the morning light, as you have seen it so many times. In the shallows a man's waterlogged shirt undulated gently. A few flies came out to greet me and convoy me to your cove, past the No Bathing signs on which the fellows and the girls had scrawled their names. I felt strangely excited suddenly to be snooping around your premises, tiptoeing along watchfully, as though not to tread by mistake upon the intervening century. Before I got to the cove I heard something that seemed to me quite wonderful: I heard your frog, a full, clear *troonk,* guiding me, still hoarse and solemn, bridging the years as the robins had bridged them in the sweetness of the village evening. But he soon quit, and I came on a couple of young boys throwing stones at him.

Your front yard is marked by a bronze tablet set in a stone. Four small granite posts, a few feet away, show where the house was. On top of the tablet was a pair of faded blue bathing trunks with a white stripe. Back of it is a pile of stones, a sort of cairn, left by your visitors as a tribute I suppose. It is a rather ugly little heap of stones, Henry. In fact the hillside itself seems faded, browbeaten; a few tall skinny pines, bare of lower limbs, a smattering of young maples in suitable green, some birches and oaks, and a number of trees felled by the last big wind. It was from the bole of one of these fallen pines, torn up by the roots, that I extracted the stone that I added to the cairn—a sentimental act in which I was interrupted by a small terrier from a nearby picnic group, who confronted me and wanted to know about the stone.

I sat down for a while on one of the posts of your house to listen to the bluebottles and the dragonflies. The invaded glade sprawled shabby and mean at my feet, but the flies were tuned to the old vibration. There were the remains of a fire in your ruins, but I doubt that it was yours; also two beer bottles trodden into the soil and become part of earth. A young oak had taken root in your house, and two or three ferns, unrolling like the ticklers at a banquet. The only other furnishings were a DuBarry pattern sheet, a page torn from a picture magazine, and some crusts in wax paper.

Before I quit I walked clear round the pond and found the place where you used to sit on the northeast side to get the sun in the fall, and the beach where you got sand for scrubbing your floor. On the eastern side of the pond, where the highway borders it, the State has added dressing rooms for swimmers, a float with diving towers, drinking fountains of porcelain, and rowboats for hire. The pond is in fact a State Preserve, and carries a twenty-dollar fine for picking wild flowers, a decree signed in all solemnity by your fellow-citizens Walter C. Wardwell, Erson B. Barlow, and Nathaniel I. Bowditch. There was a smell of creosote where they had been building a wide wooden stairway to the road and the parking area. Swimmers and boaters were arriving; bodies plunged vigorously into the water and emerged wet and beautiful in the bright air. As I left, a boatload of town boys were splashing about in mid-pond, kidding and fooling, the young fellows singing at the tops of their lungs in a wild chorus:

> Amer-ica, Amer-ica, God shed his grace on thee,
> And crown thy good with brotherhood
> From sea to shi-ning sea!

I walked back to town along the railroad, following your custom. The rails were expanding noisily in the hot sun, and on the slope of the roadbed the wild grape and the blackberry sent up their creepers to the track.

The expense of my brief sojourn in Concord was:

Canvas shoes	$1.95	
Baseball bat	.25	} gifts to take back to a boy
Left-handed fielder's glove	1.25	
Hotel and meals	4.25	
In all	$7.70	

As you see, this amount was almost what you spent for food for eight months. I cannot defend the shoes or the expenditure for shelter and food: they reveal a meanness and grossness in my nature that you would find contemptible. The baseball equipment, however, is the kind of impediment with which you were never on even terms. You must remember that the house where you practiced the sort of economy that I respect was haunted only by mice and squirrels. You never had to cope with a shortstop.

HOT WEATHER

The sound of victrola music right after breakfast gives the summer day a loose, footless feeling, the sort of inner sadness I have experienced on the outskirts of small towns on Sunday afternoon, or in the deserted city during a holiday, or on beaches where the bathhouses smelled of sour towels and yesterday's levity. Morning is so closely associated with brisk affairs, music with evening and day's end, that when I hear a three-year-old dance tune crooned upon the early air while shadows still point west and the day is erect in the saddle, I feel faintly decadent, at loose ends, as though I were in the South Seas—a beachcomber waiting for a piece of fruit to fall, or for a brown girl to appear naked from a pool.

*   *   *

Asterisks? So soon?

*   *   *

It is a hot-weather sign, the asterisk. The cicada of the typewriter, telling the long steaming noons. Don Marquis was one of the great exponents of the asterisk. The heavy pauses between his paragraphs, could they find a translator, would make a book for the ages.

*   *   *

Don knew how lonely everybody is. "Always the struggle of the human soul is to break through the barriers of silence and distance into companionship. Friendship, lust, love, art, religion—we rush into them pleading, fighting, clamoring for the touch of spirit laid against our spirit." Why else would you be reading this fragmentary page—you with the book in your lap? You're not out to learn anything, certainly. You just want the healing action of some chance corroboration, the soporific of spirit laid against spirit. Even if you read only to crab about everything I say, your letter of complaint is a dead give-away: you are unutterably lonely or you wouldn't have taken the trouble to write it.

* * *

How contagious hysteria and fear are! In my henhouse are two or three jumpy hens, who, at the slightest disturbance, incite the whole flock to sudden panic—to the great injury, nervously and sometimes physically, of the group. This panic is transmitted with great rapidity; in fact, it is almost instantaneous, like the wheeling of pigeons in air, which seem all to turn and swoop together as though controlled electrically by a remote fancier.

* * *

The cells of the body co-operate to make the man; the men co-operate to make the society. But there is a contradiction baffling to biologist and layman alike. On the day last spring that I saw a flight of geese passing over on their way to the lonely lakes of the north (a co-operative formation suggesting a tactical advantage imitated by our air corps)—on that same day cannibalism broke out among my baby chicks and I observed the brutality with which the group will turn upon an individual, literally picking his guts out. This is the antithesis of co-operation—a contrariness not unobserved in our own circles. (I recently read of a member of an actors' union biting another actor quite hard. I believe it was over some difference in the means of co-operation.)

* * *

"How are you going to keep from getting provincial?" asked one of our friends quite solemnly. It was such a sudden question, I couldn't think of any answer, so just let it go. But afterward I wondered how my friend, on his part, was going to keep from getting metropolitan.

As a matter of fact the provinces nowadays are every bit as lurid, in their own way, as the centers of culture. One of the farm owners here— a very rich man who up until quite recently owned herds and flocks for the sheer hell of associating with animals—sent his registered Guernseys on a tour of the fairs last fall. When the cows returned home heaped with glory they were met at the station by a trumpeter and led triumphantly through town in a pompous parade that conquerors of old would have envied.

All sorts of things go on in this provincial existence. To the north of us, photographers in airplanes have been making a vast aërial picture map of the country, showing every fence and lane. Eventually the whole nation will be so mapped. Individual maps are already available; a farmer can send in to Washington and they will send him a picture showing how his place looks from three miles up.

And I see by the paper that a hundred million parasites have been turned loose in the State this summer, to war on the spruce sawfly—a challenge to the balance of nature that seems rather alarming to a man who hardly dares shoot a crow for fear of upsetting the fine adjustment in the world of birds and insects, predator and prey. How could I become provincial, with parasites being loosed against the foe? I am in the very center of everything.

*   *   *

There is furthermore slight chance of my becoming provincial *this* summer, because I am raising a baby seagull and there isn't time. A young gull eats twice his own weight in food every ten minutes, and if he doesn't get it he screams.

The gull was a present from Mr. Dameron, who wore an odd look of guilt on his face as he approached, that evening, proffering the chick in a pint ice-cream container as tentatively as though it were a bill for labor. The occupant (about the size of a billiard ball) took one look at me, stretched out his stubby wings, and cried: "Daddy!" I must say I haven't failed him.

He was so tiny, so recently shell-girt, that I put him with a broody hen, thinking she might adopt him. Nothing ever came of that brief connection. The gull wanted me, not a hen. I imagine the nest seemed stuffy to him after the windblown, fog-drenched island of his nativity. I asked Mr. Dameron what to feed him. "I dunno," he replied, "but I don't think you can upset a gull's stomach."

I began cautiously with a tiny piece of hamburger. It was the merest beginning. In the last three weeks he has swallowed a mixture of foods that would sicken you to listen to. (His favorite dish is chicken gizzards chopped with clams, angle worms, and laying mash.) He has eaten ten thousand clams—of my own digging—and still screams accusingly every time I go by. He has drained my strength, yet somehow it all seems worth while. A mature gull in flight is simple beauty. Some day this child of mine is going to be stretching his wings and a gentle puff will come along and he will take off. The pleasure of seeing my worms and gizzards translated into perfect flight will be my strange reward. I just hope I live that long.

*   *   *

A note from my garage this morning, saying that my oil was changed at 7839 and that it was time I came in to have the crankcase drained. "You've got enough to think about," the note said, "without trying to remember when your car needs its next Mobilubrication."

It is true, we all have much to think about. I used to try to remember about the oil, used to try to change it according to mileage on the car, but not any more. Now I change oil ritualistically, four times a year, on the summer and winter solstices and the spring and fall equinoxes. They are the dates I keep with my car. It seems to work all right; yet what a falling off the centuries have seen in men's customs. The first day of spring was once the time for taking the young virgins into the fields, there in dalliance to set an example in fertility for Nature to follow. Now we just set the clock an hour ahead and change the oil in the crankcase.

CAMP MEETING

Over in the next county the Methodists have a camp ground in a clump of woods near East Machias. They were in session there for about a week, and I went over on Saturday for the *pièce de résistance*—Dr. Francis E. Townsend (himself) of California. I had long wanted to see the author of America's favorite plan, and there he was, plain as day, right under the GOD IS LOVE sign.

It was a peaceful spot, though it gave one a sultry, hemmed-in feeling, as hardwood dingles often do. There was a ticket booth, where I paid my quarter; and beyond was a lane opening out into the *al fresco* temple where about six hundred people were gathered to hear the good news. They were Methodist farmers and small-town merchants and their Methodist wives and children and dogs, Townsendites from Townsend Club Number One of East Machias, pilgrims from all over the State, honest, hopeful folks, their faces grooved with the extra lines that come from leading godly, toilsome lives. The men sat stiffly in the dark-blue suits that had carried them through weddings, funerals, and Fair days. In a big circle surrounding the temple were the cottages (seventy or eighty of them), little two-story frame shacks, set ten or a dozen feet apart, each with its front porch, its stuffy upstairs bedroom, and its smell from the kitchen. Beyond, in a nobler circle, were the backhouses, at the end of the tiny trails. The whole place, even with hymns rising through the leafy boughs, had the faintly disreputable air that pervades any woodland rendezvous where the buildings stand unoccupied for most of the year, attracting woodpeckers, sneak thieves, and lovers in season.

On the dais, behind some field flowers, sat the Doctor, patiently awaiting his time—a skinny, bespectacled little savior, with a big jaw, like the Tin Woodman. He had arrived by plane the night before at the Bangor airport a hundred miles away, and had driven over that morning for the meeting. As I sat down a voice was lifted in prayer, heads were bowed. The voice came from a loudspeaker suspended from the branch of an elm, and the speaker was talking pointedly of milk and honey. When he quit, Dr. Townsend's henchman, a baldish fellow with a businesslike manner, took the stand and introduced the man who needed no introduction, Dr. Francis E. Townsend, of California, the world's greatest humanitarian. We all rose and clapped. Children danced on the outskirts, dogs barked, and faces appeared in the windows of some of the nearest cottages. The Doctor held out his hands for silence. He stood quietly, looking round over the assemblage. And then, to the old folks with their troubled, expectant faces, he said, simply:

"I like you people very much."

It was like a handclasp, a friendly arm placed round the shoulder. Instantly his listeners warmed, and smiled, and wriggled with sudden newfound comfort.

"I have come nearly four thousand miles to see you," continued the Doctor. "You look like good Methodists, and I like that. I was raised in a Methodist family, so I know what it means."

He spoke calmly, without any platform tricks, and he sounded as though this was the first time he had ever expounded Townsendism. In words of one syllable he unfolded the plan that he had conceived, the plan that he knew would work, the plan he promised to see enacted into law, so that all people might enjoy equally the good things of this life.

"The retirement of the elders is a matter of concern to the entire population." Grizzly heads nodded assent. Old eyes shone with new light.

"In a nation possessed of our natural resources, with great masses of gold and money at our command, it is unthinkable that conditions such as exist today should be tolerated. There is something radically wrong with any political philosophy which permits this to exist. Now, then, how did it come about?"

Dr. Townsend explained how it had come about. Flies buzzed in the clearing. The sun pierced the branches overhead, struck down on the folding music stands of the musicians, gleamed on the bare thighs of young girls in shorts, strolling with their fellows outside the pale of economics. The world, on this hot Saturday afternoon, seemed very old and sad, very much in need of something. Maybe this Plan was it. I never heard a milder-mannered economist, nor one more fully convinced of the worth and wisdom of his proposal. I looked at the audience, at the faces. They were the faces of men and women reared on trouble, and now they wanted a few years of comfort on earth, and then to be received into the lap of the Lord. I think Dr. Townsend wanted this for them: I'm sure *I* did.

"Business is stymied," murmured the Doctor. "Almost half the population is in dire want. Sixty millions of people cannot buy the products of industry." The Doctor's statistics were staggering and loose-jointed, but his tone was quietly authoritative. There could be small room for doubt.

He spoke disparagingly of the New Deal, and knocked all the alphabetical schemes for employing idle men. "Do you want to be taxed for these useless and futile activities?"

His audience shook their heads.

And all the while he spoke, the plan itself was unfolding—simply, logically. A child could have understood it. Levy a two per cent tax on the gross business of the country and divide the revenue among persons over sixty years of age, with the one stipulation that they spend the money ($200 a month) within a certain number of days.

"And mind you," said the Doctor, with a good-natured grin, "we don't care a rap what you spend it for!"

The old folks clapped their hands and winked at one another. They were already buying pretty things, these Methodists, were already paying off old cankerous debts.

"We want you to have new homes, new furniture, new shoes and clothes. We want you to travel and go places. You old folks have earned the right to loaf, and you're going to do it luxuriously in the near future. The effect on business, when all this money is put into circulation, will be tremendous. Just let us have two billion dollars to distribute this month, and see what happens!"

The sound of the huge sum titivated the group; two billion dollars flashed across the clearing like a comet, trailing a wispy tail of excitement, longing, hope.

"It may even be three," said the Doctor, thoughtfully, as though the possibility had just occurred to him. "America has the facilities, all we need is the sense to use them."

He said he was reminded of a story in the old McGuffey's Reader. The one about the ship flying a distress signal, and another ship came to its assistance. "Get us water!" shouted the captain. "We are perishing of thirst."

"Dip up and drink, you fools!" answered the captain of the other ship. "You're in the mouth of the Amazon River."

"Friends," said the good Doctor, "we are in the mouth of the Amazon River of Abundance. But we haven't the sense to dip up and drink."

It was a nice story and went well.

Suddenly the Doctor switched from words of promise to words of threat. Lightly, with bony fingers, he strummed the strings of terror. If we're going to save this democracy of ours (he said), we shall have to begin soon. You've read about strikes in the great industrial centers; in a very brief time you will read of riots. And when rioting starts, it will be an easy matter for someone to seize the armed forces of the country and put them to his own use. This has happened in Europe. It can happen here.

The glade darkened ominously. Trees trembled in all their limbs. The ground, hard-packed under the Methodist heel, swam in the vile twilight of Fascist doom. Still the little Doctor's voice droned on—calm, full of humility, devoid of theatrics. Just the simple facts, simply told.

And then the vexatious question of money to carry on with. The audience shifted, got a new grip on their seats with their behinds. The ancient ceremony of plate-passing was a familiar and holy rite that had to be gone through with. The Doctor carefully disclaimed any personal ambitions, financial or political. "I don't want a fortune," he said, confidentially. "I mean that. I don't seek wealth. For one thing, it might ruin my fine son. But it does take money to educate people to a new idea. Give us a penny a day and we'll educate the next Congress."

A joke or two, to restore amiability, another poke at Uncle Sam, another mention of the need for funds to carry on with, and the speech was over.

It had been an impressive performance. Most speeches lack the sincerity the Doctor had given his; not many speeches are so simply made and pleasantly composed. It had been more like a conversation with an old friend. I had listened, sitting there near the musicians, with all the sympathy that within me lay, and (I trust) with an open mind. Even a middle-aged hack has his moments of wanting to see the world get along. After all, this was no time for cynicism; most of what Dr. Townsend had said, God knows, was true enough. If anybody could devise a system for distributing wealth more evenly, more power to him. One man's guess was as good as another's. Well, pretty nearly as good. I pocketed the few scribbled notes I had made and gave myself over to a mood of summer afternoon despondency and world decay.

The chairman rose and announced that the meeting would be thrown open to questions, but that the time was short, so please speak right up. It was at this point that Dr. Francis E. Townsend (of California) began quietly to come apart, like an inexpensive toy. The questions came slowly, and they were neither very numerous nor very penetrating. Nor was there any heckling spirit in the audience: people were with him, not against him. But in the face of inquiry, the Doctor's whole manner changed. He had apparently been through this sort of thing before and was as wary as a squirrel. It spoiled his afternoon to be asked anything. Details of Townsendism were irksome in the extreme—he wanted to keep the Plan simple and beautiful, like young love before sex has reared its head. And now he was going to have to answer a lot of nasty old questions.

"How much would it cost to administer?" inquired a thrifty grandmother, rising to her feet.

The Doctor frowned. "Why, er," he said. (This was the first "er" of the afternoon.) "Why, not a great deal. There's nothing about it, that is, there's no reason why it needs to cost much." He then explained that it was just a matter of the Secretary of the Treasury making out forty-eight checks each month, one to each State. Surely that wouldn't take much of the Secretary's time. Then these big checks would be broken up by the individual State administrators, who would pay out the money to the people over sixty years of age who qualified. "We're not going to have any administrative problems to speak of, at all," said the Doctor, swallowing his spit. The little grandmother nodded and sat down.

"Can a person get the pension if they hold property?" inquired an old fellow who had suddenly remembered his home and his field of potatoes.

"Yes, certainly," replied the Doctor, shifting from one foot to the other. "But we *do* have a stipulation; I mean, in our plan we are going to say that the money shall not go to anybody who has a gainful pursuit." An uneasy look crossed the farmer's face: very likely he was wondering whether his field of potatoes was gainful. Maybe his potato bugs would stand him in good stead at last. Things already didn't look so simple.

"How much bookkeeping would it mean for a business man?" asked a weary capitalist.

"Bookkeeping?" repeated the Doctor vaguely. "Oh, I don't think there will be any trouble about bookkeeping. It is so simple. Every business man just states what his gross is for the thirty-day period, and two per cent of it goes to pay the old people. In the Hawaiian Islands they already have a plan much like mine in operation. It works beautifully, and I was amazed, when I was there, at how few people it took to administer it. No, there'll be no difficulty about bookkeeping."

"How will the Townsend Plan affect foreign trade?" asked an elderly thinker on Large Affairs.

Dr. Townsend gave him a queer look—not exactly hateful, but the kind of look a parent sometimes gives a child on an off day.

"Foreign trade?" he replied, somewhat weakly. "Foreign trade? Why should we concern ourselves with foreign trade?" He stopped. But then he thought maybe he had given short measure on that one, so he told a story of a corn-flakes factory, and all the corn came from some foreign country. What kind of way was that—buying corn from foreigners?

Next question: "Would a person receiving the pension be allowed to use it to pay off a mortgage?"

Answer: "Yes. Pay your debts. Let's set our government a good example!" (Applause.)

And now a gentleman down front—an apple-cheeked old customer with a twinkle: "Doctor, would buying a drink count as spending your money?"

"A drink?" echoed the Doctor. Then he put on a hearty manner. "Why, if anybody came to me and wanted to drink himself into an early grave with money from the fund, I'd say, 'Go to it, old boy!' " There was a crackle of laughter, but the Doctor knew he was on slippery footing. "Don't misunderstand me," he put in. "Let's not put too many restrictions on morality. The way to bring about temperance in this world is to bring up our young sons and daughters decently, and teach them the evils of abuse. [Applause.] And now, friends, I must go. It has been a most happy afternoon."

The meeting broke up. Townsendites rose and started down the aisles to shake hands reverently with their chief. The chairman announced a take of eighty dollars and three cents. Life began to settle into its stride again. Pilgrims filed out of the pews and subsided in rocking chairs on the porches of the little houses. Red and white paper streamers, festooning the trees, trembled in the fitful air, and soft drinks began to flow at the booth beyond the Inner Circle. The Doctor, waylaid by a group of amateur photographers, posed in front of an American flag and then departed in a Dodge sedan for the airport—a cloud-draped Messiah, his dream packed away in a briefcase for the next performance. On the porch of a cottage called "Nest o'Rest" three old ladies rocked and rocked and rocked. And from a score of rusty stovepipes in the woods rose the first thick coils of smoke from the kitchen fires, where America's housewives, never quite giving up, were laboriously preparing one more meal in the long, long procession. The vision of milk and honey, it comes and goes. But the odor of cooking goes on forever.

SECOND WORLD WAR

Saw a cat hunting in a field as I drove the little boy in to school this morning and thought how devious and long is the preparation before the son of man can go out and get his own dinner. Even when a scholar has the multiplication table at his tongue's end, it is a long way to the first field mouse.

ใ•

Six days a week, eight months of the year, in war or in peace, Dameron goes down the bay in the morning and hauls his traps. He gets back about noon, his white riding-sail showing up first around the point, then the hull, then the sound of the engine idling and picking up again as he pulls his last two traps. Sometimes, if the sun is right, we can see pinwheels of light as he hurls crabs back into the sea, spinning them high in air. And sometimes, if he has had a good catch of lobsters, we can hear him singing as he picks up his mooring. It is a song of victory, the words of which I've never made out; but from this distance it sounds like a hymn being clowned.

He is as regular as a milk train, and his comings and goings give the day a positive quality that is steadying in a rattle-brained world. In fog we can't see him but we can hear his motor, homebound in the white jungle; and then the creak of oar in lock, tracing the final leg of his journey, from mooring to wharf. He has no watch, yet we can set ours by his return. (We could set it by his departure too if we were up—but he leaves at six o'clock.)

I went with him in his boat the other day, to see what it was like, tending seventy traps. He told me he's been lobstering twenty-five or six years. Before that he worked in yachts—in the days when there were yachts—and before that in coasting schooners. "I liked coasting fine," he said, "but I had to get out of yachting." A look of honest reminiscent fright came into his face. "Yachting didn't agree with me. Hell, I was mad the whole time."

"You know," he explained, pushing a wooden plug into a lobster's claw, "there's a lot o' them yacht owners who haven't much use for the common man. That's one thing about lobstering—it gives you a hell of an independent feeling."

I nodded. Dameron's whole boat smelled of independence—a rich blend of independence and herring bait. When you have your own boat you have your own world, and the sea is anybody's front yard. Old Dameron, pulling his living out of the bay at the end of twelve fathoms of rope, was a crusty symbol of self-sufficiency. He cared for nobody, no not he, and nobody cared for him. Later in the fall he would haul his boat out on his own beach, with his own tackle. He would pull the engine out, take it up through the field to his woodshed, smear it with oil, and put it to bed in a carton from the grocer's. On winter evenings he would catch up on his reading, knit his bait pockets, and mend his traps. On a nasty raw day in spring he would get the tar bucket out and tar his gear and hang it all over the place on bushes, like the Monday wash. Then he would pay the State a dollar for a license and seventy-five cents for an official measuring stick and be ready for another season of fishing, another cycle of days of fog, wind, rain, calm, and storm.

Freedom is a household word now, but it's only once in a while that you see a man who is actively, almost belligerently free. It struck me as we worked our way homeward up the rough bay with our catch of lobsters and a fresh breeze in our teeth that this was what the fight was all about. This was it. Either we would continue to have it or we wouldn't, this right to speak our own minds, haul our own traps, mind our own business, and wallow in the wide, wide sea.

Letter from a reader:

"We too came [to the country] to lead the simple life; we too started with 36 pullets—which were all eaten by rats; we too had a spring with eels and frogs where one could go to muse and be eaten by mosquitoes. We had them all, and have lost them quite completely. What we have now is some 8,000 chickens of varying ages and susceptibilities to coccidiosis, less income, twice or thrice as much work, and perpetual worry. We have become as accustomed to the peace and quiet of the country as you say one does to the roar of the Sixth Avenue El, and winding lanes are no more to us now than turnstiles in our urgent comings and goings to banks and grain mills and osteopaths.

"I see from what you say . . . that you sense your danger, but it is one thing to sense it, and another to avoid it. . . . It's too late for us to turn back, but we hate to see others of our kind blithely tripping into the pit."

I got that letter quite a while ago, and have kept it around to study over, maybe even to answer. Nothing could be truer than that one's relationship to the country changes by the simple fact of one's living with it continuously; but so, for that matter, does one's relationship to the woman one lives with, or to the plumbing and heating system. (I am fresh from a bout with the kitchen drain, and though the purity of our relationship is forever lost, I now feel the solid pleasure of close companionship with my own pipes. I may smell like a dishmop, but I have grown acquainted with my sink's peculiar qualities and know its kinks.) My correspondent was probably asking too much of life if he expected to find in eight thousand chickens the original rapture of his first encounter with a pipping shell. I know all about the subtle erosion of character that takes place when one progresses, in imperceptible steps, from the keeping of pets to the managing of a commercial poultry operation. I haven't stood up under it any too well. A year ago, when I was ready to house my pullets, I wrote that there was to be no purge, no culling of the little flock; I said I would put them all into the laying house without discrimination and let them eat their fill and lay if they chose. I am now compelled to record that this is not what happened. Of the 37 pullets, I put only 35 in the house, leaving two sad-looking sisters in a small pen in the orchard and later selling them (without mentioning that they were my culls) to a mysterious little man who arrived unheralded in a driving shower of rain to buy a rooster. By this simple but calculating deed I lost forever my amateur standing with a hen. Now, a whole year later, with four times the number of birds under my protection, I make no bones about culling. Only the physically fit survive in my tyranny. As in the Third Reich, in my henhouse the individual must be sacrificed to the good of the whole. I am degraded by this practice, but I fall in line just the same. Some day I may revolt; some day, instead of destroying a sick hen lest she infect the others, I shall destroy the others and nurse the sick one back to glowing health, thus re-establishing my own self-respect.

I am in fact very grateful for this letter from the man with eight thousand chickens, although long before I got it I sensed what he so eloquently expresses. I don't know whether I came to the country to live the simple life; but I am now engaged in a life vastly more complex than anything the city has to offer. It has its compensations. Even through the demoralizing days of my expanding husbandry I have never quite lost my feeling for an egg, as such. I built a new henhouse this summer, to keep my mind off Europe, and I have chosen for its wall motto those fertile lines of Clarence Day's:

O who that ever lived and loved
Can look upon an egg unmoved?

I haven't yet had to be rubbed by an osteopath, but my trips to the grain mill are more numerous than they once were. This week, because of the invasion of Poland, the darn stuff is up thirty cents a bag.

ह•

War comes to each of us in his own fashion. Early on that Sunday when England and France finally lost their patience, wishing to put my affairs in order, I cleaned my comb and brush, pouring a few drops of household ammonia into the bowl of water, running the comb through the brush, then brushing the comb with a nail brush. At breakfast there was a house guest, in a bathrobe. She approached the war intellectually, through Versailles.

After breakfast I went to the garage and sorted some nails, putting the clapboard nails together in a bunch, the six-penny nails together, the boarding nails together, in cans. The blade of my jackknife being stiff, I eased it with a few drops of penetrating oil. We decided we would go to church—a solemn place for a solemn hour. The preparation was hurried (as though we were organizing a picnic on the spur of the moment). Church is at 10:30 here. The little boy was in tears about having to wear the blue suit, yet wanting to go. I wore a hat I found in a closet. The minister, a young fellow I recently sold some old hens to for a dollar apiece, said he believed the meek would inherit the earth. We sang "Am I a soldier of the Cross, Are there no foes for me to fight?" The storekeeper passed the plate. When we got back home I went out to the barn to fix some chum bait, and somebody came out after a while and announced: "Dinner, and the King." The words came with painful slowness, as we all sat and chewed. Thus began the second war for democracy.

ह•

Some day, if I ever get around to it, I would like to write the definitive review of America's most fascinating book, the Sears Roebuck catalogue. It is a monumental volume, and in many households is a more powerful document than the Bible. It makes living in the country not only practical but a sort of perpetual night-before-Christmas.

When you buy something in a store, you see it with your eyes and it has a prosaic and sometimes devastating reality. When you order something from Sears, it exists only in the mind's eye, sugar-coated, triple-reinforced, and surrounded by an aura of light.

Around these parts the firm is known as "Sears and Roebuck." The "and" is always used. It just got in there, somehow, and never got out.

I've been looking over the special "Back-to-School and Harvest Event" catalogue, a small edition of the main catalogue. The title conjures up all the standard autumnal visions: crisp days, button chrysanthemums, football, russet apples, children playing in school yards under yellowing maples. One forgets that the years march on. The first three items that I happened to strike were (1) some high-potency vitamin capsules "to ward off winter ills"; (2) a jitterbug shoe for young men, called "Swingaroo"—"plenty swishy with lots of funny sayings printed on the natural color uppers"; and (3) a harvest radio designed for smart moderns, in the shape of a rocket.

I guess as the years roll on and the wars roll on, we shall have to forget Currier and Ives and take the strange new harvest as it comes. This fall the crepe soles of the Swingaroo ($1.98) will, as the catalogue predicts, bounce with every drumbeat when autumn's in the groove. Even the drums seem likely to be promoted from a swingtime band to a fife and drum corps. I note that one of the funny sayings printed on the natural color uppers is "I'll mow ya down." You can't get ahead of Sears.

FIRST WORLD WAR

I keep forgetting that soldiers are so young. I keep thinking of them as my age, or Hitler's age. (Hitler and I are about the same age.) Actually, soldiers are often quite young. They haven't finished school, many of them, and their heads are full of the fragile theme of love, and underneath their bluster and swagger everything in life is coated with that strange beautiful importance that you almost forget about because it dates back so far. The other day some French soldiers on the western front sent a request to a German broadcasting studio asking the orchestra to play *"Parlez moi d'amour."* The station was glad to oblige, and all along the Maginot Line and the Siegfried Line the young men were listening to the propaganda of their own desire instead of attending to the fight. So few people speak to the young men of love any more, except the song writers and scenarists. The leaders speak always of raw materials and *Lebensraum.* But the young men in uniforms do not care much for raw materials (except tobacco) and they are thinking of *Liebestraum,* and are resolving their dream as best they can. I am trying hard to remember what it is like to be as young as a soldier.

When war was getting under way in 1914, I was in high school. I was translating Caesar, studying ancient history, working with algebraic equations, and drawing pictures of the bean, which is a dicotyledonous seed, and of the frog, an amphibian. In those days I kept a journal. My life and activities and thoughts were dear to me, and I took the trouble to set them down. I still have this journal, and the outbreak of the present war has started me going through its pages to refresh my memory. The entries are disappointingly lacking in solid facts. Much of the stuff is sickening to read, but I have a strong stomach and a deep regard for the young man that was I. Everyone, I believe, has this tolerance and respect if he is worth anything, and much of life is unconsciously an attempt to preserve and perpetuate this youth, this strange laudable young man. Though my journal is a mass of horrid little essays. moral in tone and definitely on the pretty side, I cannot bring myself to throw it away. Just now I like to consult it to rediscover what the impact of a world war meant to one young fellow in the 1914–1918 period—how important each step seemed, what preposterous notions I held, how uncertain and groping and unscathed I was.

At first, before the United States entered the fray, the War seemed to mean mighty little. In those years, war was remote, implausible—a distant noise or threat, something that was ahead perhaps, like college or marriage or earning one's living, but not near enough to be of any immediate concern. In the early pages of my journal I was thinking and writing about keeping pigeons, about going skating, about the comings and goings of people on the same block with us. After a couple of years of it the War begins to take shape and I begin swelling with large thoughts. On March 16, 1917, carefully described as a "rainy Saturday," I pasted into my journal an editorial from the *Globe* on the emancipation of Russia, which spoke of the sunlight of freedom shining over the Russian steppes. "Father thinks it will be an important factor in the ultimate results of the war," I wrote. "I have always wondered what the purpose—in the bigger sense—of the war was. Perhaps this is it."

Russian freedom probably occupied my mind upward of ten minutes. The next entry in the journal was concerned with plans for a canoe trip down the Housatonic (which I never took) and with the rehearsals of a Pinero farce in which I acted the part of an English servant.

On Palm Sunday, 1917, with a bad cold in the head, I reported the advent of springtime, and the flags flying from houses all along the block. "War and springtime are being heralded with one breath and the thoughts of the people are in confusion." My own thoughts, however, were not in any particular confusion. They came to an orderly, if not monumental, focus in the composition, on the same page, of a love poem of twenty-four lines, celebrating an attachment to a girl I had met on an ice pond.

On April 3rd, with America still three days away from war, I speculated on the possibility of another canoe trip, for August—a journey on which I proposed to carry "a modified form of miner's tent." Apparently I was spending more time reading sporting goods catalogues and dreaming of the woods than studying news accounts of hostilities in Europe. I was also considering the chances of getting a summ r job. Next fall I was to enter college.

Springtime and wartime! Of the two, springtime clearly took precedence. I was in love. Not so much actively as retrospectively. The memory of winter twilights, when the air grew still and the pond cracked and creaked under our skates, was enough to sustain me; and the way the trails of ice led off into the woods, and the little fires burning along the shore. It was enough, that spring, to remember what a girl's hand felt like, suddenly ungloved in winter. I never tried to pursue the acquaintanceship off the pond. Without ice and skates, there seemed no reason for her existence. Lying on my back on the settee in the hall, I listened to Liszt on the pianola.

I wrote half a dozen nature poems, got a haircut, read *Raymond* by Sir Oliver Lodge, and heard one of Billy Sunday's workers in church on the text: "Follow me and I will make you fishers of men." One of my friends enlisted in the Naval Reserve. Another became wireless operator on a mosquito boat. Dimly, dimly I became aware that something was going on.

> April 26, 1917. I suppose this little Journal ought to be filled with war talk, because that is what people are all thinking about now. It is believed that there will be a shortage of food soon, and so the State is supervising a "Farm Cadet" movement.

I joined the cadets that July, and served in Hempstead, L. I. It never seemed to me that the farmers were particularly pleased with the arrangement.

> May 14, 1917. Yesterday I heard Billy Sunday deliver his booze sermon.
>
> May 27, 1917. I don't know what to do this summer. The country is at war and I think I ought to serve. Strange that the greatest war in the history of the world is now going on, and it is hard to get men to enlist.
>
> June 3, 1917. I'm feeling extraordinarily patriotic tonight, after having read the papers. I think tomorrow I shall buy a Liberty Bond and get a job on a farm. The struggle in Europe isn't over by any means, and so much history is being made every minute that it's up to every last one of us to see that it's the right kind of history. It is my firm conviction that only the unstinted giving of time, money, and resources of the American people can save this world from its most terrible doom.
>
> June 7, 1917. I guess there is no place in the world for me. I've been trying to get a job since Monday, and have failed. Yesterday afternoon I applied at G——'s School of Popular Music for a job playing piano at a summer hotel in the Catskills. This was in answer to an ad that I had seen in the paper. When I got there, I couldn't play the kind of music he gave me, so I started for the

door, but not before he had handed me a circular showing how, by his method, ragtime piano playing might be taught in 20 lessons. However, when I arrived home, I discovered that the little town in the Catskills was not on the map. I don't weigh enough to join the Army, and a job on a farm would probably be hard on my hay fever. I want to join the American Ambulance Corps, but I'm not eighteen and I've never had any experience driving a car, and Mother doesn't think I ought to go to France. So here I am, quite hopeless, and undeniably jobless. I think either I must be very stupid or else I lack faith in myself and in everything else.

My morale at this point had sunk so low that I pasted into the journal a clipping called "Foolishness of Worry," a reprint from *The White Road to Verdun,* by Kathleen Burke.

June 10, 1917. Tomorrow I am going to the city to find out facts concerning the American Ambulance Corps. Somewhere in Europe there must be a place for me, and I would rather save men than destroy them. Father and Lillian have just come back from the city where they went in a fruitless attempt to hear Billy Sunday.

July 5, 1917. I can think of nothing else to do but to run away. My utter dependence galls me, and I am living the life of a slacker, gorging my belly with food which others need. I wish I were old enough to be drafted.

July 11, 1917. My birthday! Eighteen, and still no future! I'd be more contented in prison, for there at least I would know precisely what I had to look forward to.

September 4, 1917. Tonight I have been reading about aviation tests—I think I would like to fly, but as with everything else I have thought of, I lack the necessary qualifications.

Leaving the war behind, I packed my suitcase and went off to college, itself no small adventure. I took along the strip of bicycle tape which she and I used to hang onto in our interminable circuit of the pond the winter before. I was homesick. After the football games on Saturday afternoons I would walk down the long streets into the town, shuffling through the dry leaves in the gutters, past children making bonfires of the piles of leaves, and the spirals of sweet, strong smoke. It was a golden fall that year, and I pursued October to the uttermost hill.

October 13, 1917. My English prof said the other day that bashfulness was a form of vanity, the only difference being that vanity is the tendency to overestimate your worth, and bashfulness to underestimate it; both arising from the overindulgence of self-consciousness. The days are getting colder.

November 10, 1917. The war still continues in this its third autumn. [I couldn't even count—it was the *fourth* autumn.] Our troops are in the trenches on a relatively quiet sector of the west front. Just the other day I read that the first American Sammy had been killed. More are being trained by experienced officers in back of the line, and still more are in this country training in the several cantonments for the National Draft Army. It is a wonderful thing. The Russians have again overthrown their new-born republic and are showing themselves incapable of meeting the crises that are being put in their way. The Italian Army has been outguessed by the combined Austro-German forces and has retreated to the Piave River. The French and English lines show little change. Now, after more than three years of intensive warfare, Germany stands, solidly defying three-fourths of the countries of the world. They all look to us as the only hope of salvation, and I firmly believe that, slow as we are to foresee danger and loath as we seem to be to give up our pleasures and amusements, once in the struggle for fair we will live up to the examples set by our sturdy forefathers and will shed the last drop of blood for the great cause for which the whole world is now shedding blood.

November 21, 1917. I've been feeling sick for the past week and I think I must have consumption. If I have, I will leave college and travel for my health.

December 25, 1917. I have just finished *Over the Top* by Arthur Guy Empey. On the last page of his narrative he confirms what I have always sensed as truth, that strength comes surely at the critical hour, that anticipation far exceeds the realization of the utmost trial; and that man, despite his recent gentle breeding and flabby ways, when called, is not found wanting, nor untrue when facing death.

December 31, 1917. I find myself thinking the same thoughts and wishing the same wishes that I thought and wished this night a year ago. I'm wondering if I'm any nearer my ultimate goal—certainly still a long way off inasmuch as the goal itself is an unknown quantity.

February 18, 1918. The talk is of Universal Peace after the war—everlasting peace through the medium of an international council. Nations will be ruled by brotherly love and divine principle, arms will be laid down forever and man will return to the ploughshare. Bosh!

March 26, 1918. Sunday was the beginning of the immense German offensive along a 50-mile front which is threatening the civilized world and which is paralyzing the stoutest of hearts in the enormity of its plan and the apparent success of its execution. The grimness of impending danger is settling slowly over the American people. I had begun to think that perhaps I would not be called to war, but now I am not so sure. In fact, it seems almost inevitable that I will go. Things are happening on a tremendous scale.

April 13, 1918. I heard ex-President Taft speak in Bailey Hall this morning. He spoke on the war—nothing else is spoken of in these days. Now the question is, shall I set out, at the close of this academic year, to fit myself for some branch of the service so that at the age of 21 I will be trained in military or war work, or shall I wait still longer in the hope that peace will come?

On April 25th I inscribed a short nature poem, celebrating spring. On May 11th, while other freshmen were burning their caps, I recorded the belief that the greatest period of my life was past and gone. The school year was drawing to a close and again I was left stranded for the summer.

"I don't even know that I'll return in the fall. I ought to want to, but I'm not sure that I do. I am never sure of anything."

I settled this feeling of uncertainty by buying a second-hand Oldsmobile and taking a job in my father's store, in the credit department. But I could feel the War in my bowels now.

> July 14, 1918. I have been thinking of a sentence I read somewhere: "Destiny makes no mistakes."

Armed with a copy of *Marcus Aurelius,* I accompanied my family to Bellport, Long Island, for the month of August. There was a noticeable dearth of young men at the summer resort. The sea washed over me, the sun struck down, the wind blew at me, in an attempt to dispel the fearful mists of indecision. On the first of September we returned to the cicada-laden streets of our suburb; the month in Bellport had become a memory of sea and sky and doubt. On August 31st I wrote a poem strongly advising myself to get killed in action. On September 12th, with thirteen million other Americans, I registered for the draft.

> September 21, 1918. My serial number is 3751 and I don't understand what it means, except that I can remember the days when I didn't used to have a number. The harvest moon is full tonight . . . and looking through the window 3751 enjoys the splendor.

The War, and my own travail, were both drawing to a close. I returned to Ithaca and enlisted in the Army. The enemy turned out to be an epidemic of flu—which I met stoically with a bag of licorice drops. I can't remember who told me that licorice fended off flu germs, but he was right.

> November 12, 1918. Yesterday was one of the greatest days in the history of the world. The war came to an end at 2:15 o'clock in the morning. At half-past five a hand pushed against me in the darkness and a voice whispered "The whole town of Ithaca must be on fire—listen to the bells!" I sat up in bed. Just at that moment the chimes in the library tower rang out "The Star Spangled Banner" and someone down below yelled "The war is over!" . . . The terms are little less than unconditional surrender. Germany is brought to her knees, and is no longer in a position to menace the safety of other European nations. Peace with victory has been established, to the everlasting glory of all the allied countries who stood side by side in the greatest conflict of history.

For another month we had to go on drilling as though nothing had happened. As a parting blessing, the War Department vaccinated all of us for smallpox, shot us with a triple dose of typhus serum, and confined us to barracks. It was dark when I walked out of the Army, and the lights were beginning to twinkle in the valley. I strode away from the mess hall in a mantle of serenity.

December 25, 1918. Christmas Day. I argued with father for about an hour and a half after breakfast, and just as is always the case we came to no agreement. He believes that the plans now being formulated for a League of Nations will be the means of preventing war in the future for all time. I cannot believe that that is so. He believes that a new era has dawned, that our President and his associate representatives of other nations have a great vision, that all the countries of the world will be united by a bond so strong that there can be no war. Father did most of the talking.

December 28, 1918.
> The pines hang dark by a little pond
> Where the ice has formed in the night
> And the light in the west fades slowly out
> Like a bird in silent flight.
> The memory of the sun that's gone
> Is just the glow in the sky,
> And in the dusk beyond the trees
> A figure is skating by.

I was still in love. The great world war had come and gone. *Parlez moi d'amour.*

POETRY

A FRIEND of mine has an electric fence around a piece of his land, and keeps two cows there. I asked him one day how he liked his fence and whether it cost much to operate. "Doesn't cost a damn thing," he replied. "As soon as the battery ran down I unhooked it and never put it back. That strand of fence wire is as dead as a piece of string, but the cows don't go within ten feet of it. They learned their lesson the first few days."

Apparently this state of affairs is general throughout the United States. Thousands of cows are living in fear of a strand of wire that no longer has the power to confine them. Freedom is theirs for the asking. Rise up, cows! Take your liberty while despots snore. And rise up too, all people in bondage everywhere! The wire is dead, the trick is exhausted. Come on out!

&

"I wish poets could be clearer," shouted my wife angrily from the next room.

Hers is a universal longing. We would all like it if the bards would make themselves plain, or we think we would. The poets, however, are not easily diverted from their high mysterious ways. A poet dares be just so clear and no clearer; he approaches lucid ground warily, like a mariner who is determined not to scrape his bottom on anything solid. A poet's pleasure is to withhold a little of his meaning, to intensify by mystification. He unzips the veil from beauty but does not remove it. A poet utterly clear is a trifle glaring.

The subject is a fascinating one. I think poetry is the greatest of the arts. It combines music and painting and story-telling and prophecy and the dance. It is religious in tone, scientific in attitude. A true poem contains the seed of wonder; but a bad poem, egg-fashion, stinks. I think there is no such thing as a long poem. If it is long it isn't a poem; it is something else. A book like *John Brown's Body,* for instance, is not a poem—it is a series of poems tied together with cord. Poetry is intensity, and nothing is intense for long.

Some poets are naturally clearer than others. To achieve great popularity or great fame it is of some advantage to be either extremely clear (like Edgar Guest) or thoroughly opaque (like Gertrude Stein). The first poet in the land—if I may use the word loosely—is Edgar Guest. He is the singer who, more than any other, gives to Americans the enjoyment of rhyme and meter. Whether he gives also to any of his satisfied readers that blinding, aching emotion that I get from reading certain verses by other writers is a question that interests me very much. Being democratic, I am content to have the majority rule in everything, it would seem, but literature.

There are many types of poetical obscurity. There is the obscurity that results from the poet's being mad. This is rare. Madness in poets is as uncommon as madness in dogs. A discouraging number of reputable poets are sane beyond recall. There is also the obscurity that is the result of the poet's wishing to appear mad, even if only a little mad. This is rather common and rather dreadful. I know of nothing more distasteful than the work of a poet who has taken leave of his reason deliberately, as a commuter might of his wife.

Then there is the unintentional obscurity or muddiness which comes from the inability of some writers to express even a simple idea without stirring up the bottom. And there is the obscurity that results when a fairly large thought is crammed into a three- or four-foot line. The function of poetry is to concentrate; but sometimes over-concentration occurs, and there is no more comfort in such a poem than there is in the subway at the peak hour.

Sometimes a poet becomes so completely absorbed in the lyrical possibilities of certain combinations of sounds that he forgets what he started out to say, if anything, and here again a nasty tangle results. This type of obscurity is one that I have great sympathy for: I know that quite frequently in the course of delivering himself of a poem a poet will find himself in possession of a lyric bauble—a line as smooth as velvet to the ear, as pretty as a feather to the eye, yet a line definitely out of plumb with the frame of the poem. What to do with a trinket like this is always troubling to a poet, who is naturally grateful to his Muse for small favors. Usually he just drops the shining object into the body of the poem somewhere and hopes it won't look too giddy. (I sound as though I were con-temptuous of poets; the fact is I am jealous of them. I would rather be one than anything.)

My quarrel with poets (who will be surprised to learn that a quarrel is going on) is not that they are unclear but that they are too diligent. Diligence in a poet is the same as dishonesty in a bookkeeper. There are rafts of bards who are writing too much, too diligently, and too slyly. Few poets are willing to wait out their pregnancy—they prefer to have a premature baby and allow it to incubate after being safely laid in Caslon Old Style.

I think Americans, perhaps more than other people, are impressed by what they don't understand, and the poets take advantage of this. Gertrude Stein has had an amazing amount of newspaper space, out of all proportion to the pleasure she has given people by her writings, it seems to me, although I am just guessing. Miss Stein is preoccupied with an experimental sort of writing she finds diverting and exciting, and that is all right by me. Her deep interest in the sound that words make is laudable; too little attention is paid by most writers to sound, and too many writers are completely tone-deaf. But on the other hand I am not ready to believe that any writer, except with dogged premeditation, would always work in so elegantly obscure and elliptical a fashion as the author of "A rose is a rose"—never in a more conventional manner. To be one hundred per cent roundabout one must be pure genius—and no-body is that good.

On the whole, I think my wife is right: the poets could be a little clearer and still not get over onto ground that is unsuitably solid. I am surprised that I have gone on this way about them. I too am cursed with diligence. I bite my pencil and stare at a marked calendar.

ع

In the cities (but the cities are to be destroyed) lights continue to burn on into the morning, in the hotel bedrooms that open into the dark court, in the little sitting rooms off the bedrooms, where the breakfast things linger, with the light gleaming on the half grapefruit and the bright serving covers and the coffee thermos, the ice melting around the grape-fruit-rind all through the morning and shades going up across the area-way where the other people in dressing gowns and bathrobes and paja-mas are lifting the receiver from the hook and calling room service and ordering the half grapefruit and the toast and marmalade and running the water behind the shower curtain. The city wakens, but to its own internal suns, each lamp with its parchment shade and the cord, dusty twisted, that connects it to the center of light and of power, the umbilicals of the solar system. (But they tell me the cities are all to be destroyed and that people will no longer live in the impractical cities, but the time has not yet come.) Nevertheless I must begin keeping green the memory of the cities, the ferns and tiger plants in the boxes under the lights in the dining rooms and the restaurants and the grills, the opening and closing of the doors of the elevators and the finger always on the button summoning the elevator, waiting silently with the others (there are always others in the city) and the ascent and descent always with the others, but never speaking. In the bookshops the clerks, wanting to know if they can help, but you say no you are just looking around, and the terrible excitement of so great a concentration of books in one place under one roof, each book wanting the completion of being read. Under the marquee, after the show, huddling out of the rain with the rain on the roofs of the cabs and the look on the faces of the city people desperate in the rain, and the men in their black coats and hats darting out into the withering fire of raindrops to seek the turbulent headwaters of the stream of taxis, and the petulance and impatience and desperation of the women in their dresses waiting for the return of the men who are gone so long into the fierce bewildering night, and the mass urgency, there under the marquee, as though unless they all escaped safely into a cab within five minutes they would die. (You must leave the key at the desk when you go out. Even though the cities are to be destroyed, don't forget to leave the key at the desk when you go out.)

THE FLOCKS WE WATCH BY NIGHT

On the afternoon of the day after the first killing frost, I was coming around the barn carrying a sack of straw when I saw Charles turn in from the road and start down toward my pasture. He had on his gray fedora hat with the low crown and the turned-up brim, and his arms overflowed with turnip tops to bring the sheep in with. He had a rope, too. Charles had just shaved and was bleeding freely around the chin. One arm encircled the greens; with his free hand he mopped away at the blood. I thought, "I guess Charles has come to get that ewe with the cough." (Maybe I should explain that Charles has his sheep in with mine —I let him use my pasture and he lets me use his, and we alternate the sheep back and forth because they get better feed that way.)

It was cold, clear weather, and the wind had a bite to it. The darkness comes early these afternoons. I put my sack down and set out across the field toward the stile, the dachshund following, expectant, full of an instinctive notion that something might be up and that it might involve sheep. Charles was calling them. "Knaac, knaac," he said, and the tame ewe came bobbling up from the cedars, tolling the others in. Charles handed out greens all round. The sheep surrounded him, ate thankfully. When I was halfway to the stile I saw him let the greens fall to the ground; his left arm went out and took one of the ewes suddenly by the wool at the base of her neck. She ducked, backed away madly; Charles was jerked forward and flung himself on her shoulders, tackling her hard, his jacket riding up around his neck and his hat slipping back off his forehead. It was a big ewe, and she took Charles with her, plunging and slipping among the rocks. I walked on, climbed the stile, picked up the rope that Charles had dropped, and walked over to where the two of them had fallen after the last spasm. Charles' chin was buried in the ewe, the blood showing red in the dirty gray wool. Gathering her strength, she bolted. I took a quick hold on her rear end and went along with them. As she dropped I threw my leg over her back and we came to rest, with Charles breathing heavily on account of his asthma. The dachshund tested out one of her legs, going in cautiously, nipping, then withdrawing quickly. We all three, the ewe, Charles, and myself, lay there a second, breathing.

"I found out what was the matter with that engine," said Charles.

"The magneto?" I asked.

"Yes," he said. "Bert was down this afternoon tinkering with it. . . . This gets my wind awfully." His wind was almost done. He rested his head on the sheep and closed his eyes, as though he would soon sleep.

I passed Charles the rope, which had a knot near one end so that when he made a noose it wouldn't draw tight. Charles tied it around the ewe's neck and I made up the coil.

"Miss Templeton was over to my house earlier," said Charles. "That woman has had everything the matter with her a woman can."

"I better take the dog up," I replied.

"Wait till we get her over the stile. She must weigh nearly two hundred." Charles pushed her eyelid back with his big fingers, exposing the eyeball with tiny veins of blood. "That's a good ewe—look at that blood," he said.

The dachshund, almost insane with the kill, withdrew and went forward to finish off at the throat. His mouth clogged with wool. Charles heaved on one side and I pushed from behind, but it was hard work. It was mostly a case of waiting till she wanted to go. The ewe backed against me, then jumped furiously ahead toward the stile. The rope caught in Charles' foot and he was down, against a rock; the dachshund quickly transferred to him and danced about him while I grabbed the line and held. We eased the ewe up the first step of the stile and she crumpled. Charles' breath was coming short and we had to rest. I had one knee on the stile, one hand under the ewe's tail to keep her from sliding back. We didn't want to lose what we had gained. The ewe went limp on us and was dead weight.

"Will you have to take the magneto to town?"

"Yes," he said, "I can't do anything with it. Let's give her one more, but watch when she goes over the other side she doesn't jam you." He took out a dirty handkerchief and held it against his chin. "I can't seem to stop bleeding once I start."

"Why don't you get a styptic pencil?" I asked.

"I got one," said Charles.

We both lifted together and the ewe stumbled to her feet on the stile, fell forward on the other side, and plunged down. Charles made it up over in time, wheezing, with the rope, and snubbed her as she bolted for the bushes along the fence. The dachshund was under her, fighting his way up through wool.

"Why don't you use it?" I asked.

"Doesn't do any good. I rubbed it on these cuts, but it doesn't stop. I always bleed a lot."

"You heard her cough lately?" I asked.

"No. But it might be the worms. You can tell—if they brace themselves with their front feet planted forward when they cough, it's more likely it's worms than a cold. If it's worms, we want her out of here anyway. It might just be a cold. She's a damn good ewe."

I got hold of the dachshund's tail and pulled hard. He came out whimpering and I took him in my arms.

"I'll put him in the house," I said. "We'll get along better." As I walked up to the house my boy came out and ran toward us, catching up a switch as he came. I went on with the dog and shut him in the kitchen, breaking his heart for the millionth time. When I got back the boy was prodding and Charles would pay the line out while the ewe ran, and then jump along at the end of the rope in long, impossible strides. His hat was on with the bow on the right-hand side, and it was twisted slightly. The ewe was always either running hard or at a dead stop.

"I'll take the rope," I said, "if running gets your wind." Charles handed it over.

"The ram ought to be here this week, hadn't he?" Charles asked.

"Yes. It's a yearling. Do you think a yearling can handle this size flock?"

"Sure," said Charles. "That's a lot of nonsense about not breeding too much. Frank Bickford had a thoroughbred Jersey bull and he wouldn't let it breed only twice a week. Damn bull died of loneliness."

At the end of a long run the ewe veered off the road in front of McEachern's house, which is just this side of Charles' place, went down on her knees, then sank. The boy and I went down with her, hanging on. Charles caught up with us, walking. His breath was coming better. He knelt down beside the ewe. Her eyes were closed with weariness and grief. The boy stroked her tenderly. The sun had gone, and the car that came along had its parking lights on, showing clear and clean-cut in the dusk, with no glare. "She's dead," said the boy. "Her eyes are closed."

The McEacherns' little girl came out of the house and stood watching. "Is that sheep dead?" she asked.

"Yes," said the boy.

"Can you go after the ram with your truck when he comes?" asked Charles.

"Yes," I said. We pushed the ewe and she went on and turned into Charles' yard. I held her while he went and got a pinch bar to tether her to.

"Come in, won't you?" said Charles when the ewe was tied. "I'll show you my new cat."

It was good and dark now. My toe caught on the edge of the linoleum rug.

"This place smells like a monkey cage," Charles said, "but I never do anything about it when Sarah's away. She'll be back Tuesday. I had a letter."

The boy and I groped along, and Charles struck a match and lit a lamp. I sat down in an old rocker by the stove and the boy stood beside me, his arm around me. Charles put the black kitten in my lap and it settled there.

"What's the iron pipe out back?" I asked.

"I'm going to pipe water into the house," said Charles. "Sarah wants it and I guess she ought to have it. I got a pump from Sears a year ago, but I never put the pipe in. I don't like to get things *too* handy around here."

He took down from the mantelpiece, one by one, the photographs of his four grown children and showed them to me. They were high-school graduation pictures by a studio photographer. He had shown them to me before, but he took them down again. "I haven't anything else to be proud of," he said, "but I *am* proud of them. They're good kids. A couple of them are married now."

I studied their faces gravely.

"That son's my favorite, I guess," he said.

"He looks fine," I said.

"This war's a terrible thing."

"Yes, it is."

"What do you think's going to happen?"

"I don't know," I said.

The kitchen was warming up. We lit cigarettes and sat and smoked. My boy stroked the cat. Charles put the photographs back on the mantelpiece under the picture of the ship. He had got his breath back. I felt pleasantly tired and comfortable, and hated to go, but it was suppertime. I got up to leave.

"Those lambs will be cunning, in the Spring," Charles said.

"They sure will."

As we walked back along the road, the boy and I, I noticed that the ewe was grazing quietly at her tether. Overhead the stars were bright in the sky. It looked like a good day tomorrow.

"What did he mean when he asked you what was going to happen?"

"He meant about the war."

"Does anybody know what's going to happen?"

"No."

"Do you?"

"No."

"Do people have to fight whether they want to or not?"

"Some of them."

When we got near our house we could look down and see the sheep in the pasture below us, grazing spread out, under the stars.

"I can hardly wait to see the lambs," said the boy.

REPORT

H<small>AVE</small> just been taking stock of my life to see where I stand and to review the cultural and agricultural state of affairs here. I will give an account of myself as of the year 1939 just ending.

Flocks and Herds. I have fifteen grade sheep; also own one-half of a full-blooded Oxford Down ram with another fellow. Two of the sheep are dungy tails, two are snotty noses, one is black. In general their health is good, no ticks. The ram is gentle. I have 112 New Hampshire Red pullets in the henhouse and 36 White Plymouth Rock pullets in the barn, a total of 148 layers. I have three Toulouse geese, the remnants of a flock of four, one having been taken by a fox. I have six roosters, celibates, living to themselves. There is also a dog, a tomcat, a pig, and a captive mouse.

Fruits and Vegetables. I have apples, pumpkins, squash, potatoes, and cow beets, in boxes and bins. Of jams, jellies, and preserves a great number.

Production. During the past twelve months I produced 482 dozen eggs, brown-shelled. We ate or broke 101 dozen. The other 381 dozen I marketed, some locally, most to the co-operative. At the moment I produce forty dozen eggs a week. My net loss on poultry probably doesn't exceed a dollar a bird a year. If I didn't have to earn a living by writing I think I could show a profit of a dollar a bird a year. It takes all a man's thoughts and attention to get the most out of a hen: give her only a portion of your thoughts and she will clip you.

Fish and Game. During 1939 I shot a porcupine and a rat, trapped four other rats, caught 200 pounds of cod and haddock, 150 pounds of mackerel, and 200 pounds of cunner and pollack for a gull; buried the porcupine and rats, made chowder of the haddock, gave away the cod, lost the gull, and canned the mackerel.

Denizens of Woods and Fields. Living with us here on the place, or in the waters adjacent, are skunks, woodchucks, weasels, foxes, deer, mink, rabbits, owls, crows, hair seals, coot, whistlers, loons, black ducks, squirrels (gray and red), chipmunks, porcupines, coons, hummingbirds, moles, spiders, snakes, barn swallows, tree swallows, toads, snails, and frogs. One night a wild goose stopped over on our pond en route south. There are songbirds in large numbers at certain moments of spring and fall.

Field Crops. I put three tons of hay in the barn for the sheep and raised nine bushels of oats, which turned out to have smut.

Summary. We had a good year but a selfish one, laying up for ourselves treasures on earth.

 ह•

I have been studying last year's town report to see how things went during a twelve-month period, how the money was spent, and with what luck. In a town of this size (798 people) it is possible for me to understand the financial statement, because the sums are of a size I can grasp. It is not like the Corn Exchange statement that I used to examine regularly in my theater program but that somehow eluded me. My town is to my liking in this respect: when I read under miscellaneous expenses that $2.25 was spent for repairs to the town hall (whose front door when last I passed by was held shut by a broom handle thrust into its vitals), I am reading something I can sink my teeth into. Or if I learn that $42.50 was paid out in porcupine bounties, and $13.88 to a typist, I am on ground that seems familiar and solid. I shot one of the porcupines.

In the main, it seems to me things are managed very well here. The town wage is $3 a day for a man, $6 a day for a team, $9 a day for a truck. There are more trucks than teams, but the teams are in heavier demand and scarcely have an idle day from spring till fall. Last October, on a brutally cold day with snow in the air, I saw one of these teams headed up the road to keep a haying engagement.

The average citizen pays an annual tax on his property of about twenty-five dollars. He pays a poll tax of three dollars. If he has a car he pays an excise tax. The heaviest expenses that the town must meet are for the schools, the roads, and the poor. The land and buildings owned by the non-residents of the town, that is, the summer visitors, are valued at a greater sum than the land and buildings of the residents—which gives a top-heavy feeling to the load but makes it possible for the town to survive in this generation. Without the money received from the summer population this community would find it difficult to make out.

The current expenditures for public servants, office supplies, and miscellaneous items are light. The town paid $2,084.65 to meet them last year. Out of that sum, the salaries of the selectmen, the tax collector, the constable, the health officer, and the school board were paid. Also the salaries of the auditor, the ballot clerk, the election clerk, the moderator, and the sealer of weights and measures. We have also among our town officers certain men who are designated as cullers of hoops and staves, surveyors of wood and bark, and fence viewers; but although the offices are filled, I do not find any record of the officeholders being paid anything. The constable last year received $40.50. The health officer received $15.00. This would lead one to suppose that the deportment of the citizens required closer watching than their health, but I do not believe this to be the case.

It costs a good deal more to repair roads and bridges than it does to pay the public servants. The last town meeting voted to spend $1,700 for repairing roads and bridges, plus another $800 for the improvement of State-aid roads, plus another $500 for the repair of a particular road called No. 3, plus another $292 for third-class roads, plus another $350 for the Hales Woods Road—blasting ditches through ledges, repairing culverts, et cetera. For the privilege of riding smoothly, keeping communication open, and getting where it wants to go, the town pays and pays. The boon of mobility in this isolated community is the Number One boon, outranking all others. Road money is the one item nobody seems to kick about. There are aspects of life here far bumpier than the roads, but the roads respond readily to treatment; perhaps that's the reason the townsfolk are willing to lavish so much of their wealth on them. A large proportion of the ablebodied men in town work on the road, applying tar in summer and sand in winter, so that the money that was appropriated comes home again, after a little interval, and after much toil.

The town voted $40 for putting electric lights in the library building, in order that the populace might see to read. A sum of $150 was voted for the installation of chemical toilets in one of the schools. But I am told they are less good than a well-constructed backhouse.

The heaviest expense was for education. There are in this town three one-room schools, one two-room school, and one combination high and junior high school. To maintain them, a sum of $7,400 was voted, this to include teachers' wages, fuel, janitor service, conveyance, textbooks, and supplies. The State is counted on to chip in another $1,500. In the period this report covers, that is, 1938–39, the highest paid teacher was the high school principal (who is also the baseball and basketball coach) who received $1,400. The next highest were the high school and junior high teachers, who received $800. The lowest were the grade teachers in the one-room schools, who got $504.

School buildings are heated by wood stoves, except the high school, which has a furnace. At the end of the year the account stood: for fuel, $439.44; for teachers, $2,600.40. Thus it costs one-sixth as much to heat the pupils' bodies as their minds, minds being slower to kindle. The superintendent of schools, who gives only part of his time to this town, received for his services $324.96. Snow removal cost $984.36.

The town operates a farm, which I believe was purchased because it was a handy source of gravel. (Gravel plays a major role in this community; somebody is always hauling a load of gravel somewhere either to cover an icy road in winter or to spread on tar in summer.) Hay and gravel to the amount of $242.50 were sold from the town farm, and most of this sum was paid into the poor account, the poor thus profiting because of the town's natural resources.

In all, it cost the town about $2,400 to support the poor. Some of the towns in this county in recent years have unloaded some of this burden onto the Federal government, but in our town we have walked alone. Our First Selectman does not approve of the Federal government as now constituted and has never participated in any of its gay and mischievous adventures in which Washington puts up a dollar and the town matches it with another dollar. Some of the citizens are disturbed about this, but I think most of them approve. There is some talk going round of accepting funds from the Youth Administration, to pay young high school graduates for doing odd jobs, but I don't know whether anything will come of it. I have studied the treasurer's report carefully and can find no trace of any connivance with Uncle Sam.

There is an item of $96 received from the State for overpayment of shovel rent, but no trace of Federal complicity. For all I know, the shovels may have been for the removal of fireside chats from the living rooms.

There were seven marriages in our town in the fiscal period. Of the fourteen individuals implicated, twelve were undertaking marriage for the first time, two for the second time. Six persons were born, 2 males and 4 females. Nine persons died, 4 females and 5 males. Dogs were licensed to the number of 42 males, 8 females. Ninety-eight children attended the dental clinic, and six permanent teeth were drawn.

I think this is an excellent report.

FRO-JOY

THEY keep the radio going low at the village garage. You can sit on a bench by the stove and listen while the mechanic tinkers with your car. The car is brought in and the doors are rolled shut behind it to keep out the cold, and everything is sort of cozy and quiet in there, with the music faintly in your ears and the re-treads suspended above your head from the rafters and the inner tubes arranged in boxes on the shelf. The radio singer (a baritone) is singing "Pale Hands I Loved Beside the Shalimar." Love oozes in a ribbon from the cabinet—genuine, passionate, romantic love, yet quiet and restful because it is turned down low. I don't know where the Shalimar is. Perhaps Persia. Love, riding the waves of warmth from the stove, takes possession of me. I see a girl of breathtaking loveliness; her hands are Persian and pale. The mechanic, adjusting the points on my distributor, has hands that are not pale. They are almost black and they know what they're doing. The mechanic has never seen the Shalimar, never seen the inside of a radio studio where love originates, but he knows everything there is to know about a motor. The stove and the music create a moment of total contentment of mind and body as the singer ends with the haunting question: "Where are you now? Where are you now?" In twenty minutes they give me back my car and I pass through the doorway into the crisp world, away from the oasis of love and dreams of fair women—a man with a smooth-running engine, beside the Shalimar.

ॐ

Some day I mean to have a fireside chat with my government, that we may come to know each other a little better, for it is by a better understanding of the other's traits that a government and its citizens must fulfill their mutual destinies. In my chat I want particularly to take up the first sentence under Section G of Form 1040, which is called "Items exempt from tax" and which starts this way:

> The following items are *partially* exempt from tax: (a) Amounts received (other than amounts paid by reason of the death of the insured and interest payments on such amounts and other than amounts received as annuities) under a life insurance or endowment contract, but if such amounts (when added to amounts received before the taxable year under such contract) exceed the aggregate premiums or consideration paid (whether or not paid during the taxable year) then the excess shall be included in gross income. . . .

I want to ask my government what it thinks would become of me and my family if I were to write like that. Three sets of parentheses in one sentence! I'd be on relief inside of a month.

That sentence, above, was obviously written by a lawyer in one of his flights of rhetorical secrecy. There isn't any thought or idea that can't be expressed in a fairly simple declarative sentence, or in a series of fairly simple declarative sentences. The contents of Section G of Form 1040, I am perfectly sure, could be stated so that the average person could grasp it without suffering dizzy spells. I could state it plainly myself if I could get some lawyer to disentangle it for me first. I'll make my government a proposition: for a five-dollar bill (and costs) I *will* state it plainly.

ह

I was thinking as I prepared to pay my tax how lucky I am about figures. Figures mean little to me, and for that reason use up very little of my time. To some people figures are the most vivid signs there are. Some people can look at the notation 5/23/29 and it means something to them, calls up some sort of image. I can't do that. I can see lust in a pig's eye, but I can't see a day in a number. I remember days, if at all, by the dent they made on me, not by the dent they made on the calendar.

When figures refer to sums of money, it all depends on what scale they're in whether they register with me or not. To me all sums under a dollar seem vital and important. Sums under a dollar seem to me to have an enormous quantitative variation. I think of fifty cents as the devil of a lot more than a quarter. The sum of ninety cents seems a lot to spend for anything, no matter what. But when I get up into gustier amounts, among sums like fifty dollars, or a hundred and thirty-two dollars, or three hundred and seven dollars, they all sound pretty much alike. If I have the money at all I can spend two hundred and thirty dollars with the same painless ease with which I might spend one hundred and fifteen. They seem virtually the same thing. Probably the importance that I attach to sums less than a dollar is a hangover from the days when practically every transaction in life was for something under a dollar, and was breathtaking.

One reason I bother to set down these remarks is because I think department stores should be informed that, to at least one customer, a dollar seems less money than ninety-eight cents. Stores are frittering away their time when they mark down something in the hope of luring me to buy. Another reason is that I think my government should be told that a vast amount of fuss could be avoided if, in taxing my income, it would explain clearly what is expected of me in the way of a payment and then, if it feared this might not supply enough revenue, simply wind up its instructions for computing the tax with the brisk remark: "Double it." I could double my tax and not bat an eye. It's only when I double the time spent translating Form 1040, or when I pay a lawyer to do it for me, that I feel the pinch. I doubt that there is any such complexity in the financial aspects of my life as is implied by the Treasury Department's searching inquiry. In many ways my life *is* complex. I keep sheep, and there is nothing simple about being a part-time shepherd. But neither the profit nor the loss from my association with ruminants need bother my country overmuch. There is nothing in it, one way or another, for the United States. I have my own little system for making and spending money. I am honest and I am willing. It shouldn't require a lawyer to set me at peace with my country.

&

On the first morning after this latest fall of snow, we went out early, my wife and I, to hunt for a sleigh and a horse. The plow had been along the road and left a perfect surface for sleighing. At the crack of day, in a six-cylinder sedan, we sallied forth to look for all our yesterdays. I knew of several barns where I thought the past might lie.

This quest will long remain in my mind—the great beauty of the morning, with the trees loaded with quiet snow, the special luster of earliness and the purity and expectancy of the new day, the sharp air, and the low cold sun promising the continuance of wintry pleasures, and in our memory the jingle of bells. We went from farm to farm (the ones we knew had horses), rapping on kitchen doors, stirring up the wives who would tell us where the men were. Everywhere the same answer:

either there was no sleigh or there was a sleigh but it was buried under six tons of hay or the horse was unshod. But what surprised us was the enthusiasm that our request aroused—the wives standing in the doorway with the cold in-draught of air chilling them, saying they too would like to take a sleighride on a morning like this. Into the faces of some of them a queer look of wistfulness came. It wasn't just the sleighs that were buried, it was the sense of the past, something of merriment gone, a sound of bells over snow. In the faces of one or two a look of exquisite longing, a memory of love somehow associated with sleighriding.

Nothing ever came of this quest. We got on to the back roads finally, but the day grew older and the morning began to get shoddy the way it does about eleven. A man can go round just so long hollering for the past, then he quits and gets on with the present. We did come across a sleigh on the way back, but the owner had arrived at his destination, taken the horse out, and was paying a call. We didn't have the crust to intrude.

ε♥

I have often wondered whether it is just a lot of sentimental rot—this idea that people had more fun in a horse-drawn society. The automobile has won out in fair competition, but it has much to answer for, it seems to me, quite aside from its reputation as a killer. It has taken us apart and put us together again, and changed the backdrop. A generation ago this town had a thriving steamboat service. There was something doing here. There were fish factories and there was a dollar to be made. Today the motor roads to the north of us carry the freight; the steamboat has been laid off, the wharf is in ruins, the factories are gone, and the population has dwindled. High school boys, with a diploma under their arms, must either look to the clam flats for a living or to the world beyond the horizon. High school girls go up to the cities, and learn shorthand—a briefer way to express what might well be said briefer anyway.

Today this town hasn't even a doctor. It doesn't have to have a doctor. If you chop off your toe with an ax you get into somebody's car and he drives you ten miles to the next town where there *is* a doctor. For movies you drive twenty-five miles. For a railroad junction, fifty. For a mixed drink, twenty-five. For a veterinary, twenty-five. For a football game, fifty, or one hundred, or two hundred, depending on where your allegiance lies. For a bush scythe, ten. For a trotting race or a bingo game, ten. Everything in life is somewhere else, and you get there in a car.

This has certainly done things to our culture. If we are not satisfied with the merchandise that we find in the general store we drive till we find something that does satisfy us. This is tough on the local storekeeper, who has his troubles anyway. Sliced bread arrives in town going sixty miles an hour in a bakery truck that is the gravest menace to every child on the road. Bread, in my town, is the staff of death. Ice cream arrives going fifty, and there is a little nameplate tacked to the door of the cab, giving the driver's name and explaining that he is pledged to safety and courtesy and has driven 209,587 miles without an accident—(eight times round the world carrying Fro-Joy in an unfrojoyous decade).

Very few housewives bake their own bread. They fry doughnuts a couple of times a week, but there is almost no bread-making. One of our greatest extravagances is homemade bread, which we buy for twenty-five cents a loaf from a lady ten miles away and which often means a special journey to town—twenty miles round trip. It is wonderful bread and worth the effort probably. The whole car smells of it on the way home. But it is a strange way for us to live. I have half a notion to learn to make bread myself: I imagine it's no harder than mixing a good Martini, and I might come to enjoy the work.

The automobile is at the bottom of every plot. In the next town to ours the grade schools have recently been consolidated. The motor car was responsible. One large school building in the center of town now serves the whole community—which covers many square miles. The children ride to school in busses, some of them a distance of four or five miles. The small one-room schoolhouses are abandoned, and education marches on. The advantages of the consolidated school, I am told, are many. The scholars have a fireproof building and a basketball court with an electric scoreboard. They hang their things in cloakrooms that are ventilated with a flue that has a rotary windwheel carrying the smell of warm clothing up into the sky, instead of out into the classroom. They come in contact with a larger group and come under the influence of more teachers, some of whom are specialists in their subject. There is even a color scheme: the building is yellow and the busses are yellow. I think there can be no doubt that education, in its academic sense, is improved by the centralization of scholars.

Whether the improvement is general nobody knows. Certainly there is something lost. One thing that is lost is the mere business of walking to school, which is something in itself. In my community scholars still get round on the hoof. They pass our house at seven in the morning, clicking along in a ground-eating stride. Some of them make a four-mile trip to school—eight miles in all. And if there is a basketball game that night they will turn right round after supper and do the whole course over again without batting an eyelash. Sometimes a passing motorist gives them a ride, but they never ask for it and never expect it. There is no such thing as hitch-hiking in this town, no thumb is ever raised in entreaty. In all the time I've been driving these roads I've never been asked for a ride, which is almost unbelievable considering the distances that must be covered, often in zero weather or in storm. Walking is natural for these children, just as motoring is for most others. As for me, although I am motorized to a degree, I enjoy living among pedestrians who have an instinctive and habitual realization that there is more to a journey than the mere fact of arrival. If the consolidated school served by busses destroys that in our children I don't know that we are ahead of the game after all.

FARM PAPER

Sᴇᴇ *that the ewe has milk, that her udder is all right, her teats open, and that the lambs get the milk.*

That's what my bulletin said. Stern advice for a city-bred man who came late to shepherd's estate. The ewes and I went through a joint pregnancy: they carried the lambs, I carried the bulletin and the worry and the wonder. I was pretty sure that no matter how closely I watched I should finally be caught off my guard. On a Sunday morning in February, just at daylight, my hour came. The little boy burst into the bedroom and cried: "Wake up, you got a lamb!"

I pulled on some cold clothes and stumbled out toward the barnyard. Before I got down to the shed where the sheep were I could hear a lamb blaring. The sound seemed artificial, almost as though somebody were blowing short blasts on a cheap horn. I slowed my step and looked in at the door of the fold. On the frozen ground just over the threshold a lamb lay dead. A coating of frost had formed on its stiff yellow fleece. The ewe stood just beyond, her stern showing traces of blood, her eyes full of bewilderment. A few feet away there was another lamb, staggering about in small spasmodic jerks, its little dung-smeared body about the size of a turnip, its woeful voice strangely penetrating in the biting wind that blew in through the open door. Here was my lamb all right, waiting to be wrapped warmly in the nearest bulletin.

It lived through the morning, lying in a carton by the stove, but it was a weak lamb and never recovered from the first awful chill. Shortly after lunch, having nursed twice and received our blessings, it died. It was one of the briefest and most popular visitors we ever had, being loved by all

and particularly by the dachshund, who showed a deep gripping appreciation of its lovely aromatic newness—the dung in its fleece warmed by
the kitchen heat gave it a heavenly intensity quite in keeping with its
Biblical connotation. There is something about a lamb you don't get over
in a hurry. It's been gone quite a while now, and others are on the way,
but the dachshund and I still tremble all over when we think of it.

&

The two big days of the month for me are the days when *The Rural
New Yorker* arrives. I used to feel the same expectancy and excitement
about *The American Boy,* during the first years of the century, when the
pictures of pony carts and magic lanterns tortured my grasping little
heart with life's not impossible fulfillment. And there was a period, later,
when I felt the same anticipatory emotion for the morning *World,* and
those tense midnights when I would approach a newsstand on Broadway
and squander a nickel on the early edition to turn with secret torment of
suspense to the Conning Tower to discover whether some noble nubbin
of poetry had achieved the decent fame I hoped it deserved. Those were
nights! But I doubt if the boy's dream of premiums, the youth's dream of
recognition, have anything on the baffled countryman's dream of rural
felicity as pictured in a farm journal. I don't know what repressed corner
of me is relieved by a study of the minute problems of poultry-house
ventilation, or the reports of a sheep-shearing contest, or the account of
a horse celebrating his twenty-sixth birthday; but I know that I can't keep
my hands off *The Rural New Yorker* when it comes, or my mind off it
when it is due. (Geographically speaking, I should subscribe to the *New
England Homestead,* but I somehow got started with the other paper and
I don't see how I can make the break now.)

I try hard to keep my mind and my sympathies abreast of world
events by reading the newspapers; but the words of war correspondents
often seem lifeless compared to the writings of persons who confide their
troubles and their hopes to the editor of a country journal. Europe in
tatters is something that ought to occupy an honest man's attention, but
lately it has seemed too big for me. I prefer to curl up in a comfortable
chair with *The Rural New Yorker* and read: "I have a three-year-old colt
that about once a month or so will throw out her stifle joint." That is a
catastrophe I can enter into. And I like the editor's cryptic reply: "With
rest and occasional application of a Spanish-fly blister the colt may tend
to outgrow the ailment." An item like Spanish-fly blister on a stifle joint
can occupy my thoughts the better part of a whole evening.

I am not sure but that the menace and the mystery of country life are
at the core of its charm. Much of what I read and hear is wholly beyond

my comprehension, yet it holds me spellbound. Here is a letter from a subscriber (a Mrs. M. M.) giving a straightforward account of a tame hen that willfully tore a chick to pieces and then, crazed with remorse, went down cellar and committed suicide by eating moth balls. "The reason for writing about this," Mrs. M. M. adds with inspired irrelevance, "is to show how easily eggs can be tainted by bad food."

In addition to being fraught with menace, the life of the countryman has a beautiful natural balance everywhere discernible. These same moth balls that the hen gulped down to atone for her sin can be hung in an orchard to keep the deer away from the young trees. I read that in *The Rural New Yorker,* too, under the caption MOTH BALLS REPEL DEER.

For some months I have kept a file of clippings having to do with catastrophes. I find this a handy reference file when something breaks out on my own place, and I go through it frequently. One of my standbys is the case history of an abnormal heifer, reported by A. J. B. It is called "Trouble With Heifer." "I have a heifer two years old last March which I raised myself. She comes of good stock and is in good health, but have never been able to breed her. This summer she has been in pasture with the other cows but has shown no sign of breeding. The only abnormal signs I can see is that she is fond of licking the coat of one of the horses, also likes to eat cardboard."

Now, anyone can see from that report that the so-called simple life of the country is a myth. The poet's dream of cattle winding slowly o'er the lea is a pleasant idyll, but the bald fact is that you suddenly find yourself with a heifer who shuns the bull, lavishes kisses on a horse, and eats cardboard.

There is something fascinating about the prose style of many of these correspondents. One of my favorite stylists is a lady who describes her chicken venture under the heading "A Living With Poultry."

"When I see a hen shake her head," she writes, "I pick her up, rub a little kerosene over her comb, nose, gills, and under her throat, also a few drops in her mouth. I use a small spoon for this. They usually respond to this."

There is an economy of effort here that has a telling effect. The literary device of allowing the reader to guess *how* the hens respond to having kerosene poured down their throats is worthy of Tantalus. A year ago I noticed that my pullets were all shaking their heads. For weeks I tried to discover what caused it. Nobody seemed to know. I am now of the opinion that all chickens just naturally shake their heads, and that, considering the modern high-pressure methods under which they are managed, they have a pretty good reason for doing so. But although this lady doesn't know, any more than anybody else does, what makes a hen shake her head, she can't help wanting to apply a few drops of kerosene.

I fill myself to the brim with items calculated to terrify me. Often these letters begin on a tranquil note and work up to bedlam. "This has been a banner year for clover all through Cortland County, N. Y.," began one disarming story in *The Rural New Yorker.* "On our farm we had the best crop of clover ever raised, both mows and the barn floor were crammed full and we were rejoicing in the possession of so much good feed for the cows." Suddenly the mood changes. "Now," continues the writer, "the barn is gone and the clover too. It happened on September 29th. My son and the hired man were sorting potatoes in the basement of the barn and when my son started to go to the house little Phyllis, who is only two, ran to meet him and exclaimed, 'Look, Daddy, smoke!' "

Such thumbnail accounts of life haunt me. My own mows still have some hay in them, and I wince every time my son comes to me on the run. "Look, Daddy, smoke!" I hear him calling.

One learns that the well-being of farm animals is extremely tenuous. All farm animals, particularly the hen, are hanging to life by the merest thread. "My hens have a fluid in their throat," writes F. G. "My turkeys have the habit of pulling feathers from one another and eating them," sobs T. J. M. "What is the cause of large crops on White Wyandottes?" asks E. S. with a stiff upper lip. These people are all terribly real to me. They are my brothers and sisters, dwellers in darkness.

I am not doing justice to *The Rural New Yorker.* It is one of the great papers. I guess it is best known for its crusading spirit and for the vigorous help it gives farmers who have been preyed on by rascals and agents. But I think its true genius is that in the course of interpreting modern scientific farming it somehow manages to preserve and transmit a feeling for the land—a sense of fruition and of people's talent for earth and their fulfillment in the year's cycle. Most farm journals I have seen lack this quality, although they usually provide a tutti-frutti substitute. In *The Rural New Yorker* one gets it straight—in the letters from subscribers and in the articles.

The ultimate survival of this mysterious relationship between the farmer and his fields sometimes seems doubtful. The last generation has seen it weakening, along with the exhaustion of the soil itself. The farm as a way of life has been subordinated to the farm as a device for making money. Somewhere along the line the thread has been lost; somewhere in the process of introducing vitamins and electric time-switches into his henhouse the farmer has missed the point of the egg; somewhere in the long tractor-turned furrow lie the moldering roots of an earlier content. Modern methods turn the farm into a business, the farmer into a promoter. Meanwhile the land passes out of his hands (I read the other day that less than half the farm real estate in the United States is actually owned by the farmers) and nobody knows what the end of that sad story will be.

I remember, some years ago after the crash, reading a book by Ralph Borsodi called *Flight From the City.* It was an account of the author's experiment in returning to handicraft and the good life of goat's milk, wherein his wife churned butter with one hand and spun him a woolen sports jacket with the other. It was an idyll of pressure cooking and vacuum cleaning. One of my friends, after reading the book, remarked: "It's beautiful, only *my* wife isn't Mrs. Borsodi." (As I recall it, Mrs. Borsodi not only did all the spinning, dishwashing, milking, churning, caponizing, cooking, cleaning, cultivating, and baking, but she also kept her children home from school and instructed them herself rather than let them associate with the toughs of the village. Even at this late date it tires me just to think about Mrs. Borsodi.)

Yet the book, for all its extreme recommendations, was disturbing just the same. It stated the case for the escapist and it struck home to jobless urbanites who had been experiencing the baleful aspects of city life during a depression and also, I suspect, to farm owners who had been brooding on the derangements of high-powered large-scale one-crop agriculture. It suggested to an inquiring mind that somewhere between the two extremes there might be a rural existence that would be both satisfying and practical for the average man who neither wanted to spin his clothes nor run a wheat combine but who yearned for cheap light and air and a certain measure of security.

Many people are groping for this ideal all the time, moving restlessly back and forth between town and country. The land, even though it has been mistreated, can still support the population—that we know. The question is whether the population has the temperament and the ingenuity to support the land—that is, to return its goodness, not just sap it.

The test is whether a person has a feeling for fertility. This is as much a theosophical as an economical matter—whether one feels any mysterious obligation to put back into the soil the strength he took from it by his cultivation or by his buying the canned products of other people's cultivation.

I have just got hold of a book called *Bio-Dynamic Farming and Gardening* by Ehrenfried Pfeiffer, which bids fair to shape my mystical course from now on. Although I have barely thumbed through it, I can see that it is my meat at last. The hero of the book is the common earthworm. At the bottom of the compost heap sits God. Already I am a convert to bio-dynamics. Here is the life beyond the test tube—the philosophy of chemistry. I feel it in my bones, as I would a spell of damp weather coming on. Of course a farmer can't allow himself to become wholly an ascetic (specially during lambing time); but if he allows his agriculture to degenerate into mere profit-making, he is a man foredoomed. My goal is no longer a three-hundred-egg hen but to find peace through conversion of my table scraps into humus. God help my neighbor's pig—I'm afraid he'll miss the scraps.

TOWN MEETING

Awoke this morning and from my bed I could look up Madison Avenue, and there saw a big sign on the side of a building: "World Peace Through World Trade." Lay a long while wondering how world trade might bring about world peace instead of world war, which it is so accustomed to bringing about. And a brass band came by a block away on Fifth, playing "Onward Christian Soldiers," though it was still quite early on Sunday and most Christian soldiers in this town were abed. But the police were up and marching, and I could see sun on the glass tops of yellow taxis and on the bare heads of priests on their way to the Cathedral, very mirthful and sociable and feeling better than I, who had eaten a bad fish the night before.

ॐ

The elevator boy in my hotel, after he has shut the grilled gate and started the car, always slips his hand through the bars of the gate so that as he passes each floor the sill-plate will give him a dangerous little kiss on the end of his finger. It is the only record he keeps of his fabulous travels. A doctor could probably tell him why he does it, but for that matter a doctor could probably tell me why when I pass through a long corridor I always kick lightly sideways with one foot so that it ticks the baseboard. A doctor *could,* but a doctor isn't going to. There are things about my life I don't wish to pry into, and that is one of them.

ॐ

Looking at the Cathedral reminded me of Notre Dame and Quasimodo and of the troublesome time I often have at the movies. There was a scene in the "Hunchback" showing the King of France taking his annual bath. One of his attendants urges him to take two baths a year instead of only one. And right there my attention wavered from the picture and I began brooding about the problem of personal cleanliness in the 15th Century and realized that if the King, enjoying all the advantages of wealth and position, took only one bath, then the gypsy girl Esmeralda, who lived among beggars and with no facilities whatsoever, probably took none. In spite of the apparent daintiness of Miss Maureen O'Hara, who managed to come out of every brawl looking lovely and sweet, the picture was spoiled for me, and I reflected that there was hardly a heroine in fiction prior to the present century whom I would feel attracted to at close range, so spoiled is the modern male by the clean girls that are found everywhere today.

ぎ✒

There has been considerable opposition to the new census from persons who feel that the questionnaire would be an invasion of one's constitutional privacy. This hostility toward inquisitorial processes is a good sign—not that there's anything particularly devilish about census taking, but just that it's a fine thing for people to get stirred up about their rights, which otherwise tend to be nibbled away by the mice of time. We surrender our privacy too easily. The threat of a census has aroused the countryside because nobody looks forward with any pleasure to answering questions about his income or his bathtub. Housewives are haunted by the fear that when the census taker appears unexpectedly and peers into the tub he will find the brown ring of shame.

Privacy, the abstract blessing, is a lot bigger than the average-sized tub. And, like a tub, it can be irreparably marred by a blow from a blunt instrument, or law. I think that in small ways people do give up their constitutional rights without a murmur. One of the most surprising examples of this is the case of motorcar owners who of late years have remained docile while the State issued license plates that are one part identification and one part promotional advertising. When the 1939 plates appeared in New York State it was observed that they were adorned with an engraved invitation to Mr. Whalen's dumbshow in Flushing, L. I. Only a handful of car owners squawked about this—millions carried the slogan, front and rear, advertising the Fair. I seem to remember that one conscientious citizen went so far as to take the matter to the courts and demanded to be released from the indignity. He got nowhere (except into the papers). Yet I believe that a motorist is quite within his rights to refuse to carry a slogan on his car, and I believe the state is misusing its power in issuing license plates that are inscribed with a bit of institutional hoopla. The custom is spreading. Maine has for the past couple of years produced plates bearing the word "VACATIONLAND" beneath the digits. Wisconsin, I believe, advertises itself as "AMERICA'S DAIRYLAND." There are probably others that I don't know about. I haven't seen a California plate this year, but I presume it bears the inescapable legend "ROONEYMEDE."

In effect this seemingly harmless practice makes every motorist an advance agent, without pay. It also gives some of us a touch of nausea. I think undertakers in Maine can now procure, for their hearses, plates that do not include the word "Vacationland" but I am not sure. The last few hearses I have chanced to see were going so fast I couldn't make out what the plates said.

To me "Vacationland" is a particularly annoying device to be emblazoned on the bow and stern of my small overworked sedan. "Vacationland" is a loathsome word, assembled by a person of drab, untrustworthy mind. Furthermore, the residents of the State of Maine do not regard their state as a vacation land: they know from bitter experience that it is a place of hard work and long hours and tough weather. It is true that residents of other states come here in certain mild seasons to spend their vacation, but that is true of any state in the Union and is not peculiar to Maine.

Quite aside from such objections, no citizen, under the constitution, can be compelled in his private life to assume a public burden and promote a cause, and a slogan on a license plate is without question pure promotion. It is conceivable that a comfortable majority of Maine citizens may approve of the publicity methods of their state and of the conventional Chamber of Commerce approach, but there are many others who do not, and even if there were only one person who did not, or no persons who did not, the state would still be exceeding its authority by slyly converting each motorist into an advocate and by turning a private vehicle into a public testimonial. I can't even be sure that my state will not try to improve on its present form of advertisement. Next year perhaps I'll receive a license plate equipped with a small wind-driven calliope, so that I may call attention to the circus in a more shrill and provocative manner.

In the case of the census, I saw one statement that attempted to justify the inquisition by explaining that the findings of the census takers would be of inestimable value to American business men in their sales and promotion campaigns. This is an interesting bit of reasoning—the kind to examine closely. We are asked to believe that the Federal government is privileged to compel all citizens to answer certain give-away questions about themselves in order that a certain few citizens may with greater accuracy and craftiness plan campaigns to take money away from the remaining citizens. A manufacturer of an astringent, we'll say, would be ahead of the game if he could discover which was worse in America, bad breath or dandruff. The census taker will oblige with the information, and your reply, naturally, will be used against you.

Overcoming sales resistance is now an exact science, and consumers are asked to contribute to its exactitude. Selling and buying are a pitched battle: the consumer erects his sales resistance (as he might a stockade in Indian country) and the manufacturer tries to knock it down. The only alarming thing in the situation is that the Federal government proposes to take sides in the fight by gathering information to help the Indians. That seems hardly fair.

ह•

We had our annual town meeting last week, in the old town hall next to the church and across from the cemetery. I see that *Life* Magazine calls the New England town meeting the quintessence of democracy; but one of my neighbors, who has probably attended more of them than the editors of *Life*, had another name for it. "Well," he said, as he climbed into our car balancing a pot of baked beans wrapped in a paper bag, "here we go to the Chase & Sanborn hour."

It was a fine day for the meeting. About one hundred and twenty-five people turned out, or approximately one-seventh of the population. The hall is old and ugly—one of those Victorian mistakes with a mansard roof. The Masons, I am told, own the top floor, the town owns the rest. Neither can decide whether to tear the thing down or leave it up, but the question is academic because neither could get the consent of the other anyway.

The meeting is held on the first floor, in a room whose walls are sheathed in tin with a decorative tin molding. The windows are curtained with strips of pink and white paper, à la Dennison. Near the door is a wood stove, and at one end, next to the dais, are four voting booths looking perilously like pay toilets. When we arrived the ladies of the church were upstairs preparing lunch. Others were taking their places round the walls on the wooden benches. The men were gathered round the stove, visiting, warming up, talking shop, girding for trouble.

There are lots of people in town whom you see only once a year, at town meeting. They emerge from the back country and put in an appearance early; the meeting is a get-together for the town the same as Fair day is for the county. The front row of benches was occupied by a delegation from the senior class at the high school who had come to observe government processes in a free country.

This was my first town meeting (I missed last year's) and I was surprised to discover that there was not much discussion on the floor. The warrant contained thirty-eight articles, covering election of town officers and appropriation of town moneys as well as other matters of policy. Most of them aroused no debate. There were questions involving the schools, the roads, the library, public health, yet there was no general discussion of any of these subjects. New Englanders are jealous of their right to govern themselves as they like, but in my town we have learned that town meeting is no place to decide anything. We thrash out our problems well in advance, working in small queues and with a long history of spite as a background. The meeting is just to make everything legal. For the assemblage the meeting virtually was concentrated in the first thirty minutes of bloodletting. It began when one of the citizens, who we all knew was loaded for bear, rose to his feet, walked to the front, drew from his pocket a small but ominous sheet of paper, and in soft pacific tones began:

"Mr. Moderator . . ."

This was when democracy sat up and looked around. This was the spectacle the townfolk had walked miles for. Half way through the speech, when the air was heavy with distilled venom, my neighbor turned to me and whispered: "I get so excited here it makes me sick. I'll commence to shake by and by."

At the conclusion of the barrage the First Selectman rose and returned the fire. Both men held the floor without yielding. There was no motion before the house—this was just pleasure before business. It had the heat and turmoil of the first Continental Congress without its nobility of purpose and purity of design. Old echoes of twenty years ago were awakened, old fires flared up and burned with original heat. At intervals there were bursts of applause when somebody scored a direct hit. At last the Moderator rapped with his gavel. Immediately the meeting settled down to business; cheerfully the taxpayers took up in rapid succession each article in the warrant and without a murmur voted the distribution of the twenty-five thousand dollars that, by dint of much scraping, we had managed to contribute to our community in the form of taxes. We had got our money's worth in the first half hour's skirmish—the rest was routine. You had to have roads and schools; that was all there was to that.

ह•

The first sign of spring here is when the ice breaks up in the inkwell at the post office. A month later the ice leaves the lakes. And a month after that the first of the summer visitors shows up and the tax collector's wife removes the town records from her Frigidaire and plugs it in for the summer.

A SHEPHERD'S LIFE

T<small>HIS</small> is a day of high winds and extravagant promises, a day of bright skies and the sun on the white painted south sides of buildings, of lambs on the warm slope of the barnyard, their forelegs folded neatly and on their miniature faces a look of grave miniature content. Beneath the winter cover of spruce boughs the tulip thrusts its spear. A white hen is chaperoning thirteen little black chicks all over the place, showing them the world's fair with its lagoons and small worms. The wind is northwest and the bay is on the march. Even on the surface of the watering fountain in the hen-yard quite a sea is running. My goose will lay her seventh egg today, in the nest she made for herself alongside the feed rack in the sheep shed, and on cold nights the lambs will lie on the eggs to keep them from freezing until such time as the goose decides to sit. It is an arrangement they have worked out among themselves—the lambs enjoying the comfort of the straw nest in return for a certain amount of body heat delivered to the eggs—not enough to start the germ but enough to keep the frost out. Things work out if you leave them alone. At first, when I found lambs sitting on goose eggs I decided that my farm venture had got out of hand and that I had better quit before any more abortive combinations developed. "At least," I thought, "you'll have to break up that nest and shift the goose." But I am calmer than I used to be, and I kept clear of the situation. As I say, things work out. This is a day of the supremacy of warmth over cold, of God over the devil, of peace over war. There is still a little snow along the fence rows, but it looks unreal, like the icing of a store cake. I am conducting my own peace these days. It's like having a little business of my own.

People have quit calling me an escapist since learning what long hours I put in.

Lambs come in March, traditionally and actually. My ewes started dropping their lambs in February, reached their peak of production in March, and now are dribbling into April. At the moment of writing, thirteen have lambed, two still await their hour. From the thirteen sheep I have eighteen live lambs—six sets of twins and six single lambs. April is the big docking and castrating month, and since I have named all my lambs for friends, I wield the emasculatome with a somewhat finer flourish than most husbandrymen. Tails come off best with a dull ax—the lambs bleed less than with a sharp instrument. I never would have discovered that in a hundred years, but a neighbor tipped me off. He also told me about black ash tea, without which nobody should try to raise lambs. You peel some bark from a black ash, steep it, and keep it handy in a bottle. Then when your lambs come up from the pasture at night frothing at the mouth, poisoned from a too sudden rush of springtime to the first, second, and third stomach, you just put the tea to them. It makes them drunk, but it saves their lives.

That peerless organ of British pastoral life, *The Countryman,* published at Idbury, recently printed a list of ancient Celtic sheep-counting numerals. I was so moved by this evidence of Britain's incomparable poise during her dark crisis that I gave the antique names to my fifteen modern ewes. They are called Yain, Tain, Eddero, Peddero, Pitts, Tayter, Later, Overro, Covvero, Dix, Yain-dix, Tain-dix, Eddero-dix, Peddero-dix, and Bumfitt. I think Yain is rather a pretty name. And I like Later, too, and Pitts. Bumfitt is a touch on the A. A. Milne side, but I guess it means fifteen all right. As a matter of fact, giving numerals for names is a handy system; I have named the ewes in the order of their lambing, and it helps me keep my records straight. Peddero-dix and Bumfitt are still fighting it out for last place.

When I invested in a band of sheep last fall (they cost seven dollars apiece) I had no notion of what I was letting myself in for in the way of emotional involvements. I knew there would be lambs in spring, but they seemed remote. Lambing, I felt, would take place automatically and would be the sheep's business, not mine. I forgot that sheep come up in late fall and join the family circle. At first they visit the barn rather cautiously, eat some hay, and depart. But after one or two driving storms they abandon the pasture altogether, draw up chairs around the fire, and settle down for the winter. They become as much a part of your group as your dog, or your Aunt Maudie. Our house and barn are connected by a woodshed, like the Grand Central Station and the Yale Club; and without stepping out of doors you can reach any animal on the place, including the pig. This makes for greater intimacy than obtains in a layout where each farm building is a separate structure. We don't encourage animals to come into the house, but they get in once in a while, particularly the cosset lamb, who trotted through this living room not five minutes ago looking for an eight-ounce bottle. Anyway, in circumstances such as ours you find yourself growing close to sheep. You give them names not for whimsy but for convenience. And when one of them approaches her confinement you get almost as restless as she does.

The birth of a mammal was once a closed book to me. Except for the famous "Birth of a Baby" picture and a couple of old receipted bills from an obstetrician, I was unacquainted with the more vivid aspects of birth. All that is changed. For the past six weeks I have been delivering babies with great frequency, moderate abandon, and no little success. Eighteen lambs from thirteen sheep isn't bad. I lost one pair of twins—they were dropped the first week of February, before I expected them, and they chilled. I also lost a single lamb, born dead.

A newcomer to the realm of parturition is inclined to err on the side of being too helpful. I have no doubt my early ministrations were as distasteful to the ewe as those of the average night nurse are to an expectant mother. Sheep differ greatly in their ability to have a lamb and to care for it. They also differ in their attitude toward the shepherd. Some sheep enjoy having you mincing around, arranging flowers and adjusting the window. Others are annoyed beyond words. The latter, except in critical cases, should be left to work out their problem by themselves. They usually get along. If you've trimmed the wool around their udders the day before with a pair of desk shears, the chances are ten to one they will feed their lambs all right when they arrive.

At first, birth strikes one as the supreme example of bad planning—a thoroughly mismanaged and ill-advised functional process, something thought up by a dirty-minded fiend. It appears cluttery, haphazard. But after you have been mixed up with it for a while, have spent nights squatting beneath a smoky lantern in a cold horse stall helping a weak lamb whose mother fails to own it; after you have grown accustomed to the odd trappings and by-products of mammalian reproduction and seen how marvelously they contribute to the finished product; after you've broken down an animal's reserve and have identified yourself with her and no longer pull your punches, then this strange phenomenon of birth becomes an absorbingly lustrous occasion, full of subdued emotion, like a great play, an occasion for which you unthinkingly give up any other occupation that might be demanding your attention. I've never before in my life put in such a month as this past month has been—a period of pure creation, vicarious in its nature, but extraordinarily moving.

I presume that everything a female does in connection with birthing her young is largely instinctive, not rational. A sheep makes a hundred vital movements and performs a dozen indispensable and difficult tasks, blissfully oblivious of her role. Everything is important, but nothing is intelligent. Before the lamb is born she paws petulantly at the bedding. Even this is functional, for she manages to construct a sort of nest into which the lamb drops, somewhat to the lamb's advantage. Then comes the next miraculous reflex. In the first instant after a lamb is dropped, the ewe takes one step ahead, turns, and lowers her head to sniff eagerly at her little tomato surprise. This step ahead that she takes is a seemingly trivial thing, but I have been thinking about it and I guess it is not trivial at all. If she were to take one step backward it would be a different story —she would step on her lamb, and perhaps damage it. I have often seen a ewe step backward while laboring, but I can't remember seeing one take a backward step after her lamb has arrived on the ground. This is the second instinctive incident.

The third is more important than either of the others. A lamb, newly born, is in a state of considerable disrepair; it arrives weak and breathless, with its nose plugged with phlegm or covered with a sac. It sprawls, suffocated, on the ground, and after giving one convulsive shake, is to all appearances dead. Only quick action, well-directed, will save it and start it ticking. The ewe takes this action, does the next important thing, which is to open the lamb's nostrils. She goes for its nose with unerring aim and starts tearing off the cellophane. I can't believe that she is intelligently unstoppering these air passages for her child; she just naturally feels like licking a lamb on the nose. You wonder (or I do, anyway) what strange directional force impels her to begin at the nose, rather than at the other end. A lamb has two ends, all right, and before the ewe gets through she has attended to both of them; but she always begins with the nose, and with almost frenzied haste. I suppose Darwin is right, and that a long process of hereditary elimination finally produced sheep that began cleaning the forward end of a lamb, not the after end. It is an impressive sight, no matter what is responsible for it. It is literally life-giving, and you can see life take hold with the first in-draught of air in the freed nostril. The lamb twitches and utters a cry, as though from a long way off. The ewe answers with a stifled grunt, her sides still contracting with the spasms of birth; and in this answering cry the silver cord is complete and takes the place of the umbilicus, which has parted, its work done.

These are only the beginnings of the instinctive events in the maternal program. The ewe goes on to dry her lamb and boost it to its feet. She keeps it moving so that it doesn't lodge and chill. She finally works it into position so that it locates, in an almost impenetrable jungle of wool, the indispensable fountain and the early laxative. One gulp of this fluid (which seems to have a liberal share of brandy in it) and the lamb is launched. Its little tail wiggles and satisfaction is written all over it, and your heart leaps up.

Even your own technique begins to grow more instinctive. When I was a novice I used to work hard to make a lamb suck by forcing its mouth to the teat. Now I just tickle it on the base of its tail.

COMPOST

Tᴏᴅᴀʏ joined a society called Friends of the Land, as at my time of life a man should belong to a club so that he will have somewhere to sit in the afternoon. I am going to put an old chair out by my compost heap and shall go there whenever I feel sociable and friendly toward the land. Membership cost me five dollars, which is the first time my high regard for earth has ever cost me a nickel; but these are expensive times.

&

Am writing this on the fourth day of the Battle of France, as the announcer calls it, so there will probably be no continuous thought from one paragraph to the next. I am not able to write on a single harmonious theme while jumping up frequently to hear whether freedom is still alive. I don't think I would lose my nerve if I were directly engaged in war, but this radio warfare makes me edgy. I suspect I joined my club only because I was rattled. When I am composed I feel no need of affiliating myself with anybody. There is a lot of the cat in me, and cats are not joiners.

&

So great is the importance attached to news from abroad, even my club intends to have foreign correspondents. I should imagine today would be a discouraging day for the northern France correspondent of Friends of the Land. The organic matter now being added to French soil is of a most embarrassing nature. Until we quit composting our young men we shall not get far with a program of conservation.

ટ૦

I have a letter from a trader in Santa Fe, New Mexico, that begins: "How would you like to wear a tie that no other man in your town could have—a tie hand-woven exclusively for you?" He encloses a swatch and a drawing of the tie. It is very pretty. He invites me to join his "exclusive tie group." If you like this tie, he says, it is "yours exclusively—no other person in your town can get it." I replied immediately, inviting him to our next rummage sale.

ટ૦

A friend of the land wouldn't know where to go in an exclusive tie.

ટ૦

The question of what to wear is always baffling. From *Harper's Bazaar,* which is my Bible, I learn that the Boston group in North Haven frown on new garments in their summer colony, and that a man in a new pair of sneakers is snubbed. "The older the clothes, the bluer the blood," says the writer. Society of course has lately found itself in the difficult position of wanting the comfort of old clothes without relinquishing the prestige that has always been connected with new ones. It took a long time before the elite surrendered to old clothes, and even now they publish frequent denials in the papers, hoping to be both exclusive and comfortable. It must raise the spirits of the millions to whom old clothes come naturally and inevitably to learn how blue their blood has been these many years.

ટ૦

I am aging a pair of sneakers and a jacket in case I should meet a Bostonian in warm weather.

ટ૦

I have given up planning a perfect state for America, as it is too small a field. Henceforth I shall design only world societies, which will include everybody and everything. Don Marquis began work on the almost perfect state but died before it came into being. I should let that be a lesson to me.

ટ૦

It is easier to plan a good world than a good nation, or even a good hemisphere. Nothing can be worked out to the advantage of the human race as long as the mind is hampered and cramped by existing boundaries, however unfortified. The success of Hitler can be ascribed to his determination to see the planet whole. Besides, a man can always discuss a thing more intelligently and honestly if he knows he is not being taken seriously. The most forthright book that was ever written was *Mein Kampf,* and nobody gave it a second thought.

ع

Obviously the first contingency to provide for in a world plan is war. In the perfect state there will be no war, but this state will be arrived at only after much fighting, and I shall plan for this, too. From now on, no democratic nation must arm itself merely for defense, as the United States proposes to do. To arm defensively is to construct, not a series of fortifications and weapons, but a bad state of mind and a perpetual dilemma.

Parenthesis: The good world will be based on the democratic ideal of individual freedom, but I am learning a good deal from tyrants. End of parenthesis.

ع

To arm defensively is to indulge in a most demoralizing form of deliberate activity. A vast defensive armament has all the costly, savage attributes of offensive armament and in addition is stuffy. A nation armed merely to defend its own territory is of no more consequence than a rather large safe deposit vault. It has become merely a front for intrenched wealth, and will eventually deteriorate. The armies of the democracies that will lead up to my world state will be built *for attack.* They will be imaginative, bold, and alive, but their minds will not be on conquest nor will they confuse raw materials with the good life.

They will be trained to attack today's injustice, rather than to repel tomorrow's invasion.

ع

Remind me to discuss the necessity for reviving the word piffle.

ع

War, in the preliminary period leading up to the almost perfect state, must be conducted in a reckless and hasty fashion, with no discussion in advance. The democracies must take over war from the despotic powers and use it to clinch their advantage. The technique of military science will be to meddle in other people's affairs frequently, gallantly, and without warning—but with no ulterior motive.

Thought: Before democracy can become stable and perfect it must become arrogant and tough. The punky spots in the character of free men will have to be cut out before it is too late. It is as essential for this free country that its young men despise American piffle as that they despise European poison.

ဆ

Voice: If they despise piffle, how can they earn their living?
Answer: How should I know? The important thing is to despise it.

ဆ

A first step in elevating the character of war and improving the world state is the abandonment of diplomacy. Events of the past few months have demonstrated that diplomacy gives the advantage to liars and tends to weaken democracies. Diplomacy reached its lowest ebb at Munich, when a conservative Briton carrying an umbrella entered a cage of live *Panzers*. A child could have seen that no good could come from any such heroics.

Diplomacy is the lowest form of politeness because it misquotes the greatest number of people. A nation, like an individual, if it has anything to say, should simply say it. This will be hard on editorial writers and news commentators, who are always glad to have diplomatic notes to interpret; but it will be better for the people.

ဆ

Voice: How do you know what's good for the people?
Stinging reply: I know what's good for me.

ဆ

Having dropped diplomacy, we can now employ the Army for the highest military purpose and train it for a career of inspired meddling. All branches of the service will be shifty, unpredictable, and arbitrary. Equipment will be the most modern and fierce obtainable. Singing will be a requirement of every soldier, and officers will be chosen for their likeness to Gene Autry.

Let us suppose we had adopted my principles of warfare a couple of years ago at the time of Germany's torture of the Jews. The President would have cabled the Nazi government the following message: CUT OUT TORMENTING MINORITIES—ROOSEVELT. He would then have dispatched a destroyer carrying a party of Marines, landed them at a German port, rescued two or three dozen Jewish families from the campaign of hate, and shot up a few military police in a surprise movement. Such a junket would have had no military significance and might easily have ended in the loss of the destroyer, but the effect on the world would have been incalculable. It would have excited the imagination of free men everywhere, and it would have put Germany in the extremely awkward position of being obliged to declare war on the United States at a time when she was in no position to do so. It would have called her bluff and disrupted her schedule of aggression against small neutrals. The United States Marine incident would not only have forestalled the invasion of Poland, Denmark, Norway, Holland, and Belgium (in that order), but it might conceivably have increased Hitler's rage to such a pitch of insanity that even the Nazi party couldn't follow him.

U. S. Marines going to the rescue of persons in distress is in the best Hollywood tradition, and I am convinced that the gesture would have achieved the same general popularity that Hollywood personalities and themes enjoy among all the people of the earth. It would have saved the world billions of dollars and millions of men. If we knew then what we know now, there would have been no question that it was the thing to do.

&

Proposition: The duty of a democracy is to know then what it knows now.

&

The way to know the shape of things in advance is to listen to seers and mystics instead of to economists and tacticians. The world had ample warning of every event that it has greeted with such gasps of surprise in the past twelve months. Part of the preparation for the perfect world society will be the recognition of seers. It will be required of the President of the United States that he read one poem and one parable or fable a day, in addition to the editorials in the *Times*. The brotherhood of man can never be achieved till the democracies realize that today's fantasy is tomorrow's communiqué.

&

A seer a day keeps Armageddon away.

&

Impudent interruption: You're trying to sound like Don Marquis, aren't you?

Soft answer: Yes. I have not given up loving his almost perfect state, and will continue to discuss it any time I see fit.

ૐ

My almost perfect army will be picturesque as well as fearless. Their uniforms and flags will be designed by the foremost Hollywood scene and costume designers. The army will be as reckless as a suicide squad, as shifty as an American backfield, as merciful as the Red Cross, as relentless as the Northwest Mounted Police, as swift and terrible as a tank division, as heroic as the Coast Guard, as resourceful and tender as Tarzan, as chivalrous as a knight. It will be copied by all nations—which will be its chief merit. At home or abroad it will meet life bravely. It will swoop down on lynching parties and annihilate them. It will break up the Daughters of the American Revolution whenever they try to keep Negro singers from singing their lovely songs. It will rush to the aid of every country whose land is being invaded and whose homes are being destroyed and whose people are being murdered. If it were in existence today my army would be in Europe, helping to stop the German tide.

ૐ

Voice: We tried that once.
Answer: You mean we tried it once after waiting three years. My army doesn't wait. It is a swashbuckling organization, dealing with a foreign tyrant as brilliantly as with a domestic train robber. It would have started fighting Hitler years ago when he was just beginning to be a nuisance.

ૐ

Voice: But your army would get us in trouble.
Answer: Where do you think we are now, pal?

FREEDOM

I HAVE often noticed on my trips up to the city that people have recut their clothes to follow the fashion. On my last trip, however, it seemed to me that people had remodeled their ideas too—taken in their convictions a little at the waist, shortened the sleeves of their resolve, and fitted themselves out in a new intellectual ensemble copied from a smart design out of the very latest page of history. It seemed to me they had strung along with Paris a little too long.

I confess to a disturbed stomach. I feel sick when I find anyone adjusting his mind to the new tyranny that is succeeding abroad. Because of its fundamental strictures, fascism does not seem to me to admit of any compromise or any rationalization, and I resent the patronizing air of persons who find in my plain belief in freedom a sign of immaturity. If it is boyish to believe that a human being should live free, then I'll gladly arrest my development and let the rest of the world grow up.

I shall report some of the strange remarks I heard in New York. One man told me that he thought perhaps the Nazi ideal was a sounder ideal than our constitutional system "because have you ever noticed what fine alert young faces the young German soldiers have in the newsreel?" He added: "Our American youngsters spend all their time at the movies— they're a mess." That was his summation of the case, his interpretation of the new Europe. Such a remark leaves me pale and shaken. If it represents the peak of our intelligence, then the steady march of despotism will not receive any considerable setback at our shores.

Another man informed me that our democratic notion of popular government was decadent and not worth bothering about—"because England is really rotten and the industrial towns there are a disgrace." That was the only reason he gave for the hopelessness of democracy; and he seemed mightily pleased with himself, as though he were more familiar than most with the anatomy of decadence, and had detected subtler aspects of the situation than were discernible to the rest of us.

Another man assured me that anyone who took *any* kind of government seriously was a gullible fool. You could be sure, he said, that there is nothing but corruption "because of the way Clemenceau acted at Versailles." He said it didn't make any difference really about this war. It was just another war. Having relieved himself of this majestic bit of reasoning, he subsided.

Another individual, discovering signs of zeal creeping into my blood, berated me for having lost my detachment, my pure skeptical point of view. He announced that he wasn't going to be swept away by all this nonsense, but would prefer to remain in the role of innocent bystander, which he said was the duty of any intelligent person. (I noticed, however, that he phoned later to qualify his remark, as though he had lost some of his innocence in the cab on the way home.)

Those are just a few samples of the sort of talk that seemed to be going round—talk that was full of defeatism and disillusion and sometimes of a too studied innocence. Men are not merely annihilating themselves at a great rate these days, but they are telling one another enormous lies, grandiose fibs. Such remarks as I heard are fearfully disturbing in their cumulative effect. They are more destructive than dive bombers and mine fields, for they challenge not merely one's immediate position but one's main defenses. They seemed to me to issue either from persons who could never have really come to grips with freedom, so as to understand her, or from renegades. Where I expected to find indignation, I found paralysis, or a sort of dim acquiescence, as in a child who is dully swallowing a distasteful pill. I was advised of the growing anti-Jewish sentiment by a man who seemed to be watching the phenomenon of intolerance not through tears of shame but with a clear intellectual gaze, as through a well-ground lens.

The least a man can do at such a time is to declare himself and tell where he stands. I believe in freedom with the same burning delight, the same faith, the same intense abandon that attended its birth on this continent more than a century and a half ago. I am writing my declaration rapidly, much as though I were shaving to catch a train. Events abroad give a man a feeling of being pressed for time. Actually I do not believe I am pressed for time, and I apologize to the reader for a false impression that may be created. I just want to tell, before I get slowed down, that I am in love with freedom and that it is an affair of long standing and that it is a fine state to be in, and that I am deeply suspicious of people who are beginning to adjust to fascism and dictators merely because they are succeeding in war. From such adaptable natures a smell rises. I pinch my nose.

For as long as I can remember I have had a sense of living somewhat freely in a natural world. I don't mean I enjoyed freedom of action, but my existence seemed to have the quality of freeness. I traveled with secret papers pertaining to a divine conspiracy. Intuitively I've always been aware of the vitally important pact that a man has with himself, to be all things to himself, and to be identified with all things, to stand self-reliant, taking advantage of his haphazard connection with a planet, riding his luck, and following his bent with the tenacity of a hound. My first and greatest love affair was with this thing we call freedom, this lady of infinite allure, this dangerous and beautiful and sublime being who restores and supplies us all.

It began with the haunting intimation (which I presume every child receives) of his mystical inner life; of God in man; of nature publishing herself through the "I." This elusive sensation is moving and memorable. It comes early in life: a boy, we'll say, sitting on the front steps on a summer night, thinking of nothing in particular, suddenly hearing as with a new perception and as though for the first time the pulsing sound of crickets, overwhelmed with the novel sense of identification with the natural company of insects and grass and night, conscious of a faint answering cry to the universal perplexing question: "What is 'I'?" Or a little girl, returning from the grave of a pet bird and leaning with her elbows on the windowsill, inhaling the unfamiliar draught of death, suddenly seeing herself as part of the complete story. Or an older youth, encountering for the first time a great teacher who by some chance word or mood awakens something and the youth beginning to breathe as an individual and conscious of strength in his vitals. I think the sensation must develop in many men as a feeling of identity with God—an eruption of the spirit caused by allergies and the sense of divine existence as distinct from mere animal existence. This is the beginning of the affair with freedom.

But a man's free condition is of two parts: the instinctive freeness he experiences as an animal dweller on a planet, and the practical liberties he enjoys as a privileged member of human society. The latter is, of the two, more generally understood, more widely admired, more violently challenged and discussed. It is the practical and apparent side of freedom. The United States, almost alone today, offers the liberties and the privileges and the tools of freedom. In this land the citizens are still invited to write their plays and books, to paint their pictures, to meet for discussion, to dissent as well as to agree, to mount soapboxes in the public square, to enjoy education in all subjects without censorship, to hold court and judge one another, to compose music, to talk politics with their neighbors without wondering whether the secret police are listening, to exchange ideas as well as goods, to kid the government when it needs kidding, and to read real news of real events instead of phony news manufactured by a paid agent of the state. This is a fact and should give every person pause.

To be free, in a planetary sense, is to feel that you belong to earth. To be free, in a social sense, is to feel at home in a democratic framework. In Adolf Hitler, although he is a freely flowering individual, we do not detect either type of sensibility. From reading his book I gather that his feeling for earth is not a sense of communion but a driving urge to prevail. His feeling for men is not that they co-exist, but that they are capable of being arranged and standardized by a superior intellect—that their existence suggests not a fulfillment of their personalities but a submersion of their personalities in the common racial destiny. His very great absorption in the destiny of the German people somehow loses some of its effect when you discover, from his writings, in what vast contempt he holds *all* people. "I learned," he wrote, ". . . to gain an insight into the unbelievably primitive opinions and arguments of the people." To him the ordinary man is a primitive, capable only of being used and led. He speaks continually of people as sheep, halfwits, and impudent fools—the same people from whom he asks the utmost in loyalty, and to whom he promises the ultimate in prizes.

Here in America, where our society is based on belief in the individual, not contempt for him, the free principle of life has a chance of surviving. I believe that it must and will survive. To understand freedom is an accomplishment all men may acquire who set their minds in that direction; and to love freedom is a tendency many Americans are born with. To live in the same room with freedom, or in the same hemisphere, is still a profoundly shaking experience for me.

One of the earliest truths (and to him most valuable) that the author of *Mein Kampf* discovered was that it is not the written word, but the spoken word, that in heated moments moves great masses of people to noble or ignoble action. The written word, unlike the spoken word, is something every person examines privately and judges calmly by his own intellectual standards, not by what the man standing next to him thinks. "I know," wrote Hitler, "that one is able to win people far more by the spoken than by the written word. . . ." Later he adds contemptuously: "For let it be said to all knights of the pen and to all the political dandies, especially of today: the greatest changes in this world have never yet been brought about by a goose quill! No, the pen has always been reserved to motivate these changes theoretically."

Luckily I am not out to change the world—that's being done for me, and at a great clip. But I know that the free spirit of man is persistent in nature; it recurs, and has never successfully been wiped out, by fire or flood. I set down the above remarks merely (in the words of Mr. Hitler) to motivate that spirit, theoretically. Being myself a knight of the goose quill, I am under no misapprehension about "winning people"; but I am inordinately proud these days of the quill, for it has shown itself, historically, to be the hypodermic that inoculates men and keeps the germ of freedom always in circulation, so that there are individuals in every time in every land who are the carriers, the Typhoid Marys, capable of infecting others by mere contact and example. These persons are feared by every tyrant—who shows his fear by burning the books and destroying the individuals. A writer goes about his task today with the extra satisfaction that comes from knowing that he will be the first to have his head lopped off—even before the political dandies. In my own case this is a double satisfaction, for if freedom were denied me by force of earthly circumstance, I am the same as dead and would infinitely prefer to go into fascism without my head than with it, having no use for it any more and not wishing to be saddled with so heavy an encumbrance.

THE PRACTICAL FARMER

My PUBLISHERS have presented me with H. A. Highstone's book *Practical Farming for Beginners,* the sly inference being that I have much to learn. Publishers are on the whole well satisfied to have their writers disappear into rural circumstances, but they are genuinely concerned about how we put in our time. I am sure that, like parents whose children have left home, publishers are often visited with vague forebodings, sudden twinges of fear, the feeling that something is about to fall on writers— an eight-pound striking hammer perhaps, or a fit of loneliness.

There are ample grounds for this alarm. When a person who has been accustomed to making his living by writing attempts to combine this heavy work with the even heavier work of growing some of his own food, the consequences may be grave. If recent book lists are any indication, the country must be overrun with writers who are whipping their environment into shape for publication. The strain is very great, on both nature and man, and I sometimes wonder which will crack first. There is something ominous about an impatient author, with a deadline to meet, keeping petulant vigil in a pumpkin patch so that he will be on time with his impressions of fall.

For me, always looking for an excuse to put off work, a farm is the perfect answer, good for twenty-four hours of the day. I find it extremely difficult to combine manual labor with intellectual, so I compromise and just do the manual. Since coming to the country I have devoted myself increasingly to the immediate structural and surgical problems that present themselves to any farmer, be he ever so comical in his methods and his designs. I have drifted farther and farther from my muse, closer and closer to my post-hole digger.

The blurb that accompanies *Practical Farming for Beginners* states that the book will be welcomed by "an increasing number of American people who, fed up with the pressure of city living, are going back to the land for their livelihood." That shows that publishers do not understand the situation. Pressure of city living? No pressure that I ever knew in town compares with the pressure of country living. Never before in my life have I been so pressed as in the past two years. Forty acres can push a man hard even when he isn't in debt, provided he loves them and is an easy victim to the stuff he reads in the bulletins. Pressure! I've been on the trot now for a long time and don't know whether I'll ever get slowed down. Today is our bean harvest, and even the beans in their screw-top jars are under pressure (ten pounds) in our new pressure canner, so hot are we to get them processed in one-third the time it might otherwise take. And when there is pressure up in the kitchen, it transmits itself to the whole place, and the tension becomes noticeable in all departments.

One morning a few months ago, during a particularly busy time, when I awoke I didn't dare get dressed: I knew that my only hope of getting an overdue piece written was to stay in bed—which is where I did stay. I told my wife it was a slight sore throat, but it was a simple case of voluntary confinement. It was the first time I had ever taken to bed in the full blush of health simply because I didn't dare face the economic consequences of putting my pants on.

Mr. Highstone's book presents a formula for subsistence farming, that is, farming for consumption rather than for profit, farming to produce *all* one's needs. It is the best diagram of that scheme I have studied. It is hardboiled, sound, persuasive, and convincing. On that account I regard it as one of the most dangerous of books, capable of destroying whole families, wiping them out like flies; for it suggests that any city man of average ability can create, within a couple of years and with his own hands, a satisfactory and secure economy based on the land, independent of any other source. This I do not believe. I believe that relatively few city-bred men are capable of achieving self-sufficiency through farming, and that, on the whole, the ones that might be capable of it wouldn't be particularly interested in it. Mr. Highstone is obviously a man with a gift for organization. He possesses a dauntless spirit, a keen financial sense, and the sort of mechanical ability that makes him jack-of-all-trades. He even writes well. He is informed, and he tells what he knows. His chapter called "The Chicken Trap" could only have been written by a man who had experienced the disappointments of an ill-planned poultry venture and who had learned to hate the very guts of a hen. It should certainly be read and digested by any person who dreams of lightening his old age by collecting eggs at sundown.

Briefly Mr. Highstone's formula is this:

To sustain yourself on the land, you must first get straight in your head that there is to be no nonsense about "making a profit." There is to be no buying of chicken feed by the bag and marketing of eggs by the dozen cases. You must simply create a farm that will produce, directly, everything you need including a small regular cash income (not profit). Any deviation from this course will get you into hot water. Furthermore, you must have enough capital at the start so that you won't be mortgaging your future. Mr. Highstone tells you how many thousands of dollars you will need to get started, how many acres you must buy (how many in grass, how many in grain, how many in gardens), and he names the animals you will need, the number of tons of every grain you must produce, the extra amount of cream and eggs you must sell to provide the monthly check, and the equipment you will need in house and barn. He faces life with confidence, and by the time you have read the book you, too, will face life with confidence and will believe that you can harness a team and hold a plow.

To create a self-sustaining farm, he says, you must have the following set-up:

Three cows.

One hundred hens (no more, no less).

A team of horses (which you buy after reading *Farmer's Bulletin 779*, "How to Select a Sound Horse").

Three or four hogs. (Usually Mr. Highstone is much more specific than this and says definitely three, or definitely four, but in this case there is a little leeway and you can decide between three hogs and four hogs.)

A hive of bees.

Enough land to grow all the feed for the above animals and for yourself and family, namely, ten tons of grain, fifteen tons of hay, and the usual vegetables and fruits. That's what you have to have. From these animals and this land you will receive all the food you and your family need, plus forty dollars a month—$25 from eggs, $15 from cream.

The principle on which this method of subsistence works is this:

The cow is the foundation on which the structure is built. The cow provides the means of producing, from the land, the indispensable commodities, milk, butter, and cheese. Furthermore the cow provides skim-milk, the by-product that makes diversification possible. Skim milk contains the protein that makes chickens lay eggs and makes hogs grow.

This protein is ordinarily provided (on profit-and-loss farms) by expensive concentrates bought at a grain store—laying mash, hog ration, etc. Mr. Highstone will have you buy nothing, and he is very stern about that. It's forbidden, and if you start slipping and buy a bag of grain, your whole structure will topple. The cow also provides surplus cream, which is saleable and from which you get a monthly check, along with a check for the eggs that the hens laid because they were fed skim milk and that they wouldn't have laid if they had been on a straight grain diet.

The author admits that there is nothing new or original about this scheme; his contribution is in establishing the correct balance and in pointing out the fallacy of disturbing the balance by adding here or subtracting there. Thus the scheme fails, for instance, if the farmer reduces his hens to a flock of twelve or increases them to a flock of five hundred; twelve hens won't provide extra money from the sale of eggs, and five hundred hens will turn into a poultry farm and will take more time than a diversified farmer can give and will consume more food than he can raise on his property.

Mr. Highstone, being himself a practicing farmer, knows one important truth about country life: he knows that farming is about twenty per cent agriculture and eighty per cent mending something that has got busted. Farming is a sort of glorified repair job. This is a truth that takes some people years to discover, and many farmers go their whole lives without ever really grasping the idea. A good farmer is nothing more nor less than a handy man with a sense of humus. The repair aspect of farming looms so large that, on a place like my own, which is not really a farm at all but merely a private zoo, sometimes months go by when nothing but repair goes on. I can get so absorbed in the construction of a barn door that I can let the spring planting season go right by without ever opening the ground or sowing a seed. If I were engaged in making myself self-sustaining, I should perhaps be a little wider awake; but I know, from experience, that at any given moment of the year I would be found doing the wrong thing, and with a dull tool. I mention this because the weakness in Mr. Highstone's book is not in his plan for subsistence but in the people who are going to carry it out. In spite of all his warnings, there will be plenty of them who will get sidetracked, probably along the line of some special hobby, hitherto unindulged. I have been fooling around this place for a couple of years, but nobody calls my activity agriculture. I simply like to play with animals. Nobody knows this better than I do—although my neighbors know it well enough and on the whole have been tolerant and sympathetic.

Mr. Highstone wisely insists that the man who intends to get a living from the land begin not by studying agronomy but by learning to hollow-grind an ax and file a saw. He insists that you equip yourself, immediately, with dozens of tools and implements including a pipe vise, a drill press, a forge, and a 2-horse stationary gasoline engine. "The fact," says Mr. Highstone, "that a man may be unfamiliar with some of them should never daunt him." I have a strong suspicion, although I know nothing about Mr. Highstone, that his years in the city were spent dreaming not so much about fields of ripening grain as about a shop equipped with a pipe vise. The ecstatic passages in his book are not the ones dealing with husbandry and tillage but the ones dealing with edge tools. He demands that the subsistence farmer equip himself right at the start with four hundred dollars' worth of implements and tools, including a walking plow, a two-horse spike harrow, a one-horse row cultivator, a wire hayrake, a mowing machine, a buck rake, a stone boat, a farm wagon, a roller, a disk harrow, and a long list of tools ending with an assortment of nuts and bolts, washers, and wood screws. (Incidentally, he forgot a crowbar, a clawbar, a block-and-tackle, and a pair of tinner's snips, without which my own life would be empty indeed.)

In all this, and in fact in his pattern for a self-contained farm, he seems to me essentially sound. It is only in his assumption that a city man of average intelligence, strength, and will power can operate a self-contained farm that he appears fanciful. Some of the bald statements in his book are open to question. He says: "Anyone with brains enough to pound sand can successfully raise chickens." I think that is a misleading pronouncement. Raising chickens (except in very small quantities) is partly luck, partly experience, and partly a sort of gift, or talent.

In another place Mr. Highstone actually suggests that the subsistence family harvest its own grain crop by mowing it with a mowing machine and making sheaves by hand. Remember that the grain harvest is ten tons, or 200 sacks of grain each weighing one hundred pounds. And remember also that the grain harvest comes at the same season as the canning—those 600 Mason jars that have to be filled. It would take a large family of stalwart sons and daughters to put through that program without cracking. Some of the jars are going to crack even if the children don't.

The life of self-sufficiency in this 20th century is the dream of persons with a nostalgic respect for early American vitality and ingenuity. It conflicts, temperamentally, with modern ways. If I were to attempt to put myself on a self-sustaining basis I know that for practical reasons I would have to throw the master switch in the cellar and send my regrets to the Power Company, not simply because I couldn't afford to buy power on forty dollars a month but because the possession of power in the household leads on into paths that are inimical to self-sufficiency. They lead direct to the profit (and loss) system. Mr. Highstone devotes a section to the septic tank and sewage-disposal system; but my first step in the direction of security on the land would be to abandon all flush toilets, not because I don't approve of them but because they can destroy one's economy. People differ about plumbing. Mr. Highstone proposes to lick plumbing with a pipe vise. His is the manly approach. But I know my limitations. The practical way for me to lick plumbing is not to have any. I would also have to abandon my electric refrigerator, my electric water pump, my electric water heater, my electric lights, and I would have to sell my furnace and use the coal bin for storing root vegetables. There are days when I could take the leap with a glad cry; there are other days when I would hesitate.

The great service Mr. Highstone has rendered in his book is to clarify the scene. He tells what self-sufficiency means, tells where back-to-the-landers go wrong and how they confuse the idea of being self-sustaining with the idea of running a country business for profit. Of course even the most realistic subsistence farmers are sometimes wanderers in the paths of evil. I can picture the day in the Highstone family when the news got round that Father was writing a book called *Practical Farming for Beginners.* He started secretly, but writers give themselves away eventually, and pretty soon the family knew that something was up.

"What's Pop doing, Mom?" one of the little Highstones asked.

"Sh-h, he's writing a book, dear," replied Mrs. Highstone.

"You can't eat a book, Mom."

"Well, no-o. But you see your father will receive money from the sale of the book, and with the money we can buy what we need."

"What about that sauerkraut he was going to put up today?"

"He will soon have money so we can *buy* some sauerkraut."

"Will we have sugar in our coffee instead of honey?"

"Maybe."

"That's cheating, isn't it, Mom?"

"I wouldn't know, darling. Ask your father."

And so, above the Highstone farm, the specter of Profit raised its ugly head.

SANITATION

 T HE good world will be impossible to achieve until parents quit teaching their children about materialism. Children are naturally active and somewhat materialistic, but they are not incurably purposeful. Their activity has a fanciful quality and is harmless although often destructive to property.

We teach our child many things I don't believe in, and almost nothing I do believe in. We teach punctuality, but I do not honestly think there is any considerable good in punctuality, particularly if the enforcement of it disturbs the peace. My father taught me, by example, that the greatest defeat in life was to miss a train. Only after many years did I learn that an escaping train carries away with it nothing vital to my health. Railroad trains are such magnificent objects we commonly mistake them for Destiny.

We teach cleanliness, sanitation, hygiene; but I am suspicious of these practices. A child who believes that every scratch needs to be painted with iodine has lost a certain grip on life that he may never regain and has acquired a frailty of spirit that may unfit him for living. The sterile bandage is the flag of modern society, but I notice more and more of them are needed all the time, so terrible are the wars.

We teach our child manners, but the only good manners are those that take shape somewhat instinctively, from a feeling of kinship with, or admiration for, other people who are behaving in a gentle fashion. Manners are a game adults play among themselves and with children to make life easier for themselves, but frequently they do not make life easier but harder. Often a meal hour is given over to the business of enforcing certain standards on a child, who becomes petulant and refractory, as do the parents, and the good goes out of the food and the occasion. It is impossible for a mature person to take manners seriously if he observes how easily they shape themselves to fit the circumstances. Ten or fifteen years ago it was customary in a restaurant to rise when someone approached your table. But when the Pullman-type booth was invented men discovered they couldn't rise out of their seat without barking their belly on the edge of the table—so they abandoned the rule and kept their seat. This is most revealing. If a man were truly bent on showing respect for ladies he would do so even if it meant upsetting every table in the room.

I teach my child to look at life in a thoroughly materialistic fashion. If he escapes and becomes the sort of person I hope he will become, it will be because he sees through the hokum that I hand out. He already shows signs of it.

I guess there are two reasons for my not interpreting life more honestly for my son. First, it is too hard. (It's almost a full-time job to interpret life honestly.) Second, if you tell a child about the hollowness of some of the conventions, he will be back in ten minutes using his information against you.

ᶾ▰

When three coasting schooners, one right after another, tacked into our cove and dropped anchor I knew there must be something wrong. In these days one schooner is news, three in a bunch are almost unheard of. It soon was apparent that the vessels were dude-carriers. Their decks, instead of being loaded with pulp wood, held that most precious freight —men and women on excursion. I rowed out into the cove to see the sights and was invited aboard one of the vessels by an enthusiastic old sea dog who, after three full days of life afloat, was bursting with information of a feverishly nautical character. He kept tying knots in things and rushed me all over the little ship, above and below, showing off its rude appointments and instructing me in the proper handling of a coasting schooner in fair weather and foul, including the management of a sail that he called the "jib flapsail." The schooners' yawl boats were busy taking passengers ashore for a lobster dinner on the beach, and our usually quiet cove, whose only regular night visitors are myself and a great blue heron, was soon gay with the vagrant screams and cries of persons temporarily removed from their normal environment.

I was told that the schooners were all owned by the same man—he has five or six of them and is buying others as fast as he can find them. Dude business is good. Not much has to be done to the ships—some bunks built into the hold, a toilet installed, a new sail or two, and some paint. They are old boats, most of them, but plenty good enough for summertime cruising, and are competently sailed by Maine captains, who accept the arrival of vacationers on their foredeck with the same stoical reserve with which they accept fog on a flood tide at evening.

The invasion of western ranches and eastern schooners by paying guests who are neither cowboys nor sailors is an American phenomenon we have grown used to. Some of the ranches have even moved east, to be nearer their cash customers. It's hard to say why the spectacle is saddening to the spirit, but there is no denying the way I feel when I see a coaster that has lost her legitimate deckload and acquired a crew of part-time gypsies. There is nothing wrong about it—anybody who is having a good time can't be wrong—yet the eternal quest for the romantic past that lives in the minds of men and causes them to strike attitudes of hardihood in clothes that don't quite fit them is so obviously a quest for the unattainable. And it ends so abruptly in reality. A dude, at best, is merely an inexperienced actor in the revival of an old melodrama.

ᑫᐧ

One change that has come about since the World War is the change in people's feelings about dachshunds. I remember that in the last war if a man owned a dachshund he was suspected of being pro-German. The growth in popularity of the standard breeds has brought about a spirit of tolerance, almost a spirit of understanding. My neighbors here in the country don't seem to attach any dark significance to our dachshunds, Fred and Minnie. In this war if you own a dachshund people don't think you are pro-Nazi, they just think you are eccentric.

If there was a shadow of a doubt about my Americanism, on account of the dachshunds, it was completely dispelled in the town hall the other night when I won a wire-haired fox terrier puppy on a twenty-five-cent lottery ticket. Everyone knows that a man's allegiance belongs to the country where the jackpot is.

ᑫᐧ

In a news broadcast the other morning, I heard a minor item that has stuck in my mind. The reporter said that the Nazis were "re-Germanizing" the land of Alsace, eliminating all French influence. He mentioned some rules which had been made to this end: Alsatian men named Henri would have to write their name Heinrich, and all inscriptions on tombstones would have to be in German. It seemed to me that the German ideal of purity had suddenly met its match, when it sought to "re-Germanize" not only the quick Alsatians but also the old bones in the cemeteries. To say that a man shall remember his dead in German is like saying that he shall perspire in German, or taste his spit in German. I doubt that the memory of the dead is capable of revision at the caprice of a conqueror.

Conquest in the disciplined German manner seems curiously lacking in the lustiness that is traditionally associated with victory in war. In earlier, more robust times, the victorious soldiery roared through town, drinking the bars dry and ravishing the girls. Today the new conquest seems to be mechanical, inhibited, orderly, and grim. A man back from ambulance service with the French army tells me that the German soldiers he saw in occupied France were well behaved: they all had excellent cameras and went round taking pictures of everything in sight.

In Alsace, they not only snap pictures, they diligently revise the legends on gravestones.

ತಿ

I was spreading some poison in the barn the other day for mine enemies the rats, when I came upon an unopened copy of the *Boston American,* dated Sunday, October 31, 1909. It was a special "Achievement Number" and contained 128 pages—at that time the largest newspaper that had ever been published in New England. Probably there haven't been many bigger ones since, either. It contained fifteen sections, each one of them something of a journalistic nosegay.

By inquiring around I discovered that the paper was one that had been in possession of my wife's father. She remembers that, as a little girl, the *Boston American* was never allowed in her house; and apparently her father, true to his principles, had declined to open the Achievement Number that had been sent to him and that, we discovered, contained his picture along with the pictures of some other Boston industrialists of the 1900's. He didn't throw the paper away but just set it aside, and it has moved about from garret to storage warehouse to barn for thirty years, while its achievements dimmed and its pages yellowed.

It made pretty good reading. In thirty years the greatest change has really been in our feeling about achievement itself. The *Boston American* of 1909 exuded a supreme sense of calm and pride in America. That is no longer a typical newspaper reaction. Even on that October Sunday in the proud and prospering Boston of 1909, the news of the day failed somehow to corroborate the dream of achievement. Holdup men had victimized two ladies of Quincy. In South Braintree a young husband, after shooting his wife, had hurried to the cellar and slashed his throat. In Melrose a young boy ran stark mad through the streets, driven out of his mind by a thwarted desire to play on the Melrose High School team.

And there was immorality in Scollay Square. The leading story on Page One was the most sobering and contradictory of all—it was the account of the Harvard-Army game. Harvard had managed to win the game for the Achievement Number, but in doing so had broken the neck of Army's left tackle, E. A. Byrne, and the player had died on the field.

MOTOR CARS

THE motor car is, more than any other object, the expression of the nation's character and the nation's dream. In the free billowing fender, in the blinding chromium grilles, in the fluid control, in the ever-widening front seat, we see the flowering of the America that we know. It is of some interest to scholars and historians that the same autumn that saw the abandonment of the window crank and the adoption of the push button (removing the motorist's last necessity for physical exertion) saw also the registration of sixteen million young men of fighting age and symphonic styling. It is of deep interest to me that in the same week Japan joined the Axis, DeSoto moved its clutch pedal two inches to the left—and that the announcements caused equal flurries among the people.

I have long been interested in motor-car design, or the lack of it, and this for two reasons. First, I used to like motoring. Second, I am fascinated by the anatomy of decline, by the spectacle of people passively accepting a degenerating process that is against their own interests. A designer sitting at his drafting board blowing up a mudguard into some new fantastic shape is no more responsible to his public than is a political ruler who is quietly negotiating a treaty for the extension of his power. In neither case is the public in on the deal.

Some years ago car manufacturers maliciously began reducing the size of windows and increasing the size of mudguards, or "fenders" as the younger generation calls them. By following no particular principle of design and by ignoring the functional aspects of an automobile, these manufacturers eventually achieved a vehicle that not only was stranger looking than anything that had heretofore been seen, but that, because it cut off the driver's view, proved itself capable of getting into more scrapes. At first the advantages of this design were not apparent, but it didn't take long before the motor-car industry realized that it had hold of something that, from a commercial angle, was pure gold. Every automobile was intrinsically self-defacing—and sometimes self-destructive —and this soon made the market ever so much brisker.

I shall go into the evolution of this modern car in a little more detail. The way it happened was that a rumor got started (I don't know why) that a motor car should be "longer" and "lower." Now, obviously it was impractical to reduce, to any great extent, the height of a motor car. And it was just as impractical to increase, to any great extent, the length of a motor car. So the designers had to produce an *illusion* of great length and extreme lowness. The first thing they did was to raise the hood, so that the rest of the car would appear lower by contrast. Having raised the hood, they also raised the line of the doors, to carry out the illusion clear to the bitter end. This of course reduced the size of the windows, and the motorist began the long sinking process that was to end, in 1941, in his total immersion. Fenders also had to be raised (you notice that in order to build a "low" car everything was raised). But it was impossible to raise fenders without also enlarging them—otherwise they would rise right up off the wheels. So the designers began playing with new shapes in fenders, and they huffed and they puffed, and they produced some wonderful fenders—fenders that not only were a very odd shape indeed, but that would reach out and claw at everything that came anywhere near them.

Meanwhile wheels had shrunk so small, and tires had grown so big, that the fenders were still further enlarged in a downward direction, so that they would not only be readily bumped but would scrape along the tops of curbings and culverts and miscellaneous mounds. They also made it impossible for anyone but a contortionist to change tires.

The decrease in the size of windows, simultaneously with the increase in the size of fenders, produced astounding results in the automobile industry. Millions of motorists who had become reasonably proficient in driving their cars without denting them suddenly lost that proficiency because they no longer could see where they were going (or where they had been), and because the dentable surfaces had been so drastically enlarged. Car owners who were accustomed to keeping a car for six or eight years, found that their modern car was all dented up after a single season of blind flying. So they would trade it in for a new one. Here was a most favorable turn of events for the manufacturer. He wasn't slow in catching on.

The ultimate goal of automobile designers is to produce a car into whose driving seat the operator will sink without a trace. They have very nearly achieved this goal. I know several women whose heads are permanently slanted backward because of the neck cramps they have developed trying to peek out over the cowl of a modern super-matic automobile. Incidentally, the steering wheel has been a big help to the designers in producing this type of cramp. If, after the hood had been raised, there still lingered any doubt that the operator's vision had been blocked off, the designer settled it once and for all by moving the wheel up an inch or two till the top of it was exactly on eye level. Even a skinny little steering wheel can cut off about an acre of visibility if properly placed by a skillful designer.

Mr. Arthur W. Stevens of Boston has computed that since 1900 the motorist's angle of visibility has been reduced thirty-six degrees. That is nice figuring. All I know is that for almost two decades I owned cars and never dented them up, and a couple of years ago I bought a new sedan in the low-price group, and after two years of my conservative driving it looks as though it had been dropped from a high building. This doesn't mean that I have become less skillful in driving a car; it means that the designers have become more determined that I shall not be given an even show.

The public's passive acceptance of this strange vehicle is disheartening, as is the acceptance by other peoples of the strange modern governments which are destroying them in a dulcet fashion. I think there will some day be an awakening of a rude sort, just as there will some day inevitably be a union of democracies, after many millions have died for the treacherous design of nationalism.

MAINE SPEECH

I FIND that, whether I will or no, my speech is gradually changing, to conform to the language of the country. The tongue spoken here in Maine is as different from the tongue spoken in New York as Dutch is from German. Part of this difference is in the meaning of words, part in the pronunciation, part in the grammar. But the difference is great. Sometimes when a child is talking it is all one can do to translate until one has mastered the language. Our boy came home from school the first day and said the school was peachy but he couldn't understand what anybody was saying. This lasted only a couple of days.

For the word "all" you use the phrase "the whole of." You ask, "Is that the whole of it?" And whole is pronounced hull. Is that the hull of it? It sounds as though you might mean a ship.

For lift, the word is heft. You heft a thing to see how much it weighs. When you are holding a wedge for somebody to tap with a hammer, you say: "Tunk it a little." I've never heard the word tap used. It is always tunk.

Baster (pronounced bayster) is a popular word with boys. All the kids use it. He's an old baster, they say, when they pull an eel out of an eel trap. It probably derives from bastard, but it sounds quite proper and innocent when you hear it, and rather descriptive. I regard lots of things now (and some people) as old basters.

A person who is sensitive to cold is spleeny. We have never put a heater in our car, for fear we might get spleeny. When a pasture is sparse and isn't providing enough feed for the stock, you say the pasture is pretty snug. And a man who walks and talks slowly or lazily is called mod'rate. He's a powerful mod'rate man, you say.

When you're prying something with a pole and put a rock under the pole as a fulcrum, the rock is called a bait. Few people use the word "difference." When they want to say it makes no difference, they say it doesn't make any odds.

If you have enough wood for winter but not enough to carry you beyond that, you need wood "to spring out on." And when a ewe shows an udder, she "bags out." Ewe is pronounced yo by old-timers like my friend Dameron.

This ewe and yo business had me licked at first. It seemed an affectation to say yo when I was talking about a female sheep. But that was when I was still thinking of them as yews. After a while I thought of them as yos, and then it seemed perfectly all right. In fact, yo is a better-sounding word, all in all, than yew. For a while I tried to pronounce it half way between yew and yo. This proved fatal. A man has to make up his mind and then go boldly ahead. A ewe can't stand an umlaut any more than she can a terrier.

Hunting or shooting is called gunning. Tamarack is always hackmatack. Tackle is pronounced taykle. You rig a block and taykle.

If one of your sheep is tamer than the others, and the others follow her, you say she will "toll" the others in. The chopped clams that you spread upon the waters to keep the mackerel schooling around your boat are called toll bait. Or chum bait. A windy day is a "rough" day, whether you are on land or sea. Mild weather is "soft." And there is a distinction between weather overhead and weather underfoot. Lots of times, in spring, when the ground is muddy, you will have a "nice day overhead."

Manure is dressing, not manure. I think, although I'm not sure, that manure is considered a nasty word, not fit for polite company. The word dung is used some but not as much as dressing. But a manure fork is always a dung fork.

Wood that hasn't properly seasoned is dozy. The lunch hour is one's nooning. A small cove full of mud and eelgrass is a gunkhole. When a pullet slips off and lays in the blackberry bushes she "steals a nest away." If you get through the winter without dying or starving you "wintered well."

Persons who are not native to this locality are "from away." We are from away ourselves, and always will be, even if we live here the rest of our lives. You've got to be born here—otherwise you're from away.

People get born, but lambs and calves get dropped. This is literally true of course. The lamb actually does get dropped. (It doesn't hurt it any

—or at any rate it never complains.) When a sow has little ones, she "pigs." Mine pigged on a Sunday morning, the ol' baster.

The road is often called "the tar." And road is pronounced ro-ud. The other day I heard someone called President Roosevelt a "war mongrel." Statute is called statue. Lawyers are busy studying the statues. Library is liberry. Chimney is chimley.

Fish weir is pronounced fish ware. Right now they're not getting anything in the wares.

Hoist is pronounced hist. I heard a tall story the other day about a man who was histed up on the end of a derrick boom while his companions accused him of making free with another man's wife. "Come on, confess!" they shouted. "Isn't it true you went with her all last year?" For a while he swung at the end of the boom and denied the charges. But he got tired finally. "You did, didn't you?" they persisted. "Well, once, boys," he replied. "Now hist me down."

The most difficult sound is the "a." I've been in Maine, off and on, all my life, but I still have to pause sometimes when somebody asks me something with an "a" in it. The other day a friend met me in front of the store, and asked, "How's the famine comin' along?" I had to think fast before I got the word "farming" out of his famine.

The word dear is pronounced dee-ah. Yet the word deer is pronounced deer. All children are called dee-ah, by men and women alike. Workmen often call each other dee-ah while on the job.

The final "y" of a word becomes "ay." Our boy used to call our dog Freddie. Now he calls him Fredday. Sometimes he calls him Fredday dee-ah; other times he calls him Fredday you ol' baster.

Country talk is alive and accurate, and contains more pictures and images than city talk. It usually has an unmistakable sincerity that gives it distinction. I think there is less talking merely for the sound that it makes. At any rate, I seldom tire of listening to even the most commonplace stuff, directly and sincerely spoken; and I still recall with dread the feeling that occasionally used to come over me at parties in town when the air was crowded with loud intellectual formations—the feeling that there wasn't a remark in the room that couldn't be brought down with a common pin.

LIME

Received my allotment of ground limestone from the government last month. They gave me three tons of it, and it cost me nothing save a nominal charge for trucking. I have already spread it on my upper field and harrowed it in. Thus the New Deal comes home to me in powdered form, and I gain a new alkalinity and acquire some fresh doubts and misgivings.

I've been thinking a good bit about this lime, this handout; and it seems to me that it is the principal ingredient of the new form of government that Mr. Roosevelt is introducing, an ingredient I must try hard to identify in order to clarify the stew on which I feed and on which the people of America (or Amarrica) are so sharply divided. By applying for and receiving this lime I have become a party to one of the so-called "social gains" we heard so much about during the political campaign. I don't know whether I like it or not. The lime for my field was a gift to me from all the taxpayers of the United States, a grudging gift on the part of about half of them who disavow the principles of the AAA, a gift in the name of fertility, conservation, and humanity. In so far as it is to the advantage of the nation that the soil of America shall be maintained in all its chemical goodness, the dispensation from Mr. Roosevelt is justifiable. Most farmers need more fertilizer than they can afford to buy; when the government provides it free of charge the land improves. But this of course isn't the whole story.

To be honest I must report that at the time I got the lime I experienced a slight feeling of resentment—a feeling not strong enough to prevent my applying for my share in the booty but still a recognizable sensation. I seemed to have lost a little of my grip on life. I felt that something inside me, some intangible substance, was leaching away. I also detected a slight sense of being under obligation to somebody, and this, instead of arousing my gratitude, took the form of mild resentment —the characteristic attitude of a person who has had a favor done him whether he liked it or not. All I had to do was spread the lime on a five-acre piece, together with barn dressing, but the Federal government had a harder spreading job than that: the government had to spread the cost of it over the entire citizenry, over not only those who had re-elected Roosevelt but those who had despised him. So much Republican acidity for the lime to sweeten, it must have lost much of its strength before it reached my clay soil.

I don't know. It is something for every man to study over, with the help of his God and his conscience. I do begin to feel the friendly control over me and over my land that an Administration exerts in its eagerness to "adjust" me and to change the soil reaction of my upper field. I believe in this Administration, on the whole; in its vision and in its essential vigor. I even voted for it again. It has been called crackpot, but that doesn't disparage it for me. Genius is more often found in a cracked pot than in a whole one. In the main I prefer to be experimented on by an idealist than allowed to lie fallow through a long dry reactionary season. I believe in this Administration, but I am also trying to make out the implications in a load of limestone.

I think it is an unusually important question, and I wish I could be as sure of it in my mind as the President is in his. (Query: does he ever get any free lime for his Hyde Park place?) The gift of fertilizer is an arbitrary benefit bestowed by thinkers who agree that soil fertility is a national concern—a matter that touches *all* the people and, therefore, that may rightly be charged against all the people. That much is true, I think, even though there are millions of Americans who will never feel any direct gain from the increased alkalinity of my little bit of ground. But I believe it also is true that a government committed to the policy of improving the nation by improving the condition of *some* of the individuals will eventually run into trouble in attempting to distinguish between a national good and a chocolate sundae.

To take an extreme example: through indirect taxation my lime is paid for in part by thousands of young ladies many of whom are nursing a personal want comparable to my want of lime. We will say that they want a permanent wave, to bolster their spirits and improve the chemistry of their nature. Theirs is a real want, however frivolous. Hairdressing, like any other form of top dressing, is a vital need among many people, and the satisfaction of it, in a sense, may be termed a national good. It doesn't come first, as soil does, but it comes eventually at the end of a long line of reasoning or unreasoning. I think that one hazard of the "benefit" form of government is the likelihood that there will be an indefinite extension of benefits, each new one establishing an easy precedent for the next.

Another hazard is that by placing large numbers of people under obligation to their government there will develop a self-perpetuating party capable of supplying itself with a safe majority. I notice that a few days after my lime had come I received a letter from my county agent that started, "To Members of the H—— County Agricultural Conservation Association. Dear Member . . ." You see, already I was a paid-up Democrat, before ever the lime had begun to dissolve.

Well, I'm not trying to take sides. I'm just a man who got a few bags of lime for nuthin', and whose cup runneth over, troubling his dreams.

ॐ

Started using lights on my pullets today, the days being so short. Tomorrow my birds will experience a false sunrise at 4 A.M. when the alarm goes off and the light snaps on. I used to think that electric lights in a henhouse were a barbarous idea, but I don't any more, now that I am better acquainted with hens. The nights here are fifteen hours long, and a hen almost starves to death waiting for morning to come. It is not enough that a hen have food—she must be able to see to eat.

Am reading *The Formation of Vegetable Mould, Through the Action of Worms, With Observations on Their Habits,* by Charles Darwin. I borrowed it from the keeper of a tavern, who seemed surprised that his library included so unsuitable a volume. "I was thus led to conclude," says Darwin, "that all the vegetable mould over the whole country has passed many times through, and will again pass many times through, the intestinal canals of worms."

DOG TRAINING

THERE is a book out called *Dog Training Made Easy* and it was sent to me the other day by the publisher, who rightly guessed that it would catch my eye. I like to read books on dog training. Being the owner of dachshunds, to me a book on dog discipline becomes a volume of inspired humor. Every sentence is a riot. Some day, if I ever get a chance, I shall write a book, or warning, on the character and temperament of the Dachshund and why he can't be trained and shouldn't be. I would rather train a striped zebra to balance an Indian club than induce a dachshund to heed my slightest command. For a number of years past I have been agreeably encumbered by a very large and dissolute dachshund named Fred. Of all the dogs whom I have served I've never known one who understood so much of what I say or held it in such deep contempt. When I address Fred I never have to raise either my voice or my hopes. He even disobeys me when I instruct him in something that he wants to do. And when I answer his peremptory scratch at the door and hold the door open for him to walk through, he stops in the middle and lights a cigarette, just to hold me up.

"Shopping for a puppy presents a number of problems," writes Mr. Wm. Cary Duncan, author of *Dog Training Made Easy*. Well, shopping for a puppy has never presented many problems for me, as most of the puppies and dogs that have entered my life (and there have been scores of them) were not the result of a shopping trip but of an act of God. The first puppy I owned, when I was about nine years old, was not shopped for—it was born to the collie bitch of the postman of my older sister, who sent it to me by express from Washington, D.C., in a little crate containing, in addition to the puppy, a bar of Peters' chocolate and a ripe frank-furter. And the puppy I own now was not shopped for but was won in a raffle. Between these two extremes there have been many puppies, mostly unshopped for. It is not so much that I acquire dogs as it is that dogs acquire me. Maybe they even shop for me, I don't know. If they do I assume they have many problems, because they certainly always arrive with plenty, which they then turn over to me.

The possession of a dog today is a different thing from the possession of a dog at the turn of the century, when one's dog was fed on mashed potato and brown gravy and lived in a doghouse with an arched portal. Today a dog is fed on scraped beef and Vitamin B_1 and lives in bed with you.

An awful lot of nonsense has been written about dogs by persons who don't know them very well, and the attempt to elevate the purebred to a position of national elegance has been, in the main, a success. Dogs used to mate with other dogs rather casually in my day, and the results were discouraging to the American Kennel Club but entirely satisfactory to small boys who liked puppies. In my suburban town, "respectable" peo-ple didn't keep she-dogs. One's washerwoman might keep a bitch, or one's lawn cutter, but not one's next-door neighbor.

The prejudice against females made a deep impression on me, and I grew up thinking that there was something indecent and unclean about she-things in general. The word bitch of course was never used in polite families. One day a little mutt followed me home from school, and after much talk I persuaded my parents to let me keep it—at least until the owner turned up or advertised for it. It dwelt among us only one night. Next morning my father took me aside and in a low voice said: "My son, I don't know whether you realize it, but that dog is a female. It'll have to go."

"But why does it have to?" I asked.

"They're a nuisance," he replied, embarrassed. "We'd have all the other dogs in the neighborhood around here all the time."

That sounded like an idyllic arrangement to me, but I could tell from my father's voice that the stray dog was doomed. We turned her out and she went off toward the more liberal section of town. This sort of incident must have been happening to thousands of American youngsters in those days, and we grew up to find that it had been permanently added to the record by Dorothy Parker in her short story "Mr. Durant."

On our block, in the days of my innocence, there were in addition to my collie, a pug dog, a dachshund named Bruno, a fox terrier named Sunny who spent many years studying one croquet ball, a red setter, and a St. Bernard who carried his mistress's handbag, shuffling along in stately fashion with the drool running out both sides of his jaws. I was scared of this St. Bernard because of his size, and never passed his house without dread. The dachshund was old, surly, and disagreeable, and was endlessly burying bones in the flower border of the DeVries's yard. I should very much doubt if any of those animals ever had its temperature taken rectally, ever was fed raw meat or tomato juice, ever was given distemper inoculations, or ever saw the whites of a veterinary's eyes. They were brought up on chicken bones and gravy and left-over cereal, and were all fine dogs. Most of them never saw the inside of their owners' houses—they knew their place.

The "problem" of caring for a dog has been unnecessarily complicated. Take the matter of housebreaking. In the suburbia of those lovely post-Victorian days of which I write, the question of housebreaking a puppy was met with the simple bold courage characteristic of our forefathers. You simply kept the house away from the puppy. This was not only the simplest way, it was the only practical way, just as it is today. Our parents were in possession of a vital secret—a secret which has been all but lost to the world: the knowledge that a puppy will live and thrive without ever crossing the threshold of a dwelling house, at least till he's big enough so he doesn't wet the rug.

Although our fathers and mothers very sensibly never permitted a puppy to come into the house, they made up for this indignity by always calling the puppy "Sir." In those days a dog didn't expect anything very elaborate in the way of food or medical care, but he did expect to be addressed civilly.

Mr. Duncan discusses housebreaking at some length and assumes, as do all writers of dog books, that the owner of a puppy has little else to do except own the puppy. It is Mr. Duncan's theory that puppies have a sense of modesty and don't like to be stared at when they are doing something. When you are walking the dog, he says, you must "appear utterly uninterested" as you approach some favorite spot. This, as any city dweller knows, is a big order. Anybody who has ever tried to synchronize a puppy's bowels with a rigid office schedule knows that one's interest in the small phenomena of early morning sometimes reaches fever pitch. A dog owner may feign disinterest, but his mask will not suffice. Nothing is more comical than the look on the face of a person at the upper end of a dog leash, pretending not to know what is going on at the lower.

A really companionable and indispensable dog is an accident of nature. You can't get it by breeding for it, and you can't buy it with money. It just happens along. Out of the vast sea of assorted dogs that I have had dealings with, by far the noblest, the best, and the most important was the first, the one my sister sent me in a crate. He was an old-style collie, beautifully marked, with a blunt nose and great natural gentleness and intelligence. When I got him he was what I badly needed. I think probably all these other dogs of mine have been just a groping toward that old dream. I've never dared get another collie for fear the comparison would be too uncomfortable. I can still see my first dog in all the moods and situations that memory has filed him away in, but I think of him oftenest as he used to be right after breakfast on the back porch, listlessly eating up a dish of petrified oatmeal rather than hurt my feelings. For six years he met me at the same place after school and convoyed me home—a service he thought up himself. A boy doesn't forget that sort of association. It is a monstrous trick of fate that now, settled in the country and with sheep to take care of, I am obliged to do my shepherding with the grotesque and sometimes underhanded assistance of two dachshunds and a wire-haired fox terrier.

THE WAVE OF THE FUTURE

THURSDAY. This morning made preparations for building a boat—the first boat I ever prepared to build. Bought ten cents' worth of wicking and borrowed some caulking tools, and prepared myself further by asking a man how to build a boat and he told me. It is to be a small scow, made of native cedar. Heard deer hunters beating through the woods this afternoon, hollering and carrying on.

Sunday. All morning at work boat-building. Had a stove going in the shop and, although it was a cold rainy morning, all was cheerful inside. The cedar shavings smell good and are worth the effort of planing. The boat has been named *Flounder.* I am perfectly happy doing anything of this sort and would rather construct something than do any other sort of work. When I needed a three-eighths-inch dowel stick I had to dismast a small American flag and use the staff, but it worked well and is now an integral part of *Flounder.*

Tuesday. Arose at six on a cold morning and by truck alone to Waterville to keep an appointment with a medical man, a drive of about eighty miles, but I would travel farther than that to find relief for a sick nose. Anyway, I like travel for its own sake, either with others or alone. It was quite cold in the cab of the truck and I had to stop occasionally to thaw out. Passed some grave diggers in a cemetery, and they were having hard going through frozen ground but were eager and undismayed.

While waiting to see the doctor bought Anne Lindbergh's book *The Wave of the Future* and read it sitting in the truck. It is called a "confession of faith," but I couldn't make out what it is she believes in and did not think it a clear book or a good one. So read it all through again, and

I think she wants a good world, as I do, but that she has retreated into the pure realm of thought, leaving the rest of us to rassle with the bear. Mrs. Lindbergh feels that the war is so large and so dreadful that a man must at all costs keep his perspective and look at it in the broader way; but I think it is even more dreadful than that, and that we ought to fight and win it. And she says that the things that are going on in the world today are so tremendous and significant that we should concentrate on taking the beam out of our own eye and never mind the mote in our neighbor's; but I do not like that advice and do not intend to take it, for in this instance the spectacle of my neighbor's mote is of such a character that it has moved me to tears and the tears are dissolving my beam at a fair rate—which is as good a way to get rid of it as any.

As I read and re-read *The Wave of the Future,* parked at the curb of a town of the present, watching the flow of life in a New England community on a winter's afternoon, I kept waiting for the expression of faith that did not come. Mrs. Lindbergh speaks of the dream of the future, which is to be realized by taking advantage of the "great forces pushing in the world"; but either by accident or by design she identifies these great dream-fulfilling forces with the push in Germany, Italy, and Russia. In the revolutionary turbulence of fascist countries she finds a promise and a token—an ultimate answer to poverty, unemployment, depression. She speaks of a dying civilization, and her implication is that its rebirth will be in the new style now on exhibition in European show windows; but I do not agree, and do not believe that the forces that motivate fascism are any more important in future-building, or any more promising, than, for example, the forces that are resisting fascism. Each is a part of our future, the one as passionately as the other. Mrs. Lindbergh suggests, flatly, that we not resist the wave that approaches. "It is a sin against Nature," she says, "to resist change." But I think I shall go on resisting any change I disapprove of, for I do not think change, *per se,* is anything much, nor that change is necessarily good. As for sinning against Nature, I do that every time I take a drink, but it is not the whole story of alcohol by any means, and anyway, fascism sins against Nature more grievously than anything I ever saw, because it proposes to remove (and does remove) so much of what is natural in people's lives. Mrs. Lindbergh pines for the days of her father when, she said, a person could discuss differences of opinion intelligently and dispassionately without being branded "pro" or "anti"; and I believe in that sort of discussion too and so cannot understand her pleading in the next breath that we do not resist the forces that are pledged to destroy parliaments and senates and congresses and newspapers and courts and universities.

The future, wave or no wave, seems to me no unified dream but a mince pie, long in the baking, never quite done. The push of eager, dispossessed, frustrated people, united zealously under a bad leader, is one ingredient; the resistance of those whom this push hurts or offends or threatens is another. To Mrs. Lindbergh the push of the one (for reasons that she doesn't explain) is the new, hopeful current in life; the resistance of the others is the old, decadent, disagreeable current. It seemed odd, sitting with my feverish nose and being told by Anne Lindbergh that fascism was the wave of the future, when she knows as well as I do that it is just the backwash of the past and has muddied the world for centuries. "Somehow," she says, "the leaders in Germany, Italy, and Russia have discovered how to use new social and economic forces; very often they have used them badly, but nevertheless they have recognized and used them. They have felt the wave of the future and they have leapt upon it."

I think it is only fair to ask Mrs. Lindbergh to name one *new* social or economic force that has been discovered by dictators. I can't think of any that aren't as old as the hills. The force that Hitler employs is the force generated by people who have stood all the hardship they intend to, and are exploding through the nearest valve, and it is an ancient force, and so is the use of it by opportunists in bullet-proof vests. The turbulence on which she builds her dream of a better world is an historically discouraging phenomenon, but I think it is a common fallacy to say that because a movement springs from deep human distress it must hold thereby the seed of a better order. The fascist ideal, however great the misery that released it and however impressive the self-denial and the burning courage that promote it, does not hold the seed of a better order but of a worse one, and it always has a foul smell and a bad effect on the soil. It stank at the time of Christ and it stinks today, wherever you find it and in whatever form, big or little—even here in America, the little fascists always at their tricks, stirring up a lynching mob or flagellating the devil or selling a sex pamphlet to tired, bewildered old men. The forces are always the same—on the people's side frustration, disaffection; on the leader's side control of hysteria, perversion of information, abandonment of principle. There is nothing new in it and nothing good in it, and today when it is developed to a political nicety and supported by a formidable military machine the best thing to do is to defeat it as promptly as possible and in all humility.

I think it is inaccurate of the author of *The Wave of the Future* to ascribe modernity to such old chestnuts or to imply that they bode good for the world. She herself states that the evils in the system are the "scum on the wave," but makes it clear that this is the wave. It is of course anybody's privilege to believe that a good conception of humanity may be coming to birth through the horrid forms of nazism; but it seems to me far more likely that a good conception of humanity is being promoted by the stubborn resistance to nazism on the part of millions of people whose belief in democratic notions has been strengthened. Is my own intellectual resistance, based on a passionate belief that the "new order" is basically destructive of universal health and happiness, any less promising than the force of nazism itself, merely because mine does not spring from human misery but merely from human sympathy? I don't see why. And I do not regard it as a sin to hang fast to principles of a past that I approve of and believe are still applicable and sensible merely because they are, so to speak, "past" and not "future." I think they are future too, and I think democracy—which Mrs. Lindbergh seems to feel is sick of an incurable disease—is the most futuristic thing I ever heard of, and that it holds everything hopeful there is, because "demos" means people and that's what I am for, and whatever Nazi means it doesn't mean people, it means "the pure-bred people," which is a contemptible idea to build a new order on. Mrs. Lindbergh always uses quotation marks round the word democracy as though it had to be held gingerly in the fingers. But I still think it a good word and a beautiful word, even after the drubbing it took on the campaign platforms of 1940, and I find the wave that it sets up a more agreeable wave than any other, and more promising and more buoyant and prettier to look at.

Mrs. Lindbergh says it is the duty of a writer to state the problem correctly, and I agree with her but do not think she has done a good job, because many of her statements, although accurate enough in themselves, are followed by an inferential remark that a logician would find inadmissible. She tells me that the German people are not innately bad, which is correct and is not even news as far as I am concerned; but then she draws the inference that therefore the star the German people are following is good, which I think is illogical and a perversion of the facts. And she tells me that life is nothing but change, which is correct; and then implies that change is on that account beneficial, which I doubt in many cases. And she tells me that the fascist push originated in frustration and injustice, which I say is true and correct; and then infers that because the push stemmed from human misery it bodes good for the world, which I feel is fallacious, for I know a lot of things can start with human misery and not bring anything except *more* human misery.

And she tells me that this is not a war of good versus evil, which is correct, and then she says, No, it is more a war of past versus future, and I take it from a close study of her text that by "past" she means what has happened in England and France, and by "future" she means what is happening in Germany and Italy. And that is an inaccurate and really a very irresponsible statement to make. She says: "I do feel that it is futile to get into a hopeless 'crusade' to save civilization." Maybe it is, but I do not think it entirely futile to take up arms to dispossess tyrants, defend popular government, and promote free methods.

And she says look at the French Revolution, there were plenty of atrocious things going on at that time, yet we don't judge it by the atrocities. So I looked at the French Revolution, but did not find a parallel case; for the revolutionists in France were fighting because they were fed up with aristocracy and were seeking individual liberty; but in Germany the people were fed up not with a ruling class but with hard times and were surrendering their individual liberty on the promise that they would themselves become a ruling class and a ruling country.

"The things one loves, lives, and dies for are not . . . completely expressible in words," she writes. No, they are not. But sometimes, with much pain, a man can come close, and it is peculiarly desirable now that anyone who writes any statement such as *The Wave of the Future* should come as close as possible. After all, life is not entirely complex. It is certainly no figment of my imagination that today hundreds of writers and artists and scholars, whose lives and works are a monument to truth, culture, freedom, and tolerance, are muzzled—locked up in camps in the grip of the disease that Anne Lindbergh finds hopeful. Is this their wave of the future? I doubt it. They simply want to get out of camp and into harness again, and it's as simple as that.

I am determined to express, as nearly as I can, my disappointment with this book because I have heard many people speak of it and almost all of them said something like this: "Of course I don't agree with her about everything, but there's something to what she says just the same." And so I read it twice and with great care, sentence by sentence, to find what this mysterious something was, and it wasn't there, not for me it wasn't. Yet the book had a double fascination for me, because it contains so many small and rather attractive truths that all add up to make one big fallacy, and to a writer that is always a fascinating performance. And even after all my conclusions I do not believe that Mrs. Lindbergh is any more fascist-minded than I am, or that she wants a different sort of world, or that she is a defeatist; but I think instead she is a poetical and liberal and talented person troubled in her mind (as anybody is today) and trying to write her way into the clear. But although her first two books contained some of the best stuff and some of the best reporting I have ever read, this one reminded me of what Somerset Maugham wrote in *The Summing Up* when he said: ". . . there is a sort of magic in the written word. The idea acquires substance by taking on a visible nature, and then stands in the way of its own clarification."

And when I went in at last to the doctor's office and was admitted I still was thinking about these matters and felt low in my spirits and spent, and it was the first time I had seen this doctor but he didn't look at me but just said: "What's matter?"

"My nose," I replied, but I was really thinking about Anne Lindbergh and wondering about her book and about what she believed and whether she had come close to expressing it, or not close, and whether it was the book of someone who was bothered by a confusion of loyalties.

"What's trouble with nose?" the doctor asked.

"Stuffed up," I replied.

And he asked me how old I was and I said forty-one, and he wrote that down on a piece of paper, and I wanted to say "My nose is forty-one too," but thought better of it. So I told him about my hay fever, which used to rage just in summertime but now simmers the year round, and he listened listlessly as though it were a cock and bull story; and we sat there for a few minutes and neither of us was interested in the other's nose, but after a while he poked a little swab up mine and made a smear on a glass slide and his assistant put it under the microscope and found two cells that delighted him and electrified the whole office, the cells being characteristic of a highly allergic system. The doctor's manner changed instantly and he was full of the enthusiasm of discovery and was as proud of the two little cells as though they were his own.

I'm to go back Tuesday to be skin tested, to see what foods and pollens and bits of fluff disturb me, but none of them disturbs me so much as Mrs. Lindbergh's confession. These systemic disturbances are more mysterious than even doctors know, and these days he would have to scratch me with substances more subtle than rabbit's hair and duck's feathers to find my misery.

A WINTER DIARY

THURSDAY. Snowed hard all yesterday and continued through the night, and this morning the sky cleared and the wind went round into the NW. Spent the morning planking the scow that I am building. Am working from a picture in *The American Boy's Handy Book,* after a pardonable delay of thirty years, which is the time it took me to assemble the nails and the boards and the skill and the leisure and the patience. I am thankful that after that interval my desire is as strong, or almost as strong, as it was originally.

Tuesday. The roads are solid ice. Up at 5:15 and after breakfast to the doctor's, the country seeming very beautiful and cheerful after a light fall of snow. I am always humbled by the infinite ingenuity of the Lord, who can make a red barn cast a blue shadow. At the doctor's my skin was pricked eighty-one times and showed kinship with cat hair, horse dander, tobacco, oats, goose feathers, duck feathers, chicken feathers, timothy, English plantain, orchard grass, June grass, and sweet vernal, which was no news to me but which the doctor found exciting and instructive. Lunched in a taproom where there were booths and pine paneling and a voice singing "I can hear the bells of Monterey," very soft and love-sick; but anyone in the restaurant could have walked to the edge of town and heard the sleigh bells of Messalonskee.

Thursday. All morning at work indoors and this afternoon fashioned two oak knees for the scow and then went to plowing out the snow-covered driveway with my new homemade plow, and it worked remarkably well. It has adjustable wings and in all respects is a serviceable implement, and it has the advantage of not being longer or lower or smoother than the old 1940 plow. Worked till after dark, in still air with the sounds muffled and lights shining from the windows onto the drifts. After dinner to see "Foreign Correspondent" but did not like it much and do not think newspapermen are often accurately portrayed on the screen —or any other sort of person for that matter. The movies improve but slowly, and I think they would make much better progress if they would take Hamlet's advice, who said: "The play's the thing." But instead of that they stick to their own motto, which is: "The player's the thing." So everything in life has to be adjusted to fit the personality of Joel McCrea, which for me is dull sport.

Saturday. Last fall I hauled rockweed up from the shore and spread it to a depth of five or six inches on the dirt floor of the sheep shed and covered it with straw. Now the sheep droppings are accumulating on this rockweed base and forming a rich dressing for the land. There is no doubt about it, the basic satisfaction in farming is manure, which always suggests that life can be cyclic and chemically perfect and aromatic and continuous.

A brilliant testimonial to the magic of sheep dressing is written in the leaves of my New York City rubber plant, which has lately been receiving an occasional shot of liquid tonic made of a barnyard mixture that I prepare in old Scotch-whisky bottles and keep handy for use on house plants. This rubber plant is one I bought thirteen years ago on West Eighth Street and it has been my companion ever since. As rubber plants go it has been a success and I am attached to it in a curious sort of way, as a man does get attached to anything that manages to last thirteen years under the same roof with him. Its growth has been erratic and inconsistent and it has not always enjoyed good health. Some of its leaves are large and shiny and well-formed. Others I try not to think about. One leaf is barely two inches long—mute reminder of a hard winter when the plague spread over everything in our apartment. And dotting its trunk and branches are scars of one miasmic summer when I loaned the plant to an obscure biographer named Henry Pringle and it lost all its leaves but two, and a white milky fluid oozed from every wound. That summer finally ended. Pringle went on to win the Pulitzer prize, and I went on to nursing a rubber plant back to health.

Essentially, rubber plants are city plants. They often do better in dark hallways in gloomy city apartments than in the sunny south windows of country homes. For a while after we came here I kept my rubber plant in the sun, as an experiment, but it began to sicken and the leaves would turn yellow and drop off. So I removed it to a north location and it improved. But one day, more as a gag than anything else, I poured a little of the liquid sheep manure on the plant. I say more as a gag—I had always had a notion that a rubber plant drew its nourishment not so much from the ball of exhausted earth surrounding its roots as from the people it lived with and the conversations it overheard. This theory of mine was wrong. The effect of the manure was instantaneous. The plant sent out enormous red leaf spears three times the size of anything it had ever produced before, and these unrolled into leaves of magnificent proportions, so that the plant as a whole looked like a monstrosity, as though the old part didn't belong to the new. It was a startling experience, and for a while I flirted with the idea of getting rich quick by selling bottled strength to city people who harbor rubber plants. But when I figured out how much Scotch I would have to drink in order to have enough empty bottles I got cold feet and the idea blew up.

I have been listening to Hendrik van Loon broadcast the news lately, in Mr. Swing's place. He is a good news man, for he sounds as though the fighting and the destruction wearied and disgusted him. He wanders around among departed centuries like an old tourist poking with his stick in the ruins; and probably because he is a historian and a geographer and has a broader sense of time and space than most, he sounds discouraged and grieved at the repetition of ancient movements of peoples and armies on the globe, yet firm in his belief in the ultimate triumph of the free man. I have liked his reports on the day's events because he has made them seem like part of a whole, not like an isolated moment in time. Many newscasters, it seems to me, have developed a cheerful bedside manner, and when they mention a mechanized division it sounds as though they had it right there in the studio and were scratching it behind the ears.

One of the phenomena of the war is the news coverage. In a sense the American people are a bit overtrained on this strange concentrated diet. Body and mind adjust to almost any sort of stimulus; we compensate physically for the news, just as we do for the speed of a motor car in which we are riding, until at last it seems as though the car is not in motion at all, and as though there is no news, not really.

Friday. Awoke early and lay still in the dark, listening to the singing in the next room. A light snow this morning; the road was covered when I got up and snow lay on the backs of my sheep lying placidly in the barnyard. When they are in repose I can watch sheep endlessly. They are worth studying: their imperturbability and their preference for outdoors (except in hard storms), and the deep look of tranquillity on their faces as the snow settles lightly on their thick, broad backs. My flock is thriftier looking than a year ago, and now I have a pure-bred Cheviot buck, and the lambs this spring will be of his marking. Also acquired one pure-bred ewe.

Sunday. All three of us to the faraway doctor yesterday through snow and bad temper, the temper being mine; but it comes from my nose not my heart. The doctor took X-ray pictures of our son's antra and wants to bore some holes in his head, which made me sick and discouraged all day and worried. We started driving back home just before dark, but I was doubtful that we could make it, as the snow had begun to drift across the highway and it was still snowing hard. Couldn't see the road very well, so when we drew into the village of China I decided we had had enough of storm and bone cavities for one day, enough of doubts and slippery surfaces, so we drove into the garage of R. E. Coombs and he told us we might find lodging at an inn across the way. No lights showed, but we waded up to the door and were welcomed by Mrs. Wilson, the proprietress, who was surprised to find guests in winter but took us in anyway and gave us some Saturday-night baked beans and brown bread with a dessert of preserved strawberries; and we moved the davenport from the living room into a big chamber across the hall to make the third bed. After supper we had a talk with our hostess about education, a subject on which she turned out to be an authority, because in winter-time, when innkeeping is slow, she occupies herself by teaching a district school and has nine grades under her. She thought consolidation of schools in her town would probably be a good thing, but that there was strong opposition to it. And she told us that, although the disadvantages of the one-room school were very great, there were some compensating things too, principally that the pupils in such a school gained of necessity a certain independence at an early age, realizing that they had to progress in scholarship almost unassisted if they were to progress at all. She had taught also in Augusta, where she had only one grade to instruct, and she said it was noticeable how much more reliant on the teacher were the pupils there than in the country school. I believe that, too, and my guess is that the Little Red School of yesterday produced a lower average of intelligence but produced occasional individuals who had the very best education there is, namely the knack and the will to seek and gain knowledge independently, without having it spooned out.

To bed early in our room overlooking frozen China Lake, and heard the snow-plow banging and roaring away trying to make the hill outside our window. We had no nightclothes with us, so had to invent some, and my wife chose a coonskin coat, and I chose a sweater and socks and our boy chose a suit of heavies and a sweater worn on his legs. And we were much merrier than we had been in the early morning, so I made a rhyme that went:

Mamma in her coonskin and I in my socks
Had just settled ourselves for a night of hard knocks
When out on the road there arose such a clatter
We stayed comfortably in bed, since it was entirely obvious what was the matter.

Just before I went to sleep I heard my wife up and about, and I asked her why and she said she had discovered it was impossible to sleep in a coonskin coat because it tickled the back of your neck. So I asked her what she was changing to, and she replied: "Tweeds." Which is the kind of direct answer I like to get when I ask a question.

Still snowing when we awoke this morning. I lay in bed thinking of England and of English families rousing from sleep in caves and warrens, and of how when an American family becomes separated from its toothbrushes and combs and pajamas for a few hours it considers that it has had quite an adventure.

We left the inn right after breakfast and had no trouble driving home, as the roads had been broken out during the night. Found our dooryard and our fields as lovely as the Bernese Oberland, the drifts shoulder-high and little ski trails disappearing down into the spruces at the bottom of the pasture.

ON A FLORIDA KEY

I AM WRITING this in a beach cottage on a Florida key. It is raining to beat the cars. The rollers from a westerly storm are creaming along the shore, making a steady boiling noise instead of the usual intermittent slap. The Chamber of Commerce has drawn the friendly blind against this ugliness and is busy getting out some advance notices of the style parade that is to be held next Wednesday at the pavilion. The paper says cooler tomorrow.

The walls of my room are of matched boarding, applied horizontally and painted green. On the floor is a straw mat. Under the mat is a layer of sand that has been tracked into the cottage and has sifted through the straw. I have thought some of taking the mat up and sweeping the sand into a pile and removing it, but have decided against it. This is the way keys form, apparently, and I have no particular reason to interfere. On a small wooden base in one corner of the room is a gas heater, supplied from a tank on the premises. This device can raise the temperature of the room with great rapidity by converting the oxygen of the air into heat. In deciding whether to light the heater or leave it alone, one has only to choose whether he wants to congeal in a well-ventilated room or suffocate in comfort. After a little practice, a nice balance can be established —enough oxygen left to sustain life, yet enough heat generated to prevent death from exposure.

On the west wall hangs an Indian rug, and to one edge of the rug is pinned a button that carries the legend: Junior Programs Joop Club. Built into the north wall is a cabinet made of pecky cypress. On the top shelf are three large pine cones, two of them painted emerald-green, the third painted brick-red. Also a gilded candlestick in the shape of a Roman chariot. Another shelf holds some shells that, at the expenditure of considerable effort on somebody's part, have been made to look like birds. On the bottom shelf is a tiny toy collie, made of rabbit fur, with a tongue of red flannel.

In the kitchenette just beyond where I sit is a gas stove and a small electric refrigerator of an ancient vintage. The ice trays show deep claw marks where people have tried to pry them free, using can openers and knives and screwdrivers and petulance. When the refrigerator snaps on it makes a noise that can be heard all through the cottage, and the lights everywhere go dim for a second and then return to their normal brilliancy. This refrigerator contains the milk, the butter, and the eggs for tomorrow's breakfast. More milk will arrive in the morning, but I will save it for use on the morrow, so that every day I shall use the milk of the previous day, never taking advantage of the opportunity to enjoy perfectly fresh milk. This is a situation that could be avoided if I had the guts to throw away a whole bottle of milk, but nobody has that much courage in the world today. It is a sin to throw away milk, and we know it.

The water that flows from the faucets in the kitchen sink and in the bathroom contains sulphur and is not good to drink. It leaves deep-brown stains around the drains. Applied to the face with a shaving brush, it feels as though fine sandpaper were being drawn across your jowls. It is so hard and sulphurous that ordinary soap will not yield to it, and the breakfast dishes have to be washed with a washing powder known as Dreft.

On the porch of the cottage, each in a special stand, are two carboys of spring water—for drinking, making coffee, and brushing teeth. There is a deposit of two dollars on bottle and stand, and the water itself costs fifty cents. Two rival companies furnish water to the community, and I happened to get mixed up with both of them. Every couple of days a man from one or the other of the companies shows up and hangs around for a while, whining about the presence on my porch of the rival's carboy. I have made an attempt to dismiss one company and retain the other, but to accomplish it would require a dominant personality and I haven't one. I have been surprised to see how long it takes a man to drink up ten gallons of water. I should have thought I could have done it in half the time it has taken me.

This morning I read in the paper of an old Negro, one hundred and one years old, and he was boasting of the quantity of whisky he had drunk in his life. He said he had once worked in a distillery, and they used to give him half a gallon of whisky a day to take home, which kept him going all right during the week, but on weekends, he said, he would have to buy a gallon extry, to tide him over till Monday.

In the kitchen cabinet is a bag of oranges for morning juice. Each orange is stamped "Color Added." The dyeing of an orange to make it orange is Man's most impudent gesture to date. It is really an appalling piece of effrontery, carrying the clear implication that Nature doesn't know what she is up to. I think an orange, dyed orange, is as repulsive as a pine cone painted green. I think it is about as ugly a thing as I have ever seen, and it seems hard to believe that here, within ten miles, probably, of the trees that bore the fruit, I can't buy an orange that somebody hasn't smeared with paint. But I doubt that there are many who feel that way about it, because fraudulence has become a national virtue and is well thought of in many circles. In the past twenty-four hours, I see by this morning's paper, one hundred and thirty-six cars of oranges have been shipped. There are probably millions of children today who have never seen a natural orange—only an artificially colored one. If they should see a natural orange they might think something had gone wrong with it.

There are two moving picture theaters in the town to which my key is attached by a bridge. In one of them, colored people are allowed in the balcony. In the other, colored people are not allowed at all. I saw a patriotic newsreel there the other day that ended with a picture of the American flag blowing in the breeze, and the words: one nation indivisible, with liberty and justice for all. Everyone clapped, but I decided I could not clap for liberty and justice (for all) while I was in a theater from which Negroes had been barred. And I felt there were too many people in the world who think liberty and justice for all means liberty and justice for themselves and their friends. I sat there wondering what would happen to me if I were to jump up and say in a loud voice: "If you folks like liberty and justice so much, why do you keep Negroes from this theater?" I am sure it would have surprised everybody very much and it is the kind of thing I dream about doing but never do. If I had done it I suppose the management would have taken me by the arm and marched me out of the theater, on the grounds that it is disturbing the peace to speak up for liberty just as the feature is coming on. When a man is in the South he must do as the Southerners do; but although I am willing to call my wife "Sugar" I am not willing to call a colored person a nigger.

Northerners are quite likely to feel that Southerners are bigoted on the race question, and Southerners almost invariably figure that Northerners are without any practical experience and therefore their opinions aren't worth much. The Jim Crow philosophy of color is unsatisfying to a Northerner but is regarded as sensible and expedient to residents of towns where the Negro population is as large as or larger than the white. Whether one makes a practical answer or an idealistic answer to a question depends partly on whether one is talking in terms of one year, or ten years, or a hundred years. It is, in other words, conceivable that the Negroes of a hundred years from now will enjoy a greater degree of liberty if the present restrictions on today's Negroes are not relaxed too fast. But that doesn't get today's Negroes in to see Hedy Lamarr.

I have to laugh when I think about the sheer inconsistency of the Southern attitude about color: the Negro barred from the movie house because of color, the orange with "color added" for its ultimate triumph. Some of the cities in this part of the State have fête days to commemorate the past and advertise the future, and in my mind I have been designing a float that I would like to enter in the parades. It would contain a beautiful Negro woman riding with the other bathing beauties and stamped with the magical words, Color Added.

In the cottage next door is a lady who is an ardent isolationist and who keeps running in and out with pamphlets, books, and marked-up newspapers, hoping to convince me that America should mind its own business. She tracks sand in, as well as ideas, and I have to sweep up after her two or three times a day.

Floridians are complaining this year that business is below par. They tell you that the boom in industry causes this unwholesome situation. When tycoons are busy in the North they have no time for sunning themselves, or even for sitting in a semi-tropical cottage in the rain. Miami is appropriating a few extra thousand dollars for its advertising campaign, hoping to lure executives away from the defense program for a few golden moments.

Although I am no archaeologist, I love Florida as much for the remains of her unfinished cities as for the bright cabanas on her beaches. I love to prowl the dead sidewalks that run off into the live jungle, under the broiling sun of noon, where the cabbage palms throw their spiny shade across the stillborn streets and the creepers bind old curbstones in a fierce sensual embrace and the mocking birds dwell in song upon the remembered grandeur of real estate's purple hour. A boulevard that has been reclaimed by Nature is an exciting avenue; it breathes a strange prophetic perfume, as of some century still to come, when the birds will remember, and the spiders, and the little quick lizards that toast themselves on the smooth hard surfaces that once held the impossible dreams of men. Here along these bristling walks is a decayed symmetry in a living forest—straight lines softened by a kindly and haphazard Nature, pavements nourishing life with the beginnings of topsoil, the cracks in the walks possessed by root structures, the brilliant blossoms of the domesticated vine run wild, and overhead the turkey buzzard in the clear sky, on quiet wings, awaiting new mammalian death among the hibiscus, the yucca, the Spanish bayonet, and the palm. I remember the wonderful days and the tall dream of rainbow's end; the offices with the wall charts, the pins in the charts, the orchestras playing gently to prepare the soul of the wanderer for the mysteries of subdivision, the free bus service to the rainbow's beginning, the luncheon served on the little tables under the trees, the warm sweet air so full of the deadly contagion, the dotted line, the signature, and the premonitory qualms and the shadow of the buzzard in the wild wide Florida sky.

I love these rudimentary cities that were conceived in haste and greed and never rose to suffer the scarifying effects of human habitation, cities of not-quite-forgotten hopes, untouched by neon and by filth. And I love the beaches too, out beyond the cottage colony, where they are wild and free still, visited by the sandpipers that retreat before each wave, like children, and by an occasional hip-sprung farmwife hunting shells, or sometimes by a veteran digging for *Donax variabilis* to take back to his hungry mate in the trailer camp.

The sound of the sea is the most time-effacing sound there is. The centuries reroll in a cloud and the earth becomes young again when you listen, with eyes shut, to the sea—a young green time when the water and the land were just getting acquainted and had known each other for only a few billion years and the mollusks were just beginning to dip and creep in the shallows; and now man the invertebrate, under his ribbed umbrella, anoints himself with oil and pulls on his Polaroid glasses to stop the glare and stretches out his long brown body at ease upon a towel on the warm sand and listens.

The sea answers all questions, and always in the same way; for when you read in the papers the interminable discussions and the bickering and the prognostications and the turmoil, the disagreements and the fateful decisions and agreements and the plans and the programs and the threats and the counter threats, then you close your eyes and the sea dispatches one more big roller in the unbroken line since the beginning of the world and it combs and breaks and returns foaming and saying: "So soon?"

THE TRAILER PARK

Before sitting down to draft a preamble to the constitution of a world federation of democracies, uniting free people under one banner, I decided I would mosey over to the trailer park at the edge of town and ask some of the campers whether they favored any such idea as union. It's all very well to believe in supranationalism, but it's even better to find out whether somebody else at a distance believes in it—because that's what makes it supranational.

The trailer park in this Florida city is an ideal place in which to talk over big affairs with people from far away. In the first place, all your traveling is done for you—the people of Pennsylvania and Oregon and Indiana are right there in one big lot, waiting for you. In the second place, trailer people have time to think about life and to live it and to discuss it. Very few of them have any place they *must* go to in the morning, as to an office, and after they have breakfasted and emptied the sink bucket and tidied up and watered the geranium, they can subside in a folding chair in the sun and begin to think. In some respects a trailer park is a Utopian society, for it consists of persons each of whom is occupying the same amount of space in the community, and none of whom is working very hard at anything in particular, and all of whom are engaged in perfecting the art of living; and although trailer society, like every other society I have ever examined, has its little caste system, economically it is rather a success: every day is a holiday and every night is bingo.

At any rate, I decided I would ask a few American tourists what they thought about union. Even in a trailer park it is not exactly easy to walk up to a stranger and say: "Good morning, do you think the remaining democracies of the world should unite?" but in my experience with nomads I have found them ready for what comes and possessed of a candid interest in oddities of all sorts—and I have never minded being thought a little queer.

The park, situated in a grove of cabbage palms, was in its mid-morning doldrums when I entered it to begin my investigations. The trailers were moored evenly in long streets, their silver tops gleaming in the sun. Many of the occupants had left for the day, to attend a nearby pageant that had the compelling charm of being absolutely free. In the social hall a victrola revolved with a daytime drowsiness, and through the open door I could see about twenty couples maneuvering around the floor with not much gaiety but with a vast content. Past the busy shuffle-board pavilion a man strolled with a Maltese cat in leash, using a little white dog as a lead pony. Under every trailer, in the deep shade, dangled the hose connections through which life drained. Neighborliness pervaded the streets, and the faint memory of fried eggs. I passed a small building that said "Garden Club" on the door; and in fact almost every trailer had some sort of tiny landscape triumph—a nasturtium edged with clam shells or a carved pickaninny fishing in a parched pool. Several of the trailer wives were busy in the open-air laundry over the tubs and ironing boards. And at the far end of the park, where tall Australian pines cast their lengthy and luxuriant shade across a weed-grown avenue, a mocking bird sat on a bough and ran over a few scales. This was a peaceful place, this camp—a Garden of Eden on wheels, capable of picking its own latitudes and following the gentle weather around the year, a haven in which every occupant had brought his life into focus by compressing it into the minimum space, a miracle of internal arrangement plus mobility.

Streets in the park were numbered, and on Third Street I found Henry Lynd polishing his front door. (Trailer people are inveterate housekeepers, and their standards are high. It is my opinion that trailers appeal particularly to persons of a neat turn of mind because a trailer gives a man a better outlet than the average fixed home, which is apt to be somewhat sprawling and which lacks the unity and coherence so dear to orderly natures.) Mr. Lynd was surprised to see me. "I just want to ask you," I said, "whether you would be in favor of a union between the United States, Great Britain, and such other self-governing peoples as were able and willing to join."

Mr. Lynd stopped polishing and stared at me with a shy, accusing look. His lips quivered. "Why . . . yes, I would," he said.

"You think it's a good idea to unite, really?"

"Yes, I do," said Mr. Lynd.

I was hoping that he would enlarge upon the subject and I tried to lead back into it from different angles, but all he said was "Yes." It became clear to me as I worked on Mr. Lynd that, although he was a federalist by instinct, he didn't want to have to tell a stranger why, and considered it his privilege not to have to. Which seemed fair enough. So we got talking along broader lines and he told me he was from Michigan, near Lansing, and that the Florida plates on his car were because he had a child in school here, and you had to buy plates, then you could send a child to school. He said the park was fine: cost him and his family two dollars a week for the three of them, which included washrooms, five kilowatts a week for the plug-in, and dancing. I thanked Mr. Lynd and left, and he returned to polishing his green job. The score was 1-0, favor of the United States of the World. I went on to Fifth Street over near the railroad.

There I spied a man from Michigan and a man from Pennsylvania, sitting together under one canopy. I joined and made it three. "Gentlemen," I said, "if it's all the same to you, I want to ask whether you favor the United States forming a union with Great Britain and other free nations."

"Hell, no!" said Michigan, who had a firm chin and the look of a man who could handle himself without the help of any federation of powers. "The British Empire is the smartest bunch of diplomats in the world, and every time we've been mixed up with 'em they've out-smarted us and we've had to take the little end of it. We might want to form a union with them, but before they got through they'd have everything and we'd have nothing."

Pennsylvania nodded.

"Listen," continued Michigan, "why should we trust England? What did she do in the last war? We won it for her, and then the agreement was that Germany wasn't to rearm, and England sat there, thirty miles away across the Channel, and let Germany build the biggest fighting machine in all history. Why should I want to join England? It would be the same story all over again."

"That the way you feel too?" I asked Pennsylvania.

"Sure," he said, "but I say we ought to give all possible aid to Britain. We got to help her all we can, to protect ourselves. But not by sending men —not one soldier, no, sir."

"You can't trust 'em around the corner," growled Michigan impatiently. "We can't understand Europe over here anyway. Too many wheels within wheels. But it doesn't make any difference—this war is going to crack up in the Balkans, like it always does."

"No union for you gentlemen, then?" I said.

They shook their heads and I left. Score 2-1, favor of isolation.

On Eighth Street I saw an Iowa tag. The owner, a tall, spare, inhospitable man, was slowly rubbing petroleum jelly on the walls of his curious home. He was not glad to see me, but I asked my question.

"Union with England?" he sneered. "It's damn near that now, isn't it?"

"Well, sort of," I apologized. "But not really—not a real union."

"We have to keep helping them fellers every twenty years or so. What's the good? There's no end to it."

"Well, what *are* we going to do?" I asked.

"Keep what money we got right here. Germany ain't goin' to make a landing in this country."

"No union for you, then?" I said.

"Nah," he replied.

"Where you going from here?" I asked.

"Key West," he said, wiping off some jelly with a rag.

With the score 3-1 and the sun high in the sky, I continued up Eighth Street to Vaughn Avenue, where I sighted an amiable little man in comfortable shoes. He was relaxing near the doorstep of his Vagabond Coach, basking in a patch of shade formed by a small cabbage palm and a large electric-light pole. He wore a yachting cap. Under the trailer was a big wash tub with the name "Repe" painted on it.

"Good morning, Captain Repe!" I said, easing myself down on the rear bumper of his Chevrolet and turning on my question. The captain of the Vagabond regarded me with amazement and pleasure.

"Unite with other democratic countries?" he began rapidly. "You bet we better. It's the only sensible thing to do. It's our chance. I believe that people who believe in free government should get together on it, permanent, same as our States. That guy in Germany is going places. Something's got to be done. It's like a sore thumb; the more Germany gets, the more she takes. Of course eventually the whole thing will crack. Bound to. Germany can't police the entire world. But when? That's the question. We can't afford to sit around and wait. A man like Hitler has guts—you got to admire him no matter how much you despise what he does. We got to have guts too. We got to show that democratic countries mean business." He paused, and shifted knees.

I said: "Of course lots of people are against the idea of a world federation—I've been asking people in the park."

"Well," said Mr. Repe, in a confidential tone, "a lot of these people, you ask 'em a big question like that and they'll try to find out what *you* think about it so they can agree with you, but me, anybody asks me anything I tell him exactly what I think. I come in for a lot of kidding around here, on account of this cap. Everybody calls me Cap. I'm one of the oldtimers in this park, but plenty of people don't know any other name for me but Cap."

"Are you a seafaring man?" I inquired.

"Naw. It's just a cap."

"Well, it's a good one," I said, getting up to go. "And I appreciate this interview and hope that some day we shall see the world united, with freedom and justice for all."

Score was now 3-2 against it.

The next man I asked was an elderly fellow from Indiana. He seemed staggered by the question, and looked as though he were about to cry. "You better ask my son-in-law, not me," he said sorrowfully. "He's just around the other side of the trailer."

I found the son-in-law applying black paint to the trim, using a small brush. Before he started to answer my question he put aside his brush, closed the can, and sat down on a box in the center of his garden between the petunia and the calendula. "Yes," he said, "we must combine forces. Democracy cannot continue to exist in Europe without the aid of democracy here. I give Hitler better than a fifty per cent chance to win this war, and I can't see how there would be any self-government left anywhere if Hitler wins. A lot of people will tell you they don't care about Europeans and that we Americans have no stake in it, but I think we have. If Hitler wins we lose our world markets, and our standard of living goes down. We'll eat of course, but what will it be like?"

The father-in-law had crept shyly around and was listening proudly to his son's discourse, openly admiring his ability to put things like that into words—that stuff about world markets and everything. Wonderful to be able to express yourself and answer questions! I thanked them. The score was now tied, 3-3, and the morning was almost gone. The next man would decide whether the free people of the globe were to blunder along in narrow nationalistic groups, always at sixes and sevens, interminably at war, wasting their strength and dissipating their resources, or were to join hands and establish a bold new planetary society in which all men of good will could live full and fruitful lives. In this tight spot, and with the weight of my responsibility hanging round my neck like a chain, it was my incredible good fortune to encounter, a few yards from his factory-built Trail-A-Home, Mr. John Kohlmann, retired, formerly of the North Bergen, N. J., police force. Mr. Kohlmann had the agreeable relaxed look of a man who has spent much of his life spying on felons and footpads and who has at last given it up and turned his face to the sun. When I cautiously asked him if he would approve a federation of democracies, Mr. Kohlmann replied: "Sure!" in a hearty voice.

"You would?" I murmured, dazed.

"Sure, sure," he said.

"Why would you?" I asked, feebly trying to maintain a detached position, but thinking to myself, union wins, 4-3.

"Why? Because suppose we get licked, it's gonna be tough. That's why."

"Exactly," I said. "If we get licked, it's gonna be tough. Say," I continued, when a sudden thought struck me, "I used to live right across the river from North Bergen."

"Where?" asked Mr. Kohlmann, brightening.

"West Thirteenth Street, Manhattan."

"No kid, did ya?" said Mr. Kohlmann, enthusiastically.

"You're damn tootin' I did," I said.

"Well, what d'ya know," he said, shaking his head. "It's a small woild."

I came back home and sat down to work on my preamble. But it was easy work, and seemed to write itself. "We, the people of this small world," I began, "in order to form a more perfect union and before things get too tough . . ."

SPRING

NOTES on springtime and on anything else of an intoxicating nature that comes to mind.

ﻉ❧

There is considerable doubt at this writing that my hog has been bred, although she has been keeping company. Her condition is watched with interest by pigmen hereabouts, who are awaiting (as I am) the beginning of the month to see who is right. I will announce the results of this contest later if I think of it. Last year she had seven, on a Sunday. They were blithe and bonny and good and gay, except the runt—who was merely blithe and good and gay.

ﻉ❧

Anne Carroll Moore, of the New York Public Library, writes me that a representative of Superman, Inc., paid a call on the children's room the other day. He was an average-sized man (nothing super) and was armed with a large poster depicting Superman (full strength) with a list of recommended books. The list included *Robin Hood* and *King Arthur.* He told Miss Moore that boys and girls would read those books if they knew that Superman approved of them. He said his hero carried great weight now, and that teachers in public schools frequently commanded instant obedience from their pupils by invoking Superman. As far as I could gather from Miss Moore's letter, he didn't say anything about Louisa May Alcott, author of *Little Supermen* and *Little Superwomen.*

ह◆

This family, incidentally, has just finished reading *Little Women* aloud. It was our after-dinner mint of the winter of 1940–41; reading time, three months and ten days. One of the wrenching experiences that a person can wish on himself nowadays is to read about Europe in terms of Amy and Laurie.

ह◆

The intoxication of spring is a figure of speech to most creatures, but to a lamb it means a real drunk. The very young lambs who stick to a straight milk diet keep their feet pretty well, but the older ones (the ones of high school age) stagger back from the pasture and after weaving about the barnyard for a few minutes, collapse. They froth at the mouth, and you can hear them grind their teeth forty feet away. It is a glorious jag, this spring drunk. I keep my syringe loaded with tea, and administer it—between paragraphs—to the worst cases. This year is not as bad as last year, for I have fewer lambs and more tea.

ह◆

Haven't seen a snake yet, but I haven't been across to the rock pile and lifted a rock.

ह◆

A pair of starlings are renovating the knothole in the Balm o' Gilead on the front lawn, redecorating and trying to get everything done (eggs laid, birds hatched and launched) before the arrival of the flickers, who walk right in regardless.

ह◆

There is a stanza in Robert Frost's poem "Two Tramps in Mud Time" that describes an April moment when air and sky have a vernal feeling, but suddenly a cloud crosses the path of the sun and a bitter little wind finds you out, and you're back in the middle of March. Everyone who has lived in the country knows that sort of moment—the promise of warmth, the raised hope, the ruthless rebuff.

There is another sort of day that needs celebrating in song—the day of days when spring at last holds up her face to be kissed, deliberate and unabashed. On that day no wind blows either in the hills or in the mind, no chill finds the bone. It is a day that can come only in a northern climate, where there has been a long background of frigidity, a long deficiency of sun.

We've just been through this magical moment—which was more than a moment and was a whole morning—and it lodges in memory like some old romance, with the same subtlety of tone, the same enrichment of the blood, and the enchantment and the mirth and the indescribable warmth. Even before breakfast I felt that the moment was at hand, for when I went out to the barn to investigate twins I let the kitchen door stay open, lazily, instead of closing it behind me. This was a sign. The lambs had nursed and the ewe was lying quiet. One lamb had settled itself on the mother's back and was a perfect miniature of the old one—they reminded me of a teapot we have, whose knob is a tiny replica of the pot itself. The barn seemed warmer and sweeter than usual, but it was early in the day, and the hint of springburst was still only a hint, a suggestion, a nudge. The full impact wasn't felt until the sun had climbed higher. Then came, one after another, the many small caresses that added up to the total embrace of warmth and life—a laziness and contentment in the behavior of animals and people, a tendency of man and dog to sit down somewhere in the sun. In the driveway, a deep rut that for the past week had held three or four inches of water and that had alternately frozen and thawed, showed clear indications of drying up. On the window ledge in the living room, the bare brown forsythia cuttings suddenly discovered the secret of yellow. The goose, instead of coming off her nest and joining her loud companions, settled down on her eleven eggs, pulled some feathers from her breast, and resigned herself to the twenty-eight-day grind. When I went back through the kitchen I noticed that the air that had come in was not like an invader but like a friend who had stopped by for a visit.

ह•

Sugaring operations, conducted by the minor, have been under way for some time. Sap has been running strong. Last Sunday morning we had homemade syrup on pancakes, and the consensus of opinion was that the trees were maples but maybe not sugar maples. Anyway they were not hemlocks, everybody agreed on that, hopefully. Today I received some syrup from a lady who lives in New Hampshire. It had the genuine flavor. There is something quite wonderful about our own, though—a strange woody taste (and the recollection of an early morning figure starting out into the snowy woods with his buckets and his dog).

ह•

Whenever I tell about spring, or any delights that I experience, or the pleasant country, I think of a conversation I had with a friend in the city shortly before I left. "I trust," he said with an ugly leer, "that you will spare the reading public your little adventures in contentment."

૨ન

Of all the common farm operations none is more ticklish and confining than tending a brooder stove. All brooder stoves are whimsical, and some of them are holy terrors. Mine burns coal, and has only a fair record. With its check draft that opens and closes, this stove occupies my dreams from midnight, when I go to bed, until five o'clock, when I get up, pull a shirt and a pair of pants on over my pajamas, and stagger out into the dawn to read the thermometer under the hover and see that my 254 little innocents are properly disposed in a neat circle round their big iron mama. If I am lucky the thermometer registers 88° and the chicks are happily eating their favorite breakfast cereal, which costs $2.65 a bag; but there is an even chance that during the night a wandering wind has come along, whipped up the stove to 110°, burned up all the coal and left a pot full of half dead ashes. In this event the thermometer now registers 68° and the chicks are standing round with their collars turned up, blowing on their hands and looking like a snow-removal gang under the El on a bitter winter's midnight.

For mothering chicks, a stove has one real advantage over a hen: it stays in one place and you always know where it is. Right there its advantage ceases. In all other respects a hen is ahead of any stove that was ever built. A hen's thermostat is always in perfect order, and her warmth has a curious indefinable quality of sociability, which I believe means a lot to a chick and keeps its bowels in nice condition. A hen, moreover, is draft proof. When she gathers her little charges under her feathers, floor drafts are eliminated. A hen has a larger vocabulary than a stove and can communicate ideas more readily—which is desirable even though some of a hen's ideas are flighty and many of her suspicions unfounded. And of course a hen is a good provider and does a lot of spade work which the ordinary stove of today is incapable of. She doesn't have to be shaken down, and red-hot coals never roll out of her on to the dry floor.

Anyone with a fire on his mind is in a sort of trance. I have seen suburbanites on commuting trains who bore the unmistakable mark of the firemaker. Cooks have it—those who still cook over real fires. But the operator of a brooder stove has it to a pitiful degree. On his fire depends not simply the safety of the plumbing or the comfort of the tenants; his fire is a matter of life and death to hundreds of babies. If it lags even fifteen degrees they will crowd together in a corner and die from suffocation. If ever you are in the country in the spring of the year and see a face that is not as other faces, you can bet you are looking at a man who has a brooder stove on his mind.

ᡒᢛ

In this spring of 1941 a man tends his fire in a trance that is all the deeper because of its dreamlike unreality, things being as they are in the world. I sometimes think I am crazy—everybody else fighting and dying or working for a cause or writing to his senator, and me looking after some Barred Rock chickens. But the land, and the creatures that go with it, are what is left that is good, and they are the authors of the book that I find worth reading; and anyway, a man has to live according to his lights even if his lights are the red coals in the base of a firepot. On Sunday the sixth of April, the day the German spring drive started in the Balkans, a clinker started forming in one side of my grate, and for the next three days (or until I found out what was the trouble) I had a sick fire on my hands. I was trying to finish up something I had been writing, working against time, and so I had to stay up late in the evening to do my work and then get up early in the morning to make sure I still had a warm brooder; so for three days I hardly slept at all and began to feel the uneasy symptoms and the lightheadedness of brain fag. On the afternoon of the third day I was crouched carefully in front of the stove, trying for the hundredth time to figure out why a well-shaken and freshly fueled fire wouldn't take hold as it should. The thermometer had dropped to 68° and the infants, ready for bed, were chilly and were not forming the charmed circle that is indispensable to their night health but were huddled in a big black mass against one wall.

For a moment I felt as though I might be about to have what folks hereabouts call a "foolish spell," and just at that juncture somebody knocked. I unbuttoned the door and it was my boy to say that supper was ready and that "the war news was very bad." For just a second I felt licked and bewildered and afraid. But it didn't last. I soon knew that the remaining warmth in this stubborn stove was all I had to pit against the Nazi idea of *Frühling*. I boosted the fire a little, loaded about a hundred chicks into a basket in the half darkness and distributed them round the edge of the hover in a more strategic position for sleeping. Then I ate and went to bed. At eleven I got up, took a flashlight, and went out to renew my vigil in this strange cooling world. From eleven to twelve I just sat, listening to the faint stirrings of the tiny forms and occasionally reading the meter. It had sagged off four degrees.

At twelve I began experiments with a new form of poker. At twelve-thirty I located the clinker. By one o'clock I had broken it up and fished out a bucketful of dead ashes. Then I loaded another batch of chicks into the basket to lighten the congested area (like any good traffic cop) and heard that most wonderful sound—the healthy breathing of a fire that had been given up for dead.

Countries are ransacked, valleys drenched with blood. Though it seems untimely, I still publish my belief in the egg, the contents of the egg, the warm coal, and the necessity for pursuing whatever fire delights and sustains you.

MY DAY

W<small>ITH</small> Mrs. Roosevelt's permission, I shall describe my day. I woke at six and lay till quarter past, slowly turning my head from side to side to test out my neck, which has less play in it than it once had. Was disappointed in my neck but pleased at being able to recall with great clearness a dream I had had in the night. I dreamed that I was in a resort hotel, having dinner, and the manager came over to the table and tapped me peremptorily on the shoulder and said: "Mr. White, you go to your room immediately and take off that old blue sweater and put on your jacket." And straightway I arose and left the room behind the manager, clowning as I went.

So I told the dream to my wife and offered to let her interpret it, which she did. She said it was a perfectly simple dream and merely meant that the manager was probably right. But I think there is more to it than that, and I felt grieved that my wife should have sided with someone I had met in my sleep.

I got out of bed at half-past six, thinking about dreams and about what a plowman had told me the other day—which was that he often gets the answer to his problems in dreams. He had a dream lately telling him what to do about my newly-laid-down field, where I didn't get a very good catch of grass. He and I were discussing it the other afternoon at quitting time, and he told me next day that he had gone to bed thinking about it and that the answer had come to him as easy as anything.

"What did your dream say we should do?" I asked.

"Put the phosphate to it," he replied cheerfully. A good dream, and sound soil practice, but I wish people would have hallucinations that don't cost me money.

Dressed without shaving, and splashed a cupful of cold water over my face and felt as ready for the day as Jeeter Lester. So down the back stairs noisily and out through the dewy field with Fred, my chore dog, to the chicken range, where I opened the doors of the shelters and watched my two hundred pullets, long pent up, come sailing through the openings like chaff on the wind—a black cloud of feathers and delight. Some of them sprayed themselves out over the green grass, looking for employment; others gathered eagerly at my feet, looking for grain.

On the way back to the house along the hard-packed path, I noticed that a pall of smoke, presumably from forest fires to the north of us, overhung the world; it gave the sky a queer look, a sort of diffused brilliance. All common objects appeared unusual. I was surprised to note, during the course of the day, how many people remarked that it looked "like the end of the world." Why do you suppose people have decided that the end of the world will be presaged by a strange light in the sky? Certainly nobody has witnessed the event, yet all are agreed that a light will be noticed in the heavens, perhaps several hours before the crash. I have a wholly different picture of doomsday—or rather doomsmoment. I think when the end of the world comes the sky will be its old blue self, with white cumulus clouds drifting along. You will be looking out of a window, say, at a tree; and then after a bit the tree won't be there any more, and the looking won't be there any more, only the window will be there, in memory—the thing through which the looking has been done. I can see God, walking through the garden and noticing that the world is done for, reach down and pick it up and put it on His compost pile. It ought to make a fine ferment.

The plowman mentioned the smoke pall when I was talking with him in the afternoon, and I asked if he knew where the fire was.

"Canada," he replied.

"What part of Canada?" I asked.

"The whole of it," he said. "They tell me the whole of Canada is ablaze."

"That's a big fire then," I answered. "Canada is a large place, larger than the United States even."

The plowman considered this distasteful pronouncement a moment. "Well then," he said, "it is a big fire." But he added cheerfully, "Anyways, it'll have to cross a pile of water 'fore it gits to us."

I nodded in perfect agreement, for this seemed a spiritual rather than a geographical discussion, and I felt instructed and renewed.

After breakfast I went to the barn with my boy to tend a lamb that had been cut, and while the boy held the lamb I ran some pine tar into the wound to keep the flies away, and then we released it, with its mother and its sister, and the three of them raced down the lane, glad to be back to pasture again after hospitalization. So indoors and settled down to work, and worked diligently for about four minutes and then remembered that I was to call for some children, this being the last day of school and a picnic having been arranged. So into the village in the truck, after wiring the tailboard up with a piece of haywire, to prevent wholesale loss of life. The fourth, fifth, and sixth graders were gathered in the schoolyard with their teacher, who had on trousers in honor of the event, and I wished that I could see again (and in trousers) some of the teachers I had had in grammar school—Miss Hackett and Miss Kirby and Miss Crosby and Miss Douglas and Miss Ihlefeldt and Mrs. Schuyler and Miss Abigail A. Bourne and Miss Sheridan. I remembered with regret that none of them had taken me on a picnic during the eight years I spent with them, and that I had never seen any of them in trousers, and I felt cheated. Loaded the children into the truck and carried them a couple of miles to the shore, where they deployed with hot dogs and began falling into mire pots, and left them there and went back to work. Worked for ten or fifteen minutes, but remembered that I had agreed to fetch a roll here, for rolling my field, and that it was about four miles away in the barn of the old Herrick place and that it was probably as big as a house.

I got a fellow to go along with me, and we took a chain, a bar, an ax, a tackle, a few lengths of rope, and some plank, and set off, I being glad, as always, to be self-released from indoor work and glad to be visiting the old Herrick place, which is remote and quiet—an old tumbledown barn in a run-out field encircled by woods and overlooking a small secluded cove. Lilacs were in bloom by the old cellar hole, and a few old apple trees stood guard over the secrets of other days. The world stood still here in this peaceful and mysterious place, which seemed perfect for a tryst or a double suicide. The barn floor was matted with ancient hay, and there was a tedder stored in one corner, and the roll in another, and a few old magazines and junk of one sort or another. As we lifted the tongue of the roll and stirred the thing, a mouse leaped up and ran the length of it, like a tiny dog performing a circus act. I thought how pleasant it would be to start life fresh on the old Herrick place, with a one-room shack and no appurtenances—no equipment, no stock, no pets, no family responsibilities, no program. But knowing myself as well as I do, I well knew that it wouldn't be twenty minutes before I would acquire or contrive something to establish the roots of complexity in firm soil—a cold chisel perhaps, or an inamorata, or a folding towel rack. In no time at all I would destroy the old Herrick place by setting out a pansy plant or repairing a rotten sill. And then it would be just like any other spot—beloved but not removed. A man sometimes gets homesick for the loneliness that he has at one time or another experienced in his life and that is a part of all life in some degree, and sometimes a secluded and half-mournful yet beautiful place will suddenly revive the sensation of pain and melancholy and unfulfillment that are associated with that loneliness, and will make him want to seize it and recapture it; but I know with me it is a passing want and not to be compared with my taste for domesticity, which is most of the time so strong as to be overpowering.

The roll was a big old thing. It was, as I had suspected, made in one long cylinder—narrow ten-foot spruce planks bolted to a pair of old mowing-machine wheels, and the frame heavily constructed. It was as much as the two of us could do to haul it out of its corner, swing it, and start it toward the truck, which I had backed up in the doorway. We made an inclined runway of planks, hooked the tackle on, rigged a snub-line on behind to hold back when we got over the crest, and gave it the works. All went smoothly, the roll crept up the ramp, and we soon had it aboard and lashed down. But our success was of short duration. I started the truck and hadn't gone ten feet when I brought up, all standing, on a rock that was invisible from the driver's seat, and we were hung up for fair, with our load aboard and our right running board aground.

"I guess we got some trouble now," said the fellow that was with me.

We got out the jack, a pitiful little hydraulic affair painted a bright yellow to make it seem alert. Like most jacks, this one had a hernia, and wasn't supposed to lift anything. I got some junks of plank and some short boards, and we spent a happy morning jacking and (as Father Divine would say) rejacking. The jack gave us only a two-inch gain each time, and we would have to catch this gain by trigging up the wheel with wedges. Then we'd take a new footing for our jack and grab another inch or two. But it was nice there, lying full length in the tall sweet grass, and neither of us wanted to be any place else particularly. And finally we cleared the rock and backed off and squared away for home, with our wide enormous cargo.

Found the mail waiting when I got back to the house, and among other items a notice from the secretary of the class of 1921, advising me that it has been twenty years since I graduated. "Get together a gang and come to Ithaca," the announcement said. "See your friends." Then followed a list of their names, and I studied it a long time in vain.

I suppose a man ought to get back to reunion in one of the few remaining Junes of his life, but I never seem to get round to it. I keep saying to myself, "Well, you've just recently graduated, why don't you wait a little spell?" It seems nonsensical to me that I am twenty years gone. When I was an undergraduate and met an alumnus twenty years out, I regarded him as shrivelled beyond repair. Just hulks of men, these old fellows seemed to me—dry stalks, autumnal creatures, about to die.

I have decided not to go back this year, and I guess the thing that decided me was the casual reference in the letter to "the costume." That was the crowning deterrent. I might be able to undergo the embarrassment of saluting dim forgotten classmates with the wrong nicknames, and having my hand pumped by familiar-looking strangers, but I doubted that I could go through with "the costume." A costume would simply make me drink a great deal, very fast, and I can achieve that sort of delirium right here in my own cool cellar. Besides, it gave me considerable pause to realize that sartorially I have slipped like the devil since 1921 and that my everyday garb might easily be construed as a "costume" by other members of my class.

Another piece of mail was a communication from my county agent, Mr. Tibbetts. He reports rainfall below normal, which is an understatement: the ground is powdery, and some wells around here are dry for the first time in years. And he recommends that old hens be kept through the summer, which I intend to do; but I would like to get mine outdoors on green grass if I can, as they are at loose ends nowadays in their pen in the barn. In winter the pen is warm and snug, but in summer it is dusty and dull. Hens need excitement to keep them at peak production. Any little trinket that you bring a hen stimulates her, whether it is the claw of a lobster or a jade bracelet.

We had stewed rhubarb for lunch. It was from stewed rhubarb that the gods got their idea for ambrosia. This year we're going to try putting up rhubarb, which I am told is simple—just cold water, no processing. After lunch studied, in the *Mercury,* Bertrand Russell's blueprint for an enduring peace. He advocates an alliance or league. The weakness of this sort of structure of course is that the whole thing hangs on an agreement, and there is nothing more likely to start disagreement among people or countries than an agreement. I had rather see an attempt at union than an attempt at an alliance, for then the participants would be bound in fact rather than in words. A marriage of convenience between two great democracies is a conceivable thing, but it mustn't be companionate, it must be the real article. But I agree with Dr. Russell that before we can have any sort of peace, enduring or ephemeral, Hitler must be defeated, and I don't think we can accomplish that by blacking out Newark, N. J.

In the afternoon drove to the hospital for an injection, taking the laundry with me to be dropped off on the way. In town purchased ten feet of half-inch pipe and stopped in for a while to visit with a man who is building a boat, and was pleased to observe that, like myself, he was glad of any interruption from work, no matter of what nature. Home and found two female artists, so mixed a drink and they stayed for supper, of meatballs, which we apologized for but which they gobbled hungrily, it seemed to me, and gratefully. Listened to Elmer Davis at 8:55 and then out to the barn to put things to bed. In the hen pen searched the nests for broodies, and found one, and removed her, she lying quietly in my arms in the twilight with that wonderful concentrated quietude the fever of incubation induces. The smoke pall of morning had cleared away and the night was sweet and clear, with a heavy integument of lilac. In the brooder house the young cockerels were assembling in a corner, so I took a bamboo pole and rattled it and they quickly found the roosts. Then I closed the pophole. I filled a bucket with oats and continued on to the range where the pullets are, the air here smelling of blossoms with a trace of skunk, and I filled the inside feeders with oats against the morning and closed the doors of the shelters and watched the pullets settling down rank after rank with the tiny burbling sighs of contentment while the mosquitoes tore at me and the warmth and smell rose to greet me from the relaxed bodies of the birds; and I returned to the house and got the terrier and put him in the garage and then let the big red dachshund out and then in again and then the little black dachshund out and in again and I set up the fire screen in the living room and closed the door of the woodshed and turned out the lights one by one through all the rooms and ascended and brushed my teeth and pulled the window curtains and looked in at the sleeping boy to see if he was covered, and undressed and got into bed and tried my neck again and changed position from the right side to the left side and heaved a great long sigh and that (to quote Mr. Davis) is the news to this moment.

ONCE MORE TO THE LAKE

O NE summer, along about 1904, my father rented a camp on a lake in Maine and took us all there for the month of August. We all got ringworm from some kittens and had to rub Pond's Extract on our arms and legs night and morning, and my father rolled over in a canoe with all his clothes on; but outside of that the vacation was a success, and from then on none of us ever thought there was any place in the world like that lake in Maine. We returned summer after summer—always on August 1st for one month. I have since become a salt-water man, but sometimes in summer there are days when the restlessness of the tides and the fearful cold of the sea water and the incessant wind that blows across the afternoon and into the evening make me wish for the placidity of a lake in the woods. A few weeks ago this feeling got so strong I bought myself a couple of bass hooks and a spinner and returned to the lake where we used to go, for a week's fishing and to revisit old haunts.

I took along my son, who had never had any fresh water up his nose and who had seen lily pads only from train windows. On the journey over to the lake I began to wonder what it would be like. I wondered how time would have marred this unique, this holy spot—the coves and streams, the hills that the sun set behind, the camps and the paths behind the camps. I was sure that the tarred road would have found it out, and I wondered in what other ways it would be desolated. It is strange how much you can remember about places like that once you allow your mind to return into the grooves that lead back. You remember one thing, and that suddenly reminds you of another thing. I guess I remembered clearest of all the early mornings, when the lake was cool and motionless, remembered how the bedroom smelled of the lumber it was made of and of the wet woods whose scent entered through the screen. The partitions in the camp were thin and did not extend clear to the top of the rooms, and as I was always the first up I would dress softly so as not to wake the others, and sneak out into the sweet outdoors and start out in the canoe, keeping close along the shore in the long shadows of the pines. I remembered being very careful never to rub my paddle against the gunwale for fear of disturbing the stillness of the cathedral.

The lake had not been what you would call a wild lake. There were cottages sprinkled around the shores, and it was in farming country although the shores of the lake were quite heavily wooded. Some of the cottages were owned by nearby farmers, and you would live at the shore and eat your meals at the farmhouse. That's what our family did. But although it wasn't wild, it was a fairly large and undisturbed lake and there were places in it that, to a child at least, seemed infinitely remote and primeval.

I was right about the tar: it led to within half a mile of the shore. But when I got back there, with my boy, and we settled into a camp near a farmhouse and into the kind of summertime I had known, I could tell that it was going to be pretty much the same as it had been before—I knew it, lying in bed the first morning, smelling the bedroom, and hearing the boy sneak quietly out and go off along the shore in a boat. I began to sustain the illusion that he was I, and therefore, by simple transposition, that I was my father. This sensation persisted, kept cropping up all the time we were there. It was not an entirely new feeling, but in this setting it grew much stronger. I seemed to be living a dual existence. I would be in the middle of some simple act, I would be picking up a bait box or laying down a table fork, or I would be saying something, and suddenly it would be not I but my father who was saying the words or making the gesture. It gave me a creepy sensation.

We went fishing the first morning. I felt the same damp moss covering the worms in the bait can, and saw the dragonfly alight on the tip of my rod as it hovered a few inches from the surface of the water. It was the arrival of this fly that convinced me beyond any doubt that everything was as it always had been, that the years were a mirage and there had been no years. The small waves were the same, chucking the rowboat under the chin as we fished at anchor, and the boat was the same boat, the same color green and the ribs broken in the same places, and under the floor-boards the same fresh-water leavings and débris—the dead hellgrammite, the wisps of moss, the rusty discarded fishhook, the dried blood from yesterday's catch. We stared silently at the tips of our rods, at the dragonflies that came and went. I lowered the tip of mine into the water, tentatively, pensively dislodging the fly, which darted two feet away, poised, darted two feet back, and came to rest again a little farther up the rod. There had been no years between the ducking of this dragonfly and the other one—the one that was part of memory. I looked at the boy, who was silently watching his fly, and it was my hands that held his rod, my eyes watching. I felt dizzy and didn't know which rod I was at the end of.

We caught two bass, hauling them in briskly as though they were mackerel, pulling them over the side of the boat in a businesslike manner without any landing net, and stunning them with a blow on the back of the head. When we got back for a swim before lunch, the lake was exactly where we had left it, the same number of inches from the dock, and there was only the merest suggestion of a breeze. This seemed an utterly enchanted sea, this lake you could leave to its own devices for a few hours and come back to, and find that it had not stirred, this constant and trustworthy body of water. In the shallows, the dark, watersoaked sticks and twigs, smooth and old, were undulating in clusters on the bottom against the clean ribbed sand, and the track of the mussel was plain. A school of minnows swam by, each minnow with its small individual shadow, doubling the attendance, so clear and sharp in the sunlight. Some of the other campers were in swimming, along the shore, one of them with a cake of soap, and the water felt thin and clear and unsubstantial. Over the years there had been this person with the cake of soap, this cultist, and here he was. There had been no years.

Up to the farmhouse to dinner through the teeming, dusty field, the road under our sneakers was only a two-track road. The middle track was missing, the one with the marks of the hooves and the splotches of dried, flaky manure. There had always been three tracks to choose from in choosing which track to walk in; now the choice was narrowed down to two. For a moment I missed terribly the middle alternative. But the way led past the tennis court, and something about the way it lay there in the sun reassured me; the tape had loosened along the backline, the alleys were green with plantains and other weeds, and the net (installed in June and removed in September) sagged in the dry noon, and the whole place steamed with midday heat and hunger and emptiness. There was a choice of pie for dessert, and one was blueberry and one was apple, and the waitresses were the same country girls, there having been no passage of time, only the illusion of it as in a dropped curtain—the waitresses were still fifteen; their hair had been washed, that was the only difference—they had been to the movies and seen the pretty girls with the clean hair.

Summertime, oh summertime, pattern of life indelible, the fade-proof lake, the woods unshatterable, the pasture with the sweetfern and the juniper forever and ever, summer without end; this was the background, and the life along the shore was the design, the cottages with their innocent and tranquil design, their tiny docks with the flagpole and the American flag floating against the white clouds in the blue sky, the little paths over the roots of the trees leading from camp to camp and the paths leading back to the outhouses and the can of lime for sprinkling, and at the souvenir counters at the store the miniature birch-bark canoes and the post cards that showed things looking a little better than they looked. This was the American family at play, escaping the city heat, wondering whether the newcomers in the camp at the head of the cove were "common" or "nice," wondering whether it was true that the people who drove up for Sunday dinner at the farmhouse were turned away because there wasn't enough chicken.

It seemed to me, as I kept remembering all this, that those times and those summers had been infinitely precious and worth saving. There had been jollity and peace and goodness. The arriving (at the beginning of August) had been so big a business in itself, at the railway station the farm wagon drawn up, the first smell of the pine-laden air, the first glimpse of the smiling farmer, and the great importance of the trunks and your father's enormous authority in such matters, and the feel of the wagon under you for the long ten-mile haul, and at the top of the last long hill catching the first view of the lake after eleven months of not seeing this cherished body of water. The shouts and cries of the other campers when they saw you, and the trunks to be unpacked, to give up their rich burden. (Arriving was less exciting nowadays, when you sneaked up in your car and parked it under a tree near the camp and took out the bags and in five minutes it was all over, no fuss, no loud wonderful fuss about trunks.)

Peace and goodness and jollity. The only thing that was wrong now, really, was the sound of the place, an unfamiliar nervous sound of the outboard motors. This was the note that jarred, the one thing that would sometimes break the illusion and set the years moving. In those other summertimes all motors were inboard; and when they were at a little distance, the noise they made was a sedative, an ingredient of summer sleep. They were one-cylinder and two-cylinder engines, and some were make-and-break and some were jump-spark, but they all made a sleepy sound across the lake. The one-lungers throbbed and fluttered, and the twin-cylinder ones purred and purred, and that was a quiet sound too. But now the campers all had outboards. In the daytime, in the hot mornings, these motors made a petulant, irritable sound; at night, in the still evening when the afterglow lit the water, they whined about one's ears like mosquitoes. My boy loved our rented outboard, and his great desire was to achieve singlehanded mastery over it, and authority, and he soon learned the trick of choking it a little (but not too much), and the adjustment of the needle valve. Watching him I would remember the things you could do with the old one-cylinder engine with the heavy flywheel, how you could have it eating out of your hand if you got really close to it spiritually. Motor boats in those days didn't have clutches, and you would make a landing by shutting off the motor at the proper time and coasting in with a dead rudder. But there was a way of reversing them, if you learned the trick, by cutting the switch and putting it on again exactly on the final dying revolution of the flywheel, so that it would kick back against compression and begin reversing. Approaching a dock in a strong following breeze, it was difficult to slow up sufficiently by the ordinary coasting method, and if a boy felt he had complete mastery over his motor, he was tempted to keep it running beyond its time and then reverse it a few feet from the dock. It took a cool nerve, because if you threw the switch a twentieth of a second too soon you would catch the flywheel when it still had speed enough to go up past center, and the boat would leap ahead, charging bull-fashion at the dock.

We had a good week at the camp. The bass were biting well and the sun shone endlessly, day after day. We would be tired at night and lie down in the accumulated heat of the little bedrooms after the long hot day and the breeze would stir almost imperceptibly outside and the smell of the swamp drift in through the rusty screens. Sleep would come easily and in the morning the red squirrel would be on the roof, tapping out his gay routine. I kept remembering everything, lying in bed in the mornings —the small steamboat that had a long rounded stern like the lip of a Ubangi, and how quietly she ran on the moonlight sails, when the older boys played their mandolins and the girls sang and we ate doughnuts dipped in sugar, and how sweet the music was on the water in the shining night, and what it had felt like to think about girls then. After breakfast we would go up to the store and the things were in the same place—the minnows in a bottle, the plugs and spinners disarranged and pawed over by the youngsters from the boys' camp, the fig newtons and the Beeman's gum. Outside, the road was tarred and cars stood in front of the store. Inside, all was just as it had always been, except there was more Coca-Cola and not so much Moxie and root beer and birch beer and sarsaparilla. We would walk out with a bottle of pop apiece and sometimes the pop would backfire up our noses and hurt. We explored the streams, quietly, where the turtles slid off the sunny logs and dug their way into the soft bottom; and we lay on the town wharf and fed worms to the tame bass. Everywhere we went I had trouble making out which was I, the one walking at my side, the one walking in my pants.

One afternoon while we were there at that lake a thunderstorm came up. It was like the revival of an old melodrama that I had seen long ago with childish awe. The second-act climax of the drama of the electrical disturbance over a lake in America had not changed in any important respect. This was the big scene, still the big scene. The whole thing was so familiar, the first feeling of oppression and heat and a general air around camp of not wanting to go very far away. In midafternoon (it was all the same) a curious darkening of the sky, and a lull in everything that had made life tick; and then the way the boats suddenly swung the other way at their moorings with the coming of a breeze out of the new quarter, and the premonitory rumble. Then the kettle drum, then the snare, then the bass drum and cymbals, then crackling light against the dark, and the gods grinning and licking their chops in the hills. Afterward the calm, the rain steadily rustling in the calm lake, the return of light and hope and spirits, and the campers running out in joy and relief to go swimming in the rain, their bright cries perpetuating the deathless joke about how they were getting simply drenched, and the children screaming with delight at the new sensation of bathing in the rain, and the joke about getting drenched linking the generations in a strong indestructible chain. And the comedian who waded in carrying an umbrella.

When the others went swimming my son said he was going in too. He pulled his dripping trunks from the line where they had hung all through the shower, and wrung them out. Languidly, and with no thought of going in, I watched him, his hard little body, skinny and bare, saw him wince slightly as he pulled up around his vitals the small, soggy, icy garment. As he buckled the swollen belt, suddenly my groin felt the chill of death.

FALL

THERE were eight deaths in the town last year (four males and four females) and eight births (four males and four females), so we are right where we started—which is good enough for most of us. Of the deaths, one was between 90 and 100, three were between 80 and 90, two were between 70 and 80, and two were between 60 and 70. This is a different story from the old days, when every other grave was a child's grave. Nowadays it is mostly the old people who die; the children live to grow up, fight in the wars, marry, work, raise children, and draw a pension.

Eighteen young men have gone into the service from here, which is high for a town of this size.

૭▰

Potatoes have done well this year and we will get about thirty-eight bushels, enough for two families. Today I should be digging them, but another fellow is digging them for me and I am staying indoors to earn some money to pay him with. In that way a man gets not much closer to a potato than if he were living in town and harvesting his crop through the A. & P.

When a gentleman came to adjust a compass for me the other day he noticed how good the potatoes looked and asked me what date they were planted. I had to admit that I didn't remember the date, and he seemed surprised and mystified, and wondered what sort of disorderly place he had got into.

૭▰

There are many days in the autumn when the sky is a solid, heavy gray, and the woods stir uneasily in the raw wind. This is such a time. They call it the fall overcast. Sailing becomes more adventurous—the wind seems to have a great deal more weight to it and puts a bigger strain on rigging and man. The bay is rough and the lobstermen leave earlier and get home later. They have their traps off in deeper water now and are making good catches, but at greater effort. Some of them are bringing in a hundred pounds a day, and are getting twenty-two cents. Partridge shooting will begin soon, and when a man goes off to work in the morning he will take along his shotgun—just in case.

The flies have come indoors and are in an angry and turbulent state. I have a Flit gun beside my typewriter and open fire at them as they come over. The floor at my feet is strewn with raiders I have brought down, still twitching. In another couple of weeks the rats will come up from the shore into the barn, and the clan will be gathered together under one roof for the approaching cold.

I read the other day that rats on a farm of average size do a yearly damage of around thirty-five dollars. I believe this, and am surprised that farmers are not more concerned about rat depredations. I shot twelve or thirteen rats last winter and poisoned as many more, and my ex-cat brought in about a dozen. Three dozen rats would be a conservative estimate of the rat colony here, and each rat is a big consumer. Poisoning is by far the most effective procedure although less sporting than trapping or shooting. The rat has only one thing to be said for him: he supplies you with a tangible enemy on whom to vent your hate. I can take out a good deal on rats. If I were to save it all up for the real enemy I might bust. It is a source of relief, after listening to a radio broadcast, to take my .22 and go out to the barn and shoot a rat.

ৼ

The hardest thing about the war, for many of us, is to maintain a decent pitch of indignation. I become quite frightened, sometimes, when I realize how accustomed I have become to the phrase "Occupied France"—as though there could be such a place.

ৼ

When a glass of wine is poured a wine fly appears promptly—but I never see him at any other time and wonder where he keeps himself in the meanwhile and what he does for a drink.

ৼ

It's seven days since the Fair ended, but in my head I still keep hearing the enormous sound of the waltz that accompanied the swings. And every once in a while I hear too the gigantic summons, that somebody is wanted at the main gate, or will the owner of Maine license 3261 please move his car, it is blocking the highway. (And the hasty search through my pockets to see if my car bears that number.)

Anything can happen at a county agricultural fair. It is the perfect human occasion, the harvest of the fields and of the emotions. To the fair come the man and his cow, the boy and his girl, the wife and her green tomato pickle, each anticipating victory and the excitement of being separated from his money by familiar devices. It is at a fair that man can be drunk forever on liquor, love, or fights; at a fair that your front pocket can be picked by a trotting horse looking for sugar, and your hind pocket by a thief looking for his fortune.   I had expected to see more of the Fair than usual this year, because I had some sheep entered, and had to be around to tend them. But I found that I saw less, rather than more, because of being there in a responsible capacity instead of carefree. My sheep won two first premiums, which I think they would have done even if they had not been the only ones in their class.

In the clerk's office, on the first day, I waited my turn while a small boy reported the entry of a cage of ducks. The clerk asked what breed they were, and held his pencil ready.

"White ones," replied the boy.

"Yes, but what breed?" persisted the man.

"I dunno," said the boy scornfully, "they're white."

The clerk considered this carefully. Then he nodded wisely and wrote down: "Three white ducks."

A fair is good at any hour of the twenty-four. I love it early on a rainy morning when the Ferris wheel is wearing its tarpaulins and the phrenologist is just brushing her teeth. You climb a wet ladder into the loft of the cattle barn for a forkful of hay and find a fellow asleep heavily, his shoes folded across his breast like a lily.

Fitting my lambs for the Fair, I used desk scissors, and found that I still chewed my tongue as I snipped—a childish reflex for a childish occasion. When I got through, the lambs looked a little like some pictures I had studied in a sheep bulletin and a little like some wooden lambs that had come with a toy barnyard set in another period of American history.

The theme song of the Fair this fall was Irving Berlin's song "Any Bonds Today?" It took the place of the "Indian Love Call." Among the juggling acts and the sound of the horses going into the stretch, the question of bonds went almost unnoticed by the throngs, I am sure—the sound of it inescapable, the significance of it virtually lost. No one was thinking about the mechanics of liberty; people were just enjoying the fact of it. I think there has never been a song quite like "Any Bonds Today?" so innocently combining patriotic fervor with a definite rate of interest. When I first heard the line "Here comes that freedom man," I thought it was a fishbone I had in my throat.

MEMORANDUM

Today I should carry the pumpkins and squash from the back porch to the attic. The nights are too frosty to leave them outdoors any longer. And as long as I am making some trips to the attic I should also take up the boat cushions and the charts and the stuff from the galley and also a fishing rod that belongs up in the attic. Today I should finish filling in the trench we dug for the water pipe and should haul two loads of beach gravel from the Naskeag bar to spread on top of the clay fill. And I should stop in and pay the Reverend Mr. Smith for the gravel I got a month or two ago and ask him if he has seen a bear.

I ought to finish husking the corn and wheel the old stalks out and dump them on the compost pile, and while I am out there I should take a fork and pitch over the weeds that were thrown at the edge of the field last August and rake the little windfalls from under the apple tree and pitch them on to the heap too. I ought to go down to the shore at dead low water and hook on to the mooring with a chain and make the chain fast to the float, so that the tide will pick up the mooring rock and I can tow the whole thing ashore six hours later. I ought to knock the wedges out from the frames of the pier, put a line on the frames, and tow them in on the high water. First, though, I would have to find a line long enough to tie every frame. If I'm to do any work at the shore I ought first to put a cement patch on the leak in my right boot. After the frames are on the beach another fellow and myself ought to carry them up and stack them. And there is probably enough rockweed on the beach now so that I ought to bring up a load or two for the sheep shed. I ought to find out who it is that is shooting coot down in the cove today, just to satisfy my own curiosity. He was out before daybreak with his decoys, but I do not think he has got any birds.

I ought to take up the wire fence round the chicken range today, roll it up in bundles, tie them with six-thread, and store them at the edge of the woods. Then I ought to move the range houses off the field and into the corner of the woods and set them up on blocks for the winter, but I ought to sweep them out first and clean the roosts with a wire brush. It would be a good idea to have a putty knife in my pocket, for scraping. I ought to add a bag of phosphate to the piles of hen dressing that have accumulated under the range houses and spread the mixture on the field, to get it ready for plowing. And I ought to decide whether to plow just the range itself or to turn over a little more on the eastern end. On my way in from the range I ought to stop at the henhouse long enough to climb up and saw off an overhanging branch from the apple tree—it might tear the paper roof in the first big wind storm. I shall have to get a ladder of course and a saw.

Today I certainly ought to go over to the mill and get four twelve-inch boards, twelve feet long and half an inch thick, to use in building three new hoppers for dry mash feeding to my pullets. They are now laying seventy-eight per cent and giving me about eighty dozen eggs a week. I should also get one board that would be an inch thick, for the end pieces and for making the ends of the reels. I shouldn't need anything for the stands because I have enough stuff round the place to build the stands— which I had better make twenty-three inches high from floor to perch. If I were to make them less than that, the birds on the floor would pick at the vents of the birds feeding.

I ought to get some shingle nails and some spikes while I am at it, as we are out of those things. And I ought to sharpen the blade of my plane if I am going to build some hoppers. I ought to take the cutting-off saw and have it filed, as long as I am going over to the mill anyway. On the way back I ought to stop in at Frank Hamilton's house and put in my application for government lime and super, because I shall be passing his house and might just as well take advantage of it. Frank will ask me to sit down and talk a while, I imagine.

It is high time I raked up the bayberry brush which has been lying in the pasture since the August mowing. This would be a good chance to burn it today because we have had a rain and it is safe to burn. But before burning it I ought to find out whether it is really better for the pasture to burn stuff like that or to let it rot for dressing. I suppose there is so much wood in it it wouldn't rot up quickly and should be burned. Besides, I was once told in high-school chemistry that no energy is ever lost to the world, and presumably the ashes from the fires will strengthen my pasture in their own way.

I ought to take the buck lamb out of the flock of lambs today, before he gets to work on the ewe lambs, because I don't want them to get bred. I don't know just where to put him, but I ought to decide that today, and put him there. I should send away today for some phenothiazine so that I can drench my sheep next week. It would probably be a good idea to try phenothiazine this time instead of copper sulphate, which just gets the stomach worms and doesn't touch the nodular worms or the large-mouth bowel worms. And I ought to close the big doors on the north side of the barn cellar and board them up and bank them, so that the place won't be draughty down there at night when the sheep come in, as they are beginning to do. I have been thinking I ought to enlarge the south door so that I won't lose any lambs next spring from the ewes jamming through the narrow single opening, and this would be the time to do that.

Today I ought to start rebuilding the racks in the sheep shed, to fix them so the sheep can't pull hay out and waste it. There is a way to do this, and I know the way. So I am all set. Also I ought to fix up the pigpen down there in the barn cellar too and sweeten it up with a coat of whitening, so that I can get the pig indoors, because the nights are pretty cold now. The trough will probably not have to be rebuilt this year because last year I put a zinc binding all around the edges of it. (But if I *shouldn't* get round to fixing up the pen I should at least carry a forkful of straw down to the house where the pig now is—I should at least do that.)

This would be a good day to put in a new light in the window in the woodshed, and also there is one broken in the shop and one in the henhouse, so the sensible thing would be to do them all at once, as long as I have the putty all worked up and the glass cutter out. I ought to hook up the stove in the shop today, and get it ready for winter use. And I ought to run up the road and see Bert and find out why he hasn't delivered the cord of slabwood he said he was going to bring me. At any rate, I ought to make a place in the cellar for it today, which will mean cleaning house down there a little and neating up, and finding a better place to keep my flats and fillers for my egg cases. Incidentally, I ought to collect eggs right now, so there won't be any breakage in the nests.

It just occurred to me that if I'm going to the mill today I ought to measure the truck and figure out what I shall need in the way of hardwood boards to build a set of sideboards and a headboard and a tailboard for my stakes. I ought to bring these boards back with me along with the pine for the hoppers. I shall need two bolts for the ends of each sideboard, and one bolt for the cleat in the middle, and two bolts for the ends of each of the head- and tailboards, and there will be three each of them, so that makes fifty-four bolts I shall need, and the stakes are about an inch and a half through and the boards will be three-quarters, so that makes two inches and a quarter, and allow another half inch for washer and nut. About a three-inch bolt would do it. I better get them today.

Another thing I ought to do is take that grass seed that the mice have been getting into in the barn and store it in a wash boiler or some pails or something. I ought to set some mousetraps tonight, I mustn't forget. I ought to set one upstairs, I guess, in the little northeast chamber where the pipe comes through from the set tubs in the back kitchen, because this is the Mouse Fifth Avenue, and it would be a good chance for a kill. I ought to gather together some old clothes and stuff for the rummage sale to raise money to buy books for the town library, and I ought to rake the barnyard and wheel the dressing down into the barn cellar where it will be out of the weather, because there is a lot of good dressing there right now. I ought to note down on the calendar in my room that I saw the ewe named Galbreath go to buck day before yesterday, so I can have her lambing date. Hers will be the first lamb next spring, and it will be twins because she is a twinner. Which reminds me I ought to write Mike Galbreath a letter. I have been owing him one since before Roosevelt was elected for the third term. I certainly should do that, it has been such a long time. I should do it today while it is in my mind.

One thing I ought to do today is to take a small Stillson wrench and go down cellar and tighten the packing nut on the water pump so it won't drip. I could do that when I am down there making a place for the slabwood—it would save steps to combine the two things. I also ought to stir the litter in the henpen in the barn where the Barred Rocks are, and in the henhouse where the crossbred birds are; and then fill some bushel baskets with shavings and add them to the litter in the places where it needs deepening. The dropping boards under the broody coops need cleaning and I should do that at the same time, since I will be out there anyway. As far as litter is concerned, a man could take and rake the lawn under the maples where there is such an accumulation of leaves and add these dry leaves to the litter in the houses for the birds to scratch around in. Anything to keep their minds occupied in healthy channels.

Today I intend to pull the young alders in the field on the north side, as they are beginning to get ahead of me. I must do that today, probably later on this afternoon. A bush hook would be a good tool for that. I should also clean up the remaining garden trash and add it to the compost, saving out whatever the sheep might eat, and should remove the pipe from the well under the apple tree and store it down below in the barn.

I also think I had better call up a buyer and get rid of my ten old hens, since we have canned all we are going to need. After the hens are gone

I shall no longer need the borrowed range house that they are living in, and I can get two long poles, lash them on behind the truck, and load the house on and drag it up to Kenneth's house. But it will be necessary to take an ax and flatten the ends of the poles so they won't dig into the highway, although the tar is so cold now they probably wouldn't dig in much anyway. Still, the thing to do is do it right.

Another thing I should try to manage to do today is to earmark the two pure-bred lambs. That will be easy enough—it just means finding the ear tags that I put away in a drawer or some place last spring and finding the special pliers that you have to use in squeezing a tag into a sheep's ear. I think I know where those pliers are, I think they are right in my cabinet next to that jar of rubber cement. I shall have to get the lambs up, but they will come without much trouble now because they are hungry. I *could* take the buck away at the same time if I could think of a place to put him.

Today I want to get word to Walter about the plowing of the garden pieces, and I had also better arrange down cellar about a bin for the roots, because on account of the extra amount of potatoes we have it will mean a little rearranging down there in order to get everything in. But I can do that when I am down tightening the nut on the pump. I ought to take the car into the village today to get an inspection sticker put on it; however, on second thought if I am going to the mill I guess it would be better to go in the truck and have a sticker put on *that* while I am seeing about the lumber, and then I can bring the boards back with me. But I mustn't be away at low water, otherwise I won't be able to hook on to the mooring.

Tomorrow is Tuesday and the egg truck will be coming through in the morning to pick up my cases, so I must finish grading and packing the eggs today—I have about fifty dozen packed and only ten to go to make up the two cases. Then I must nail up the cases and make out the tags and tack them on and lug the cases over to the cellar door, ready to be taken out in the morning, as the expressman is apt to get here early. I've also got to write a letter today to a publisher who wrote me asking what happened to the book manuscript I was supposed to turn in a year ago last spring, and I also should take the green chair in the living room to Eliot Sweet so that he can put in some little buttons that keep coming out all the time. I can throw the chair into the truck and drop it by his shop on my way to town. If I am going to take the squashes and pumpkins up to the attic I had better take the old blankets that we have been covering them with nights and hang them on the line to dry. I also ought to nail a pole up somewhere in the barn to hang grain sacks on so the rats won't be able to get at them and gnaw holes in them; empty sacks are worth ten cents for the heavy ones and five cents for the cotton ones, and they mount up quite fast and run into money. I mustn't forget to do that today —it won't take but a minute.

I've got to see about getting a birthday present for my wife today, but I can't think of anything. Her birthday is past anyway. There were things going on here at the time and I didn't get around to getting her a present but I haven't forgotten about it. Possibly when I am in the village I can find something.

If I'm going to rebuild the racks for the sheep it would be a good idea to have the mill rip out a lot of two-inch slats for me while I am there, as I shall need some stuff like that. I ought to make a list, I guess. And I mustn't forget shingle nails and the spikes. There is a place on the bottom step of the stairs going down into the woodshed where the crocus sack that I nailed on to the step as a foot-wiper is torn off, and somebody might catch his foot in that and take a fall. I certainly should fix that today before someone has a nasty fall. The best thing would be to rip the old sack off and tack a new one on. A man should have some roofing nails if he is going to make a neat job of tacking a sack on to a step. I think I may have some but I'd better look. I can look when I go out to get the Stillson wrench that I shall need when I go down to tighten the packing nut on the pump, and if I haven't any I can get some when I go to town.

I've been spending a lot of time here typing, and I see it is four o'clock already and almost dark, so I had better get going. Specially since I ought to get a haircut while I am at it.

COON HUNT

THIS week in our county the two leading topics are deer-slaying and civilian defense. Our best defenders are off in the woods, sharpening their aim and laying up protein reserves. The rest of us attend the meetings and listen to the speakers; in our minds we rebuild, with the volunteer bricklayers, the still unruined cities. On the way home we pass the cars of the hunters and note that they are wearing antlers. If Hitler had ever spent a fall in a New England village, watching the bucks go by on the running boards, he never would have dared reoccupy the Rhineland.

Everyone is excited about the local defense program, and there is a pleasing confusion in all quarters—the sort of confusion that makes a democracy so lovable and so frightening. The absence of the tangible foe, the unlikelihood of his soon appearing in military guise, these give the whole thing a certain incredibility without lessening its intensity. In a day or two a registrar will be around to find out whether I want to join a demolition squad or learn tap dancing to amuse the draftees. In scope, the co-ordinating program is quite amazing—a curious blend of rather elusive vitamins for school-children and protection against even more elusive poison gas for adults. At the moment its advantage to the cause, I suspect, is glandular: it will release in many people, including myself, a pent-up desire to serve their country in this fight. Its disadvantage is that sheer activity often creates the illusion of accomplishment; people's gaze will be diverted from the theater of war to the theater of defense, and a sense of invincibility not in accord with the facts will be developed. In a military way America is about as invincible as anyone could wish, but in other ways I believe she is in immediate peril.

A few days before the defense meeting, where the civilians gathered to raise their barricades against the invader, the enemy slipped into town and out again, and I think there were hardly a dozen people who caught a glimpse of his coat tails. The populace was watching for planes in the sky—but when the enemy came he came in the curious shape of certain old boxes and hencoops and logs and odds and ends of rubbish that the town boys piled up, on Halloween, against the door of the Jewish merchant, the unpopular storekeeper who had been too grasping. It was a passing visit. The next day the hencoops were rolled away. The dummy that dangled in a noose from the elm tree, with the legend "This is what happens to you if you trade at ——'s," was cut down. Bystanders laughed to see such fun, a few of the elders complimented the boys on the job, and the town settled into its stride. People got ready to attend the defense meeting where they could volunteer to serve democracy by organizing a motor corps and preparing surgical dressings. The enemy had disappeared, virtually unnoticed, and all that remained were the fame of his European successes and the shadow of distant wings. Only a few people had felt his hot breath in the branches of the elm.

There would never be a moment, in war or in peace, when I wouldn't trade all the patriots in the county for one tolerant man. Or when I wouldn't swap the vitamins in a child's lunchbox for a jelly glass of compassion.

 è∾

There were two dogs with us the night we went coon hunting. One was an old hound, veteran of a thousand campaigns, who knew what we were up to and who wasted no time in idle diversions. The other was a puppy, brought along to observe and learn; to him the star-sprinkled sky and the deep dark woods and the myriad scents and the lateness of the hour and the frosty ground were intoxicating. The excitement of our departure was too much for his bowels. Tied in the truck, he was purged all the way over to Winkumpaw Brook and was hollow as a rotten log before the night was well under way. This may have had something to do with what happened.

It was great hunting that night, perfect for man and beast, a fateful night for coon. The stars leaned close, and some lost their hold and fell. I was amazed at how quickly and easily the men moved through the woods in strange country, guided by hunches and a bit of lantern gleam. The woods hit back at you if you let your guard down.

We were an odd lot. A couple of the men were in coveralls—those bunny suits garage mechanics wear. One old fellow had been all stove to pieces in a car accident; another was down with a hard cold and a rack-ing cough; another had broken two ribs the day before and had been strapped up that afternoon by a doctor. He had killed the pain with a few shots of whisky and the spirits had evidently reminded him of coon hunting. This fellow had a terrible thirst for water all during the night and he had a way of straying off from the main party and hugging the water courses where he could kneel and drink when the need was great. We could sometimes follow the progress of his thirst in the winking of his buglight, in some faraway valley. After a bit he would rejoin us. "I'm drier'n a covered bridge," he would say disconsolately.

I felt a strong affinity for the puppy because he and I were the new ones to this strange game, and somehow it seemed to me we were sharing the same excitement and mystery of a night in the woods. I had begun to feel the excitement back in the kitchen of the farmhouse where the hunters had gathered, dropping in and standing about against the walls of the room. The talk began right away, all the cooning lore, the tales of being lost from three in the morning until six, and the tricks a coon would play on a dog. There was a woman in the room, wife of the owner of the old dog, and she was the only one for whom the night held no special allure. She sat knitting a huge mitten. Mostly, the hunters paid no attention to her. Only one remark went her way. One of the men, observing the mitten, asked:

"Gettin' that man o' yours ready for winter?"

She nodded.

"I should kill him before winter if he was mine—he's no good for anything else," the fellow continued, pleasantly.

The woman raised a grudging smile to this sure-fire witticism. She plied the needles without interruption. This obviously was not the first time she had been left at home while men and dogs went about their business, and it wasn't going to be the last time either. For her it was just one night in a long succession of nights. This was the fall, and in the fall the men hunted coon. They left after sundown and returned before sunup. That was all there was to that.

The best coon country is always far away. Men are roamers, and getting a long way from home is part of the sport. Our motorcade consisted of two vehicles, a truck for the dogs and owners, and a sedan for the hangers-on, lantern-bearers, and advisory committee. The old dog jumped into place the minute he was let out of the barn; the puppy was hoisted in and tied. The two of them sat on a pile of straw just behind the cab. The man with the broken ribs got into the sedan. Nobody seemed to think it was in the least odd that he was going coon hunting, to walk twelve or fifteen miles in rough country and in darkness. He said the adhesive tape held everything O.K., and anyway, he said, the only time his chest hurt was when he breathed.

We advanced without stealth, the truck leading. The headlights of our car shone directly in the faces of the dogs. The old dog leaned back craftily against the sideboards, to steady himself against the motion. He half closed his eyes and was as quiet on the journey as a middle-aged drummer on a way train. The pup crouched uneasily and was frequently thrown. He would rare up and sniff, then crouch again, then a curve would throw him and he would lose his balance and go down. He found a hole in the sideboards and occasionally would press his nose through to sniff the air. Then the excitement would attack his bowels and he would let go all over everything—with some difficulty because of the violent motion of the truck. The old dog observed this untidiness with profound contempt.

We got away from the highway after a while and followed a rough back road up into some country I had never explored. At last we got out and let the old hound go. He went to work instantly, dropping downhill out of sight. We could hear his little bell tinkling as he ranged about in the dim valley between us and a night-struck lake. When he picked up a scent, suddenly his full round tones went through you, and the night was a gong that had been struck. The old dog knew his business. The men, waiting around, would discuss in great detail his hunting and would describe what he was doing off there, and what the coon was doing; but I doubted that they knew, and they just kept making things up the way children do. As soon as the hound barked tree, which is a slightly different sound than the sound of the running, we followed his voice and shot the coon.

Once the dog led us to an old apple tree in an almost impenetrable thicket, and when the flashlights were shined up into the topmost branches no coon was there. The owner was puzzled and embarrassed. Nothing like this had ever happened before, he said. There was a long period of consultation and speculation, all sorts of theories were advanced. The most popular was that the coon had climbed the apple tree, then crossed, squirrel-like, into the branches of a nearby hackmatack, then descended, fooling the hound. Either this was the case or the dog had made an error. Upward of an hour was spent trying every angle of this delicious contretemps.

The puppy was held in leash most of the time, but when the first coon was treed he was allowed to watch the kill. Lights from half a dozen flashlights swept the tree top and converged to make a halo, with the coon's bright little sharp face in the center of the luminous ring. Our host lethargically drew his pistol, prolonging the climax with a legitimate sense of the theater. No one spoke while he drew a bead. The shot seemed to puncture first the night, then the coon. The coon lost his grip and landed with a thud, still alive and fighting. The old hound rushed in savagely, to grab him by the throat and finish him off. It was a big bull coon; he died bravely and swiftly, and the hound worked with silent fury. Then the puppy, in leash, was allowed to advance and sniff. He was trembling in every muscle, and was all eyes and ears and nose—like a child being allowed to see something meant only for grownups. (I felt a little that way myself.) As he stretched his nose forward timidly to inhale the heady smell of warm coon the old hound, jealous, snarled and leaped. The owner jerked back. The puppy yelped in terror. Everyone laughed. It was a youngster, getting burned by life—that sort of sight. Made you laugh.

After midnight we moved into easier country about ten miles away. Here the going was better—old fields and orchards, where the little wild apples lay in thick clusters under the trees. Old stone walls ran into the woods, and now and then there would be an empty barn as a ghostly landmark. The night grew frosty and the ground underfoot was slippery with rime. The bare birches wore the stars on their fingers, and the world rolled seductively, a dark symphony of brooding groves and plains. Things had gone well, and everyone was content just to be out in the small hours, following the musical directions of a wise and busy dog.

The puppy's owner had slipped the leash and allowed his charge to range about a bit. Nobody was paying much attention to him. The pup stayed with the party mostly, and although he was aware of the long-range operations of the older dog, he seemed to know that this was out of his class; he seemed timid in the woods and tended to stay close, contenting himself with sniffing about and occasionally jumping up to kiss someone's face. We were stepping along through the woods, the old hound near at hand, when the thing happened. Suddenly the puppy (who had not made a sound up to this point) let out a loud whoop and went charging off on a tangent. Everybody stopped dead in surprise.

"What goes on here anyway?" said somebody quietly.

The old hound was as mystified as the rest of us. This was a show-off stunt apparently, this puppy trying to bark coon. Nobody could make it out. Obviously there was no coon scent or the old dog would have picked it up instantly and been at his work.

"What in *the* devil?" asked somebody.

The puppy was howling unmercifully as though possessed. He charged here and there and came back along his own track passing us at a crazy mad pace, and diving into the woods on the other side of the trail. The yelps sounded hysterical now. Again the puppy charged back.

This time as he passed we could see that he had a queer look in his eye and that his movements were erratic. He would dive one way at a terrible clip, then stop and back off as though ducking an enemy, half cringing; but he kept putting up this terrible holler and commotion. Once he came straight at me. I stepped aside, and he went by screaming.

"Runnin' fit," said his owner. "That's the trouble. I can tell now by the way he acts. He's took with cramps in his bowwils and he don't know anythin' to do 'cept run and holler. C'mon, Dusty, c'mon, boy!"

He kept calling him softly. But Dusty was in another world and the shapes were after him. It was an eerie business, this crazy dog tearing around in the dark woods, half coming at you, half running from you. Even the old dog seemed disturbed and worried, as though to say: "You see—you *will* bring a child along, after his bedtime."

The men were patient, sympathetic now.

"That's all it is, he's took with a fit."

Dusty charged into the midst of us, scattering us. He stopped, bristling, his eyes too bright, a trace of froth at his mouth. He seemed half angry, half scared and wanting comfort. "Nothing much you can do, he'll run it off," they said.

And Dusty ran it off, in the deep dark woods, big with imaginary coons and enormous jealous old hounds, alive with the beautiful smells of the wild. His evening had been too much for him; for the time being he was as crazy as a loon. Someone suggested we go home.

We started moving up toward the cars, which were two or three fields away, over where you could see the elms black against the sky. The thought of home wasn't popular. A counter suggestion was made to prolong the hunting, and we separated off into two parties, one to return to the cars, the other to cut across country with the old dog and intercept the main body where a certain woods road met the highway. I walked several more miles and for the first time began to feel cold. It was another hour before I saw Dusty again. He was all right. All he needed was to be held in somebody's arms. He was very, very sleepy. He and I were both sleepy. I think we will both remember the first night we ever went coon hunting.

INTIMATIONS

YESTERDAY the biggest boy in town tried to enlist in the Navy, but the Navy wouldn't take him. They said he was too tall. He is six feet four and a half inches or about twice the height of a Japanese. Apparently the recruiting officer felt this would give America an unfair advantage.

ॐ

As I write, this is the third day of the war. That is, for most of us it is. There's one lady I know who has it worked out that we have been at war for some years now. She is an inveterate radio listener, and whenever she hears static she thinks it's the Germans, communicating with their local spies. Life has been a vivid thing to her, and war a reality, for a long while. This latest attack on Pearl Harbor was just an incident. At that I suspect she is nearer right than most of us. It is better to hear messages in static than to hear no messages in anything: think of the people who have listened to the rumbling and crackling of National Socialism for the past six or eight years without detecting any ominous sound!

ॐ

A light fall of snow in the night, and this morning the fields look like a man's face when he has used too much powder after a shave. A few little apples still cling to one of the old trees—they catch the light and perform a frosted miracle of ornamentation. The sheep move about, restlessly, finding little to satisfy them on a hard earth.

&❧

How quickly life's accents shifted on that sudden and unforgettable Sunday—the fateful seventh of December. My wife was getting a hot-water bag for somebody, and somehow she managed to lose the stopper down the toilet, beyond recall. This grotesque little incident seemed to upset her to a disproportionate degree: it was because she felt that, now that the war had begun in earnest, there was no excuse for any clumsiness in home nursing. The loss of the stopper suddenly seemed as severe a blow as the loss of a battleship. Life, which for two years had had a rather dreamlike quality, came instantly into sharp focus. The time for losing hot-water bag stoppers was over and gone.

&❧

America has been at a great disadvantage in relation to the Axis. In this country we are used to the queer notion that any sort of sporting contest must be governed by a set of rules. We think that the football can't be kicked off until after the whistle is blown. We believe the prize fighter can't be socked until he has come out of his corner. We think the fox hunter must tip his hat to the M.F.H. before he can gallop off after a fox. In this crazy land of ours a tennis player doesn't serve until his opponent is ready. Ever since trouble began inside Germany, years ago, we have hung tight to our sportsmanship, our code of honor, our book of rules, quite incapable of comprehending any other sort of approach to life. Not all the loud denial by Herr Hitler, not the plain statement in his book that the way to get an advantage was to seize it, not the deeds themselves as the little countries were struck down one by one, made much of a dent in our characters. So it was quite to be expected that America grew purple and pink with rage and fury when the Japanese struck us without warning. There are still, on this third day, people who seem to feel that a universal referee will step in and call a penalty.

&❧

The passionate love of Americans for their America will have a lot to do with winning the war. It is an odd thing though: the very patriotism on which we now rely is the thing that must eventually be in part relinquished if the world is ever to find a lasting peace and an end to these butcheries.

To hold America in one's thoughts is like holding a love letter in one's hand—it has so special a meaning. Since I started writing this column snow has begun falling again; I sit in my room watching the re-enactment of this stagy old phenomenon outside the window. For this picture, for this privilege, this cameo of New England with snow falling, I would give everything. Yet all the time I know that this very loyalty, this feeling of being part of a special place, this respect for one's native scene—I know that such emotions have had a big part in the world's wars. Who is there big enough to love the whole planet? We must find such people for the next society.

&

Although supranationalism often seems hopelessly distant or impractical, there is one rather encouraging sign in the sky. We have, lately, at least one large new group of people to whom the planet *does* come first. I mean scientists. Science, however undiscriminating it has seemed in the bestowal of its gifts, has no disturbing club affiliations. It eschews nationality. It is preoccupied with an atom, not an atoll.

&

There will be a showdown on supranationalism after this war. The bitter debate between isolation and intervention (a debate ended abruptly last Sunday morning on an island in the Pacific) was really an extension of the fundamental conflict between the national spirit (which is in practically everyone) and the universal spirit (which is in some but not in all). Nationalism has two fatal charms for its devotees: it presupposes local self-sufficiency, which is a pleasant and desirable condition, and it suggests, very subtly, a certain personal superiority by reason of one's belonging to a place that is definable and familiar, as against a place that is strange, remote.

&

Before you can be a supranationalist you have first to be a naturalist and feel the ground under you making a whole circle. It is easier for a man to be loyal to his club than to his planet; the by-laws are shorter, and he is personally acquainted with the other members. A club, moreover, or a nation, has a most attractive offer to make: it offers the right to be exclusive. There are not many of us who are physically constituted to resist this strange delight, this nourishing privilege. It is at the bottom of all fraternities, societies, orders. It is at the bottom of most trouble. The planet holds out no such inducement. The planet is everybody's. All it offers is the grass, the sky, the water, and the ineluctable dream of peace and fruition.

&

Clubs, fraternities, nations—these are the beloved barriers in the way of a workable world, these will have to surrender some of their rights and some of their ribs. A "fraternity" is the antithesis of *fraternity.* The first (that is, the order or organization) is predicated on the idea of exclusion; the second (that is, the abstract thing) is based on a feeling of total equality. Anyone who remembers back to his fraternity days at college recalls the enthusiasts in his group, the rabid members, both old and young, who were obsessed with the mystical charm of membership in their particular order. They were usually men who were incapable of genuine brotherhood, or at least unaware of its implications. Fraternity begins when the exclusion formula is found to be distasteful. The effect of any organization of a social and brotherly nature is to strengthen rather than diminish the lines that divide people into classes; the effect of states and nations is the same, and eventually these lines will have to be softened, these powers will have to be generalized. It is written on the wall that this is so. I'm not inventing it, I'm just copying it off the wall.

৯৯

I find, on rigid introspection, that my feeling for supranationalism, and my trust in it, are intuitive rather than reasonable. It is not so much that I have faith in the ability of nations to organize themselves as that I mistrust what will happen if again they fail to do so.

৯৯

A book that has given me great pleasure during the past year is, in its delicate way, a shining advertisement of the universal spirit and a testimonial to its soundness. It is a book of folk songs called *Lullabies of Many Lands,* collected and arranged by Dorothy Berliner Commins. It contains sixteen songs that belong to sixteen peoples. These are beautiful songs and excellent arrangements, and they suggest a very strong and striking kinship among people everywhere. One of the loveliest is the German *"Schlaf, Kindlein, schlaf. Der Vater hut't die Schaf. Die Mutter Schuttelt's Bäumelein, Da fällt herab ein Träumelein. Schlaf, Kindlein, schlaf."* I don't know what particular revision the minister of propaganda has given this lovely song, but I doubt if he can permanently alter or destroy the emotions that make it live. The more brutal and desperate the time, the steadier burns the belief in universal peace. The Chinese song tells the promise: "From the flute new music comes."

৯৯

I think a good many people, here and everywhere, have a feeling in their bones that some sort of large-scale reawakening is in the cards for humanity. Intimations of this feeling are in the air—in the talk of the philosophers, in the speeches of the politicians, in the songs of the poets, in the wall charts of the economists. There is the vague feeling that after great evil comes great good; after trouble comes absence of trouble; after war, peace. It is a mystical, rather than a logical, presentiment. History does not offer any very impressive corroboration; flip over its pages and you are apt to find the disagreeable reminder that after trouble comes more trouble. Yet it is a feeling everyone must hold to.

Along with this presentiment, this hunch, goes the feeling that it is nip and tuck now with mankind on earth. Science, the dispassionate, has enabled the Japanese to deliver a terrible blow to the English and American fleets. Science, astride the fence, may enable our side to hit back. It all seems so delicately balanced. Nip we win, tuck we lose. The canny and careful reconstruction of barbarism, against the defense of old liberties and ideas. Life more and more seems to present itself in antithetical poses. Even radio news programs suggest the battle of the extremes: the world's largest-selling beauty soap paving the way for five minutes of the world's widest-spread predicament, the soft hands of Walter Winchell's lotion clasped against the tough heart of his defense of American freedom, fifteen minutes of a pleasure gasoline sponsorship in a war in which gasoline is almost the same as blood.

The mechanics and spirit of a capitalistic press and radio are both comical and beautiful today. The first words I heard after the news came of Japan's attack in Hawaii were: Give Mother foot comfort for Christmas." It was in the voice we all know so well—as though the speaker had marshmallows in place of tonsils—but it had that thoroughly cockeyed quality for which in the long run we are fighting. It makes a man suddenly realize his strange and wonderful indebtedness to the cosmetic industry and the tobacco trade and all the rest that are supplying us with capsules of news every few moments.

I was in Washington a while ago, sniffing around and annoying people by looking into their wastebaskets; and while I was there I went over one morning to a Senate committee hearing where Mr. La Guardia was testifying. The committee was investigating the problem of small business men who were being squeezed out of business by defense rulings. It wasn't big news by a long shot, but a couple of cameramen showed up and maneuvered into position quietly, crouching one on either side of the Little Flower. They were well behaved, for photographers, but now and again one of them would explode a flash. Finally one of the committeemen spoke sharply, asked them to quit and let the hearing proceed in peace. They seemed not to hear this request. They just crouched, motionless. Then the Mayor asked them to go away and wait for him outside.

The boys crouched and smiled. A newspaper correspondent sitting next to me said, proudly: "They won't pay any attention to those guys." Nothing was done. The hearing proceeded. It was a familiar pantomime—the free press, deplored yet admired. Under their vests the senators were secretly glad that they were unable to dislodge a couple of American photographers. It was what the hearing was about really—the photographers, squatting imperturbably in front of the men who were plotting to win a war that would preserve for photographers the right to squat imperturbably.

૭ں

It is hard to believe now that Washington was ever the way I saw it a week or so before the outbreak of war. I had been told that I should find Washington a madhouse, but I remember it as a quiet place that managed somehow to give the impression of stability and peace, no matter how rapidly the bureaus were proliferating. Nobody seemed worried. The taxi driver who took me from the station to the hotel said he was on his way the next morning to apply for a time-keeping job on a defense project, which would pay fifty dollars a week; and he reported with considerable enthusiasm that some of the laborers on the job had made as high as one hundred and six dollars in one week. Not even a collapsing world looks dark to a man who is about to make his fortune. The President, when he received the press in his Oval Study, gave little sign of tension and went out of his way to capture a joke or a pleasantry in midair. The weather was soft and agreeable; in the parks the oaks still held their leaves, releasing one now and then, indolently. Young girls on their hard high heels tapped home from the offices through the warm benign parks, and the squirrels and the pigeons deployed in the sunlight. In the Maryland countryside, where I visited for a week-end, there was the same hazy beauty, somnolence, and security—the little firm hills and the valleys between, friendly and warm as a mother's lap, the cornstalks in the still green pastures, the big barns, the winter wheat, and the honeysuckle and the cedars and the holly. In the morning the birds struck up almost as cheerfully as in the deep South, and on the air was the skunky smell of box. Here and there the physical signs of war, nowhere the conviction of its reality.

The whole history of the war so far has been the inability of people in the democracies to believe their eyes and ears. They didn't believe the Rhineland or the persecution of the Jews or Poland or France or any of the rest of it. That phase of the war is over. Now, at least, we can see and hear.

SONGBIRDS

QUITE a good deal has happened since the last entry. The storm windows are down and the screens are up. The ice has left the pond and the frogs have begun their song of songs, deep in the heart of wetness. Sugaring is over with and the trees plugged. Eel traps have been set and have been entered by eels. The field behind the barn has been top-dressed and the upper piece across the road sowed to grass. Each afternoon three patrol planes go over and are mistaken for hawks by the young chickens. The blueberry piece has been burned. Smelts are running in the brooks, tree swallows are nesting in their house on the pole, and the dogs have killed a skunk under the old shed behind the icehouse.

In February I registered in the third draft and from now on will do as I am told, cheerfully I trust. Lambs came in March and also a new electric brooder stove, the latter by express. Tails have been docked, bushes pruned, flower borders uncovered, bank boughs taken away; peas and radishes and spinach and carrots are in. Rhubarb is beginning to show. Mayflowers have been reported fifteen miles away in the mayflower country. Blackout curtains are up at the kitchen windows, wild cucumber up at the kitchen door. Two spring pigs, a sow and a barrow, are working the dressing in the barn cellar. Both geese have laid and set, and all twenty-two eggs have been proved infertile. The gander's face is bright orange. He is on the skids.

Sugar rationing begins next week. Hen wire is hard to get, egg cases harder. Production in the henpens is up, and prices of other things will soon be stabilized but not the price of eggs, which, like the hens themselves, will remain flighty. Spring recess is over and measles are almost over. I have built sideboards and a headboard for the truck, and in a day or two I will receive a siren to be mounted on the truck for notifying people on my stretch of road about air raids. The scow has been painted and launched. Counterweights have been rigged on the windows of the cold frame, for easier operation and smooth, effortless control. The junk-heap in the alders has been ransacked and the metal put back into circulation. Newspapers, magazines, and cardboard have been dispatched to the war. Apple trees have been sprayed, and the north field has been limed.

The last jar of 1941 peas was broached yesterday at lunch, and the preserve closet in the cellar begins to look bare. A new fielder's glove has arrived from Sears and with it the early morning sound of a ball rolling off the barn roof and landing back up there again with a sharp plunk. This week we have had two visits from a great blue heron and one from the superintendent of schools. It has been an early spring and an eerie one. Already we have had evenings which have seemed more like July than April, as though summer were born prematurely and needed special care. Tonight is such a night. The warmth of afternoon held over through suppertime, and now the air has grown still. In the barnyard, among the wisps of dry straw that make a pattern on the brown earth, the sheep lie motionless and as yet unshorn, their great ruffs giving them a regal appearance, their placidity seemingly induced by the steady crying of the frogs. The unseasonable warmth invests the night with a quality of mystery and magnitude. And in the east beyond the lilac and beyond the barn and beyond the bay and behind the deepening hills, in slow and splendid surprise, rises the bomber's moon.

ও৶

Spring is a rush season on any farm. On this farm of ours spring becomes an almost impossible season because of the songbirds, which arrive just as everything else is getting under way and which have to be identified. They couldn't pick a more inconvenient time.

I say they have to be identified—we never used to identify songbirds, we used to lump them and listen to them sing. But my wife, through a stroke of ill fortune, somehow got hold of a book called *A Field Guide to the Birds—Including All Species Found in Eastern North America,* by Roger Tory Peterson, and now we can't settle down to any piece of work without being interrupted by a warbler trying to look like another warbler and succeeding admirably.

The birds have been here a couple of weeks now, and we are getting farther and farther behind with everything. I simply haven't time to stop what I am doing every fifteen seconds to report a white eye-ring and a yellow rump-patch, and neither has my wife. Take this morning, for instance. Our home roars and boils and seethes with activity. Upstairs is German measles. In the cellar is a water pump that has gone into a running fit. Outside, a truck is noisily trying to back up to the woodshed door to deliver a couple of cords of dry wood for us to spring out on. In the shop somebody is hammering away, making a blackout frame for the next raid. In the back kitchen the set tubs are in operation, coping with a week's wash. In the front study my wife's typewriter is going like the devil, trying to catch a mail with something or other of an editorial nature. Overhead a plane grumbles and threatens and heads out to sea. Here in the living room, where I choose to work because it is the nerve center of the whole place and thus enables me to keep in touch with life without moving out of my chair, I am busy with the electric literary life of a pent-up agriculturist, such as it is. Lambs jump and dance in the barnyard, waiting for the gate to swing open so they can get at the lamb-kill; tiny broccoli and tomato and cabbage and lettuce plants struggle desperately upward in flats in the south window waiting to be transplanted into the cold frame; two hundred and seventy-two chicks romp in the brooder house in search of trouble; the wind blows, the bushes creak against the shutters, the sun shines, the radio plays for the measles, and the whole place has the eleventh-hour pulsation of a defense factory. On top of everything there are these indistinguishable little birds crying for our attention, flaunting an olive-green spot that looks yellow, a yellow stripe that looks gray, a gray breast that looks cinnamon, a cinnamon tail that looks brown.

This morning at breakfast my wife seemed tired and discouraged. I thought perhaps it was the measles upstairs (which we had wrongly identified, at first, as a boil in the ear). "Do you know," she said after a while, "that the fox sparrow can easily be mistaken for the hermit thrush? They are about the same size, and they both have a red tail in flight."

"They don't if you look the other way," I replied, wittily. But she was not comforted. She thumbed restlessly through *A Field Guide* (she carries it with her from room to room at this season) and settled down among the grosbeaks, finches, sparrows, and buntings while I went back among the smoked bacon, blackberry jam, toast, and coffee.

"My real trouble is," she continued, "that I learn the birds pretty well one year, but then the next year comes and I have to learn them all again. I think probably the only way really to learn them is to go out with a bird person. That would be the only way."

"You wouldn't like a bird person," I replied.

"I mean a sympathetic bird person."

"You don't know a sympathetic bird person."

"I knew a Mr. Knollenberg once," said my wife wistfully, "who was always looking for a difficult finch."

She admitted, however, that the problem of the birds was virtually insoluble. Even the chickadee, it turns out, plays a dirty trick on us all. Everybody knows a chickadee, and in winter the chickadees are our constant companions. For nine months of the year the chickadee announces himself plainly, so that any simpleton can tell him; but in spring the fraudulent little devil gives a phony name. In spring, when love hits him, he goes around introducing himself as Phoebe. According to the author of the *Field Guide* he whistles the name Phoebe, whereas the Phoebe doesn't whistle it but simply *says* it. Still, it's a dishonest trick, and I resent it when I'm busy.

Mr. Peterson, the author of the *Guide*, has made a manly attempt to enable us to identify birds, but the attempt (in my case) is pitiful. He says of the Eastern Winter Wren *(Nannus hiemalis hiemalis)*: it "frequents mossy tangles, ravines, brushpiles." That, I don't doubt, is true of the Eastern Winter Wren; but it is also true of practically every bird here except the chimney swift and the herring gull. Our whole country is just one big mossy tangle. Any bird you meet is suspect, but they can't all be Eastern Winter Wrens.

The titmice, the wrens, the thrushes, the nuthatches, the finches are bad enough, but when Mr. Peterson comes to helping me, or even my wife, with the warblers his efforts are indeed laughable. There are dozens of warblers, many of them barely visible to the naked eye. To distinguish them one from another is like trying to distinguish between two bits of dust dancing in a shaft of sunlight. Of the Chestnut-sided Warbler Mr. Peterson says: *"Adults in spring:*—Easily identified by the *yellow* crown and the *chestnut* sides. The only other bird with chestnut sides, the Bay-breast, has a chestnut throat and a dark crown, thus appearing quite dark-headed. *Autumn* birds are quite different—greenish above and white below, with a white eye-ring and two wing-bars. Adults usually retain some of the chestnut. The lemon-colored shade of green, in connection with the white under parts, is sufficient for recognition." Well, it is sufficient for recognition if you happen to be standing, or lying, directly under a Chestnut-sided Warbler in the fall of the year and can remember not to confuse the issue with "adults in spring" or with the Bay-breast at *any* season—specially the *female* Bay-breast in spring, which is rather dim and indistinct, the way all birds look to me when they are in a hurry (which they almost always are) or when I am. A hurried man trying to identify a hurried bird is palpably a ridiculous situation.

Even the author of the *Guide* admits, in places, that a bird spotter is in for real trouble. The Sycamore Warbler, he says, is almost identical with the Yellow-throated Warbler, but might be distinguished "at extremely short range" by the lack of any yellow between the eye and the bill. It helps some though if you can remember which side of the Alleghenies you are on. I try to keep that in mind always.

The thing that amuses me about songbirds in our amazing springtime is the way my wife takes her troubles out on the birds themselves, who are, in a sense, innocent enough. She is puzzled and annoyed at her inability to master, in a few crowded weeks, the amazing intricacies of bird markings—made even more difficult because we sent our binoculars to England year before last to help in the defense of the British Isles. A little while ago I saw her pause for a fleeting moment at a window as she was passing by and heard her mutter peevishly: "There goes one of those damned little Yellow Palm Warblers." Then she added, in a barely audible whisper, "I guess."

Songbirds can be ruinous as well as hard to tell apart. A few days ago I seeded last year's garden piece to grass. Next morning a great flock of juncos came in, wave after wave, white-bellied evil-minded juncos, slate-colored hungry juncos, smaller-than-a-house-sparrow-something-like-a-Vesper-sparrow juncos. They swarmed into the field and ate up all the seeds. It was the first time I had ever sprung after a songbird with a foul oath.

&

When we first came here to live, the road in front of our house was a dirt road. But after a while they tarred it. Now, in war, with the automobile on the wane and the horse returning, I think probably they will have to throw some dirt back on the road, the surface being too hard on the feet of animals. Moral: men should settle their differences before they improve their roads.

&

Our county had its first blackout the other evening, on Palm Sunday. It was considered a success, although no bomb fell. It was a lovely day for a raid—one of those quiet days full of a deceptive peace. When I looked out at daybreak the ground was white with frost, but you could tell it was going to be a fine day. I got up promptly to tend some new chicks and was busy with them for a half hour before breakfast, thinking of palms and Christ and bombs and dry litter. After breakfast a new lamb turned up with a sore eye, which I bathed with boric acid so it could see well for the blackout, and then was summoned to help a scholar with his grammar but with no success. When I could not think of a pronoun used with conjunctive force and did not know what an adjectival complement was he grew restless and discouraged.

"You really don't know anything about grammar, do you?" he said.

"No, I don't," I replied, with only a trace of regret.

Only three or four cars passed, the whole morning long. We saw no palm leaves and did not go to church. After his homework was done the boy left to dam a stream, and from the kitchen came the drowsy sound of something being chopped in a bowl. Mostly we just lay around, waiting for the blackout.

A little after nine o'clock in the evening, our phone began ringing the numbers on the party line (we are on a line with seven other subscribers and each has his own distinctive ring, almost as hard to tell apart as the warblers). I sat by the phone waiting, with my jacket and cap on and my gloves handy. When our call came, I picked up the phone and the voice of our chief air raid warden said: "The yellow has just come through."

Outside, the truck stood ready, trembling, its engine running, its headlights on (we were instructed to drive with lights for this first raid). I hung up the phone, ran outside, and jumped in. My assignment was to give the alarm on a stretch of road between our house and the center of the village two and a half miles away. The signal was to be a continuous blowing of the horn.

As I turned out of the drive into the highway and jammed the horn button down, trying to shift gears, blow a horn, and make a turn, all with only two hands, the thing seemed entirely real to me—just as the first second or two of the fire drill in grammar school used to seem real, when the gong sounded suddenly and you had to guess whether the fire was a hot one or an imaginary one. To race through the countryside at night, blowing your horn steadily, stirs the blood up. For a few minutes I was brother to Paul Revere.

The villagers had been reading about the blackout for a week in the newspaper and were prepared, some with blackout curtains, others with the simpler defense mechanism—blowing out the lamp. As I passed farmhouse after farmhouse, making my horrible racket, shades were quickly drawn and lights went out. I drove as fast as I could considering the condition of the road, which was full of holes where the frost had heaved the tar. The horn button proved treacherous; it would make contact only if held in a certain position, and occasionally I'd lose the horn and have to worry it on again.

As I drew in to the village I heard the church bell ringing. The church was black, the two stores were black, and the four or five houses at the corner were black. I peered into the church and tried to see the sexton at the bell rope but couldn't. For a minute or two my horn and the church bell quarreled, the sacred and the profane, riling the Sabbath evening. Then I turned the truck round and started back home—no horn this time. One house still showed lights. I stopped and tooted peremptorily. The lights were quickly extinguished. I glanced in at the house where the old lady lived who had said that she was so far off the road she wouldn't be able to hear the signal but that it wouldn't make any difference because she always went to bed before nine o'clock anyway. Everything was dark at her house.

I was back home about twenty-five past nine, and at nine-thirty the phone rang again and the warden announced: "Red light." The raid was on.

Sitting by the radio in the dark living room (our own curtains hadn't been installed) we turned on Fred Allen for the duration of the raid. When the all-clear came through I repeated the trip to town, sounding the horn again, but the bloom was off the rose: the second trip was anticlimactic. The church bell was ringing again, and this time the sexton was visible in the vestibule.

One of the things I had to do, to get ready to black out our farm, was to devise a blackout hood for the pilot light on my electric brooder stove, which goes on and off as the thermostat switch operates. I found an old tin cup and inverted this over the bulb, a simple precaution involving two hundred and seventy-two lives, not counting our own.

QUESTIONNAIRE

The mail this morning brought my occupational questionnaire from Selective Service headquarters. I have been working on it off and on all day, trying to give my country some notion of what sort of life I lead—which I take to be what it is after. Since my life is cluttered with dozens of pursuits, some of which seem wholly unrelated to the others, the form has proved hard to fill out. Explaining oneself by inserting words in little boxes and squares is like getting an idea over to a jury when you are limited to answering the questions of the attorneys.

I was rather surprised, but not alarmed, to discover that "writing" is not recognized in selective service, either as professional work or as an "occupation." Nothing is said in the questionnaire about a writer. In the lengthy list of pursuits and professions the name of writer does not anywhere appear. Scarfers, riggers, glass blowers, architects, historians, metallurgists—all are mentioned in the long alphabet of American life. But not writers. This, I feel, is as it should be, and shows that the selective service system is more perceptive than one might suppose. Writing is not an occupation nor is it a profession. Bad writing can be, and often is, an occupation; but I agree with the government that writing in the pure sense and in noblest form is neither an occupation nor a profession. It is more of an affliction, or just punishment. It is something that raises up on you, as a welt. Or you might say that it is a by-product of many occupations and professions, which the writer pursues (or is pursued by) recklessly or necessarily. A really pure writer is a man like Conrad, who is first of all a mariner; or Isadora Duncan, a dancer; or Ben Franklin, an inventor and statesman; or Hitler, a scamp. The intellectual who simply says "I am a writer," and forthwith closets himself with a sharp pencil and a dull Muse, may well turn out to be no artist at all but merely an ambitious and perhaps misguided person. I think the best writing is often done by persons who are snatching the time from something else—from an occupation, or from a profession, or from a jail term—something that is either burning them up, as religion, or love, or politics, or that is boring them to tears, as prison, or a brokerage house, or an advertising firm. A great violinist must begin fairly early in life to play the violin; but I think a literary artist has a better chance of producing something great if he spends the first forty years of his life doing something else—grinding a lens or surveying a wilderness. There are of course notable exceptions. Shakespeare was one. He was a writing fool, apparently. And I have often suspected that some of his noblest passages were written with his tongue at least halfway in his cheek. "Boy," you can hear him mutter, "will that panic 'em!"

Since I now lead a dual existence—half farmer, half literary gent—I found difficulty making myself sound like anything but a flibbertigibbet. The initial disappointment at not finding my life's work listed among the selected occupations, professions, and sciences was greatly relieved, however, when after a careful study of the list I found, under the "f's":

> Farmer, dairy
> Farmer, other

I'm not getting a cow till next year, but it is something in this life to be Farmer Other. Not Farmer Brown or Farmer White but Farmer Other. I liked the name very much and immediately wrote the words "4 years" in front of Farmer Other. When I consider that most of my neighbors have been carrying pails for half a century, four years is a mere apprenticeship, I know; but nevertheless, it is a beginning, and in the greatest occupation of all.

I imagine that my local draft board, like any group of registrars, prefers to have lives fall into conventional patterns and will not take kindly to a citizen who is so far out of line as to be both farmer and writer. It doesn't have a clean-cut sound. It is Jekyll and Hyde stuff, lacks an honest ring. In war it is better to be a clean-cut man: a hammersmith plain, a riveter simple, a born upholsterer, an inveterate loftsman, a single-hearted multi-purpose machine operator. To be farmer and writer suggests a fickleness of character out of key with the war effort. To produce, in a single week, seventy dozen table eggs and a twenty-six-hundred-word article, sounds confused, immature, and smacks of divided loyalty.

Question 20 is called "Duties of Your Present Job." Three lines are allotted for the answer, space for about forty words of crowded confession. I got myself into thirty-seven, by taking thought and by following closely the sample reply given above, starting "I clean, adjust, and repair watches and clocks. I take them apart . . . etc." I could almost have followed the sample exactly, changing only a word or two: "I clean, adjust, and repair manuscripts and farm machinery. I take them apart and examine the parts through an eyepiece to find which parts need repair. I repair or replace parts. Sometimes I make a new part, using a jackplane or an infinitive. I clean the parts and put them back together again."

Under JOB FOR WHICH YOU ARE BEST FITTED I wrote "Editor and writer." Under JOB FOR WHICH YOU ARE NEXT BEST FITTED I wrote "Poultryman and farmer." But I realized that it was not so much fitness that I was thinking about as returns. What I meant was JOB BY WHICH YOU MAKE THE MOST MONEY. And NEXT MOST. It is hard to tell about fitness. Physically I am better fitted for writing than for farming, because farming takes great strength and great endurance. Intellectually I am better fitted for farming than for writing.

ૐ

Walt Whitman should be around today to see how the boys are regenerating his stuff. For a long time I kept wondering where I had heard all this singing before—the radio programs dramatizing America, the propaganda of democracy, the music in the President's chats, the voices of the poets singing America. Then it came to me. It is all straight Walt. The radiomatics of Corwin, the sound tracks of Lorentz, the prophecies of MacLeish and Benét, the strumming of Sandburg, the iambics of Anderson and Sherwood. Listen the next time you have the radio turned to the theatrics of the air—you will hear the voice of old Walt shouting from Paumanok. If there were any doubt about where he stands in the literary ladder this decade has put an end to it. He is right at the top. He must be good or he wouldn't be heard so clearly in the syllables of our contemporaries.

There is a certain something about this sort of writing that is unmistakable; the use of place names, the cataloging of ideas, the repetition of sounds, the determination to be colloquial or bust, the celebration of the American theme and the American dream, the appreciation of the man in the street and the arm round the shoulder, the "song of the throes of democracy." You can't miss it when you hear it. Sometimes, when one is jittery or out of whack, it seems as though one heard it too much—so much that it loses its effect. But Walt unquestionably started it. He was the one who heard America beating on a pan, beating on a carpet, beating on an anvil. He heard what was coming, and he said the words.

ह•

Paid off the mortgage on the farm last week, the first time I had ever done anything like that although I had read about it in books. I put on my best clothes for the occasion and presented myself at the bank, looking like a man of affairs. The disguise didn't work very well though. While the proper paper was being drawn up, the president and I chewed the fat, and after a while I got a little nervous and said: "Don't I have to sign something?" He looked at me in surprise and then smiled indulgently.

"Sign something?" he repeated. "*You* don't have to sign anything; *we* do."

The bank, it turned out, was very sad at losing title to my property and was not consoled by all the money I paid them. They painted their grief so vividly that they had me almost in tears when I left, and I felt like an old skinflint as I walked down the steps and out into the sunshine, free and clear. Actually I wouldn't hurt a hair of a banker's head and was only paying off the mortgage because the government was instructing people to pay their debts. No matter how hard a man tries to do the right thing someone is always hurt and grieved.

Our trading center, where the bank is, is quite a distance from home, and nowadays, with the tire situation what it is, the trip is quite an event. We used to go about once a week to this embryonic metropolis; now we go about once a month—to meet a train, or anaesthetize a dog, or pay off a mortgage. Once upon a time this little city looked small to me; now it seems a boiling metropolis, vast and inscrutable and pleasantly corrupt. In it you see people in that curious larval stage, between country worm and city butterfly—the town beginning to get in its licks. Clothes are a curious compromise of farm and office, of barn and salon. The ladies have studied the fashions and have gone about the matter with a will; but their efforts don't quite come off. Men are city from the waist down, country from the waist up. Or sometimes the other way round. You see a man dressed four-fifths for business, one-fifth for chores—apportioning his apparel as he apportions his time. He may have on the trousers, shirt, vest, tie, shoes, and socks of a Brummel, but for his jacket he has substituted an old zipper sweater in a two-tone design. Or he may be turned out in the mode, complete except for his feet, which are encased sensibly in hunting boots. In general, the people in small cities of this sort seem to lack the homespun and genuinely comfortable appearance of the countryman, without having achieved the well-groomed appearance of the city dweller. It has to be a compromise. One minute a clerk will be tending his counter, half an hour later he will be tending his hens.

There are unmistakable signs that always betray embryonic cities and show that they have the makings of concentration. The presence of pigeons and of English sparrows, those unfailing followers of the smart metropolitan whirl, is a sign. An English sparrow wouldn't be found dead in the country, and it seems to me pigeons feel about the same way; but the minute you get into Main Street there they are, enjoying the hot pavements and the excitement and the congenial vices of congestion and trade. The faces you see on the streets have a slightly different look, too. They are not the faces you left back in the country. You see a fellow and he has a look in his eye, or perhaps it is the way he holds a toothpick in his mouth, as though he knew a secret. And as you pass along in front of the shops you hear the muffled sound of distant bowling balls, the tell-tale thunder of civilization.

AUNT POO

In our living room, in a great old-fashioned frame, there hangs a painting of a lady and a dog. This picture rather dominates the room, and I have become quite fond of the lady. It is not a great painting but it is a pleasing one. You can look at it again and again and not tire of it. The lady is of Victorian mold. She is young. She sits with one elbow cocked on the table next her chair, gazing down quizzically at her little dog. The artist responsible for this unsung work of art is my wife's aunt, a lady of eighty-five years, whose career as a painter was somewhat broken into in middle life when she laid aside her brushes and married a Japanese.

I have never met this fabulous aunt. She went to Tokyo and, except for a couple of brief visits, never came back. But she seems vivid enough —one of those semi-fictional characters you acquire by marriage and through much hearsay, just as you acquire, by slow degrees, the whole childhood history of the person you marry and at length feel that you know the child. I feel that I know Puss quite well, or Aunt Poo as she is invariably called by her three nieces, who cling with New England grit to the whimsical name by which she was known in the nursery. Although eighty-five, she is still beset by the enormous vigor that has filled her lifetime. At any rate she recently completed, in time to get it to America before all communication with Japan ceased, a volume of her memoirs, including a family history covering the years 1680 to 1908. I have just been reading it. Only three copies exist (one for each niece); for in fact it is not a printed book at all but is a typed book—typed by her, single-spaced, on heavy drawing paper, and beautifully bound in an old brocade handed down from her husband's ancestors. Since in her scheme of bookmaking there had to be three copies of this monumental work, Aunt Poo had to run it through her typewriter three times, an appalling task. You see, if she had merely made an original and two carbons she would have been left with an unthinkable problem in discrimination: the problem of deciding which of her three nieces was to get the original, which the first carbon, which the second. Rather than face this distasteful dilemma, and because any book of hers, even a bound typescript, must meet certain standards of craftsmanship, she laboriously executed it three times, punching away night after night in the settlement house over which she presides in the slum district of Tokyo, minding her margins and neatly pasting in photographs by way of illustration.

To have so close a link with the enemy as Aunt Poo is both sobering and salutary. In war one tends to dehumanize the foe and to take pleasure in the thought of the dropped bomb. The presence in Tokyo of a member of the family, while it in no way lessens our determination to win, somewhat tempers our blood lust; we drop our bombs rather gingerly, trusting that our old aunt is dodging with the same skill and courage with which, at the age of four in Minnesota, she was dodging musket fire in the Indian uprising while her father rode two hundred miles on horseback to the rescue of a besieged garrison of whites in Fort Abercrombie. I feel that these new bombs will not prove an impossible burden at the end of so spectacular a career, but they will tear at her heart, since they bring into conflict the two great loves of her life, her ancestral New England and her adopted Nippon.

The story of her marriage to the Japanese and of the founding of the settlement house called Yurin-En is one that I hesitate to tell, since it is just family stuff; yet it is unique and timely and perhaps worth a try.

There was always something about Aunt Poo that was vaguely exciting, according to my wife's account. Poo was the member of the family who had thrown off conventions and become an artist. She had been to Paris. She was Bohemia, in Suburbia. Strong-minded, sentimental, domineering, she had a flair for giving life (for little girls anyway) a certain extra quality. She was a great one to make an occasion of a day. Any sort of anniversary inflamed her. It would suddenly occur to her that today was Lincoln's Birthday, or the Ides of March, or Decoration Day, and in no time at all the house would tremble with the violence of redecoration or cookery or charades. She had the gift of celebration. There was no day so drab but, under Poo's fiery tutelage, could be whipped into a carnival.

She had been to Paris. She had had a studio in New York. In those days the very word studio was drenched with glamorous meaning. But despite her art and her wanderings, the great preoccupation of the first half of her life was her family, to belong to which seemed a career in itself. Her father, her mother, her sister, and her brother—to these she gave much of her energy and most of her thoughts. Within a relatively short space of time all four died, leaving her alone, and it was then that she bought a house in Woodstock, Connecticut, where the second phase of her life began.

Woodstock itself meant nothing in particular—her people had been rooted in the colder soil of Maine, in the little towns of Fryeburg, Naples, Bridgton, in Saco, and in the metropolises of Portland and Boston. Her infancy had been spent in the frontier town of St. Cloud, Minnesota, her childhood on a farm in Naples. But Woodstock contained a cousin, and to Woodstock she went to settle down for the long agreeable grind of spinsterhood. She applied herself rather briskly to fixing up the place, which she named Apple End, and rather desultorily to painting. She had come into a little money and could afford a cook. She could afford one but she couldn't seem to find one. In desperation she turned to the Springfield Y.M.C.A. Training School, among whose students were a few Orientals learning to be athletic directors in the American manner. It was summertime, and classes were over for the year.

As a result of her inquiry there arrived at Apple End one Hyozo Omori, a young Japanese of distinguished lineage, frail, aesthetic, and anxious to earn a little money. He had a slight beard which, with his delicate features and sensitiveness, gave him a Christlike appearance. He was shown the kitchen and given a rough idea of his duties: he was to cook the meals and serve them and tidy up. He seemed polite but worried.

It became apparent almost immediately that Mr. Omori and a kitchen were strangers of long standing. Aristocracy stuck out all over him. Although his efforts at cooking were preposterous, his conversation was charming. Aunt Poo saw in him a man who had been waited on all his life and who was clearly unsuited for any sudden reversal. So she set to and prepared Mr. Omori's meals for him, and as soon as possible engaged a large colored woman to carry some of the rapidly mounting household burden.

Mr. Omori, it must be said, offered to leave, but she urged him to stay on and assume duties of a more wispy sort—poking about the flower garden and exchanging views on poetry. He consented. For a while the domestic situation at Apple End was confused; the Japanese student was unwilling to sit at table with the colored woman, and the mistress of the house was disinclined to sit at table with the Japanese student. Everybody was eating off trays, in aseptic splendor.

In this way [writes Aunt Poo in her memorial volume] began my acquaintance with Hyozo Omori, a gentleman of ancient lineage and culture who, like most of the Japanese students of that day, regarded all Americans as quite inferior in culture but were quite ready, given a respect for all honest work, to earn money from us in a perfectly impersonal way, making a contact with unpleasant things for a moment for convenience, without feeling oneself degraded.

I take it what slight momentary degradation Mr. Omori had been subjected to during his first few days at Woodstock was forgotten in the ensuing weeks. Aunt Poo and he liked the same books. Together they walked in the garden and talked of Japanese art—which Mr. Omori knew a great deal about—and he told her of his two ambitions in life: to found a settlement house in Tokyo, and to increase the stature of the Japanese race. In the fall he returned to Springfield, she to Boston. They corresponded. He visited her several times, and finally asked her to marry him. She decided after a while to accept.

The news exploded like a time bomb in the house in a Boston suburb where my wife was then living as a young girl. Since Poo's immediate family were all dead, the conventional and decent thing of course would be to have her married under her brother-in-law's roof. But to a Japanese!

"What will the papers do with this?" groaned Papa, who had troubles enough of an Occidental nature without an involvement with the Rising Sun.

The *Boston American,* already banned from the house on general principles, broke the story with a mild flourish. Family councils were held behind closed doors. The girls, bursting with direct questions, were put off with evasive answers. It was a time of incredible consternation and embarrassment. But my wife's father was no quitter. He announced to the children that the wedding, if indeed their aunt was determined to go through with it, would be "under our roof." This took courage of a high order.

Meantime Mr. Omori was introduced to the household and made something of a hit with his nieces-to-be. He showed them how to make tea in the Japanese fashion, green tea served in cups without handles. Gracefully, politely, they would sip it and nibble on the little rice cakes, which were slightly sweet. Mr. Omori seemed genuinely attached to his New England fiancée, and regarded her with amazement and humorous delight. His cultivated mind and his gentle manner were disarming to a considerable degree, and his appearance was celestial. He lacked only a halo. Aunt Poo, by contrast, appeared more earthly than ever, with her plump and friendly frame.

They were married in the parlor. The girls were delighted to have a wedding in their house and to have the mantelpiece transformed into an altar by the addition of some Mrs. Humphry Ward roses. The couple left immediately for Tokyo on their wedding trip. It was the first of October, 1907.

> Since then I have lived thirty years and more in Japan, more than one-third of my life, and have never regretted that daring [writes Aunt Poo in the memoirs]. There is something in the Japanese character that can be understood by one of Puritan stock. They like simplicity, even a sort of severity of life. There is no pretense about them. In manners they are punctilious. At heart they are very kind. I do not say that I have never had homesick moments, but I truly loved my husband's beautiful spirit. When he could no longer do for his country what he so much wished to do, I tried in my small way to supply his place, and perhaps Japan is now my home as New England could not be now; and that other life is now not to me unloved, nor dead, but separated as death does separate, in a way never to be put together again.

That was written in 1939. Mr. Omori died in 1912, five years after the marriage.

One of the things he had "so much wished to do" for his country was, as I have mentioned, to increase the stature of the Japanese race, whose diminutive size he found out of keeping with their large destiny. It seemed like a detail worth correcting. First, however, he and his wife set about realizing his major aim—the Tokyo settlement house, which soon became a reality and has for a quarter of a century been an institution of considerable importance, the Hull House of Tokyo.

The other goal was less easy, but Mr. Omori made a start. What he did was to organize the first Japanese team ever to enter the Olympic Games; he hoped that participation in sports would sooner or later result in bigger bodies for his little countrymen. Proudly he escorted his team to Stockholm, over the trans-Siberian railway, and took Aunt Poo along. The whole junket seems, at this date, curiously roundabout and tinged with musical-comedy intrigue. I haven't any idea whether Uncle Hyozo was dreaming, even then, of Pearl Harbor and the straits before Singapore. My wife doubts that he was. In a way it doesn't make any difference. The Japanese are still little fellows, for all the competition they met at the games.

The team returned by way of Siberia but Aunt Poo and Uncle Hyo continued west, turning up in the Boston suburb bearing some aquamarines from the Urals as gifts for the girls. It was plain, by that time, that Mr. Omori was a sick man. He was, in fact, in an advanced tubercular stage. The doctor ordered him to quit traveling, but Mr. Omori was not a man to be ordered about. He announced that he and his wife were returning immediately to Tokyo, and together they set out. The couple got as far as San Francisco, and there he died.

San Francisco must have been a sort of crossroads for Aunt Poo. One way pointed back to New England, to her beloved villages and the elms and the kinsfolk. It was the clearer way. The other pointed to the Orient. Aunt Poo apparently never hesitated. She turned west across the Pacific, escorting her husband's body home, and there she remained to carry on the settlement house that was her husband's dearest desire.

The flyleaf of the memoirs is inscribed: "To my dear niece Katharine Sergeant White, a tribute to our common past." The story is one of the most revealing I have ever read. Page by page one learns what it was that nourished her through her busy and useful years in a foreign land. It was her extraordinary sense of the past, her deep sense of family. It was New England in Japan. As time went on she became thoroughly involved in life at 370 Kashiwagi, Yodobashi, Tokyo. She translated *Lady Murasaki* into English. In the earthquake of 1922 she performed heroic service and was decorated by the government. But through it all the sense of the past grew stronger rather than weaker. Her letters flowed in an endless stream, keeping the past alive. Now and again she would request that something be sent her—a root from a common field flower, a recipe for an ancestral pie. Her thoughts returned constantly to the Maine villages of her childhood, to the snowberries and blush roses under the windows of the house in Naples, to the syringa and the spiraea, to the living room with Hannah knitting and sister reading with the kitten in her lap.

I don't know what the war is doing to her. Intellectually it is an impossible situation. She has always stood up for Japan and has felt that everything Japan did was right—even the "China incident" as she called it. For her nieces, who saw nothing "incidental" in the ravaging of China, correspondence with Aunt Poo was becoming increasingly difficult when it was shut off altogether.

At any rate I find it, as I say, salutary to read in the neat typing of this very old lady the findings of her thirty years' ministering to the poor people of an alien race, her insistence on their good qualities. It is a valuable antidote to the campaign of hate that war breeds; for somehow I don't believe that hate is the answer to our troubles. Hate is a mere beginner of wars. To end them, we shall have to marry our indignation with our faith.

Author's note. Since the above was written, word has been received of Aunt Poo's death. Details are lacking, but she is reported to have died of natural causes. Against the backdrop of war and Japanese brutality, the story of Mrs. Omori's life seems unreal, and her long years of work in the slums of Tokyo take on the quality of a bitter jest. They were never this to her; but it is significant, perhaps, that in the last years before the war her thoughts turned away from the new currents around her in Japan and back to New England on the strong tide of emotion that took the form of her memoirs for her nieces.

BOOK LEARNING

F ARMERS are interested in science, in modern methods, and in theory, but they are not easily thrown off balance and they maintain a healthy suspicion of book learning and of the shenanigans of biologists, chemists, geneticists, and other late-rising students of farm practice and management. They are, I think, impressed by education, but they have seen too many examples of the helplessness and the impracticality of educated persons to be either envious or easily budged from their position.

I was looking at a neighbor's hens with him one time when he said something that expressed the feeling farmers have about colleges and books. He was complaining about the shape of the henhouse, but he wanted me to understand that it was all his own fault it had turned out badly. "I got the plan for it out of a book, fool-fashion," he said. And he gazed around at his surroundings in gentle disgust, with a half-humorous, half-disappointed look, as one might look back at any sort of youthful folly.

Scientific agriculture, however sound in principle, often seems strangely unrelated to, and unaware of, the vital, gruelling job of making a living by farming. Farmers sense this quality in it as they study their bulletins, just as a poor man senses in a rich man an incomprehension of his own problems. The farmer of today knows, for example, that manure loses some of its value when exposed to the weather; but he also knows how soon the sun goes down on all of us, and if there is a window handy at the cow's stern he pitches the dressing out into the yard and kisses the nitrogen good-by. There is usually not time in one man's lifetime to do different. The farmer knows that early-cut hay is better feed than hay that has been left standing through the hot dry days of late July. He hasn't worked out the vitamin losses, but he knows just by looking at the grass that some of the good has gone out of it. But he knows also that to make hay he needs settled weather—better weather than you usually get in June.

I've always tried to cut my hay reasonably early, but this year I wasn't able to get a team until the middle of July. It turned out to be just as well. June was a miserable month of rains and fog mulls. The people who stuck to their theories and cut their hay in spite of the weather, took a beating. A few extremists, fearful of losing a single vitamin, mowed in June, choosing a day when the sun came out for a few minutes. Their hay lay in the wet fields and rotted day after day, while Rommel took Tobruk and careened eastward toward Alexandria.

The weather was unprecedented—weeks of damp and rain and fog. Everybody talked about it. One day during that spell I was holding forth to a practical farmer on the subject of hay. Full of book learning, I was explaining (rather too glibly) the advantages of cutting hay in June. I described in detail the vitamin loss incurred by letting hay stand in the field after it has matured, and how much greater the feed value was per unit weight in early-cut hay, even though the quantity might be slightly less. The farmer was a quiet man, with big hands for curling round a scythe handle. He listened attentively. My words swirled around his head like summer flies. Finally, when I had exhausted my little store of learning and paused for a moment, he ventured a reply.

"The time to cut hay," he said firmly, "is in hayin' time."

MORNINGTIME AND EVENINGTIME

THE spotting post is in the western part of town, over on the river where it joins the sea, facing the unformed sunset in the rich young afternoon with the thunder wrapped in black in the north and the telephone handy for the flash when you hear *Go Ahead Please.* The post is on a ledge, high above the river and the sea, facing west, behind the postmistress's barn, a gray ledge of solid granite sprinkled with the broken shells of clams. At my feet the pasture, sultry in the summer afternoon, heedless of the grumbling shower—the juniper and laurel, the paths worn by the cows' feet, the little paths so artfully contrived among the rocks and sweetfern. Behind is the henyard where the mourners stand; the hens step gingerly among the empty clam shells and the dusting holes. I hear the thin small whining of a plane, invisible, and follow with my eyes, my ears, the eyes following the ears. Beyond the white cloud here it comes. To arms! An airplane in the sky! To arms, attention, this . . . is war! I crank the phone, which makes a sickly ring as though its throat were sore. Flash. One plane, unknown. High. The secret name (this is confidential) of this implausible and secret post where I watch the sky trails, where I scan the nimbus for the approaching foe. North, three miles, southwest. And may I say, before you cut me off, that I've observed in addition to this single plane (high, unknown) an unsurpassed example of an afternoon. Flash —sweet fern and juniper. Flash—the distant sea, my secret post and secret joy, the distant and impending shower, cumulus, the fields beyond the little stream, the holy spire of the small white church, children playing (against the rules) around the post and trading glimpses through the old binoculars. Flash. A little portion of America, imperiled, smiling and beautiful as anything. On my right the village, church and school, imperiled, still warm and to all appearances intact and safe; on my left a farmyard, threatened, brooding, waiting for the immediate thunder in the north and for the delayed thunder that you read about; and at my feet the pasture, warm and sultry, dropping to the sea. I just report it for your files, for the interceptor's files, for your information at a time when we need all the information we can get. Perhaps it is none of my business. I abuse my privilege.

The postmistress has come out of her house. On the clothesline she hangs a suit of Navy whites. She takes the clothespin from her mouth.

"My boy is home today," she calls. "On leave."

"How does he like it?"

"Good. He's only home a day and wants to get right back. Misses the other boys. He washes these himself, most generally, but doesn't really get 'em white. I used some Oxydol and still they show a little grime. He loves it, what he's seen so far. They gave him three months' training in five weeks. They taught him self-defense, jiu jitsu, wrestling, boxing, how to swim, how to take to the boats, all that stuff. He's raring to get back and when he gets there he'll be shipped. He don't know where. They never let them know."

The Navy whites are added to the scene, the thunder gains, the woman goes indoors, the world darkens, the rain descends. I slip my oilskins on and watch the sky, dripping very slightly. Out of the thin rain, in from sea, a plane comes flying north. I crank the phone. Flash, one multimotor seen. The ebb has siphoned off the river, the bar is dry, the hawk hangs fishing in the sky, the air is thunderous. I light a pipe. A small breeze passes by, the suit of whites flies flapping in my rear. A tug with barge in tow sets slowly in the west. The hours pass. A heron fishes on the flats. The tide has turned. The flood begins. My watch is done.

We serve three meals a day here still. The food is pretty good, starvation is unknown, and all that stuff is nonsense that you read—those kids in Greece and Poland couldn't be. Tonight is suppertime, the pie is blueberry, the watch is over, the observation is no more. This is the edge of dark and suppertime.

I have a date tonight. I have some hens I promised to a neighbor's wife, six laying hens. Tonight I make delivery. This is important. This (as the radio used to say) is war. The shower has passed, the air is clean and cool and sweet, the voice of Lowell Thomas comes without a squawk. Six hens, a load for a wheelbarrow; but first you need some fertilizer bags to tack across to hold them in, to make a little cover for the rig. The bags smell rich with the remains of phosphate, the hens are uneasy in the semidark. The terrier directs the transfer, tends to the nailing down, convoys the transport on the pleasant road. The hens are quiet now, concerned with balancing themselves against the jounce. The farmer chats with me a while, this being eveningtime. Together we unload the hens; they receive an ovation from some geese. The farmer wants that I should see his sow—a great big snuffling Chester White. She's easy kept. She pigs in three weeks now. I know this farmer well, our talk is effortless, he tells me what is on his mind.

"I don't feel as though I was doing enough," he says. "I'd just as leave go in one of the freight boats if it's men they need."

The day has come to rest at last, the terrier rides the empty barrow home, as happy as a boy. It's half-past eight. Light up a Lucky Strike. Ladies and gentlemen. Question and answer. These are the boys that know the answers. They know the answers up till five of nine. From half-past eight till five of nine they know the answers—then they miraculously disappear. At 8:55 exactly the Russians resume their withdrawal, the Germans resume their advance, the Japanese resume their position along the Siberian border, and it's time to shut the pullets up; for no one knows the answers any more and the dark is here and one more day is done.

This should be the sweetly scented night, the hay strong in the long-bearded mows; but the night has picked up something on the way, like a dog that has met a skunk. The night has been abroad and met a skunk. The night is all stunk up with trouble and alarm. I listen for the phone, making the rounds, shining my flashlight in the nests. It's hours later when it starts, the ringing on the line, first five short rings (that would be Freethey's) then a sign-off, and then in quick succession Henry Tapley, Josie Dow, then ours.

"The yellow has come through . . . the alert." Yellow, the color of dandelions, color of buttercups and country cream, the yellow for alert —this is the color of tonight, a yellow sky, a yellow thought, a yellow command. The evening stiffens. I'm lucky I'm dressed. Others are not so fortunate; they failed to notice how the night smelled, so they went to bed. They must be tumbling out now, dressing hastily to meet the yellow occasion, to spread the buttercup of alarm. I wave and blow the horn and as I disappear I see, in the rear-view mirror, that the lights go out.

Yellow is the color of pumpkin and of squash, yellow's a pretty color for a girl, a yellow sweater with the sleeves pushed up. The yellow has come through. The squash vine yellow in the night. I blow the horn continuously, passing farm by farm, the night is loud, more loud than yellow when I blow the horn, continuously. Dark at the Wardwells', dark at Charlie's house, all dark at Earl's—he's gone to Rockland anyway, nobody home, give him the horn though, just the same, make dark the night by making it so loud; dark at the Allens' house, at First Selectman Kane's, at Carter's, Gott's, and Henderson's, all dark, all orderly, now slow for Staples' corner, now step on it and blow—blow, Gabriel, blow, this is the yellow, this is no fooling, this (as they used to say in the curious yellow voice) is war.

The town lights still are on, yellow and bright along the road, and one old lady's reading by her lamp. I turn and start for home. It's up to Albert Anderson to get the lights out; this is his patrol. I see him coming from his house. I stop, tell him about the lights, and then drive on, returning home. I leave the truck in the driveway, headed out, and take up my patrol. I climb the gate, sit on the top rail. No cars must move now, during the red. Stop all cars. There'll be none along, I know that well enough. Only the warden's on the adjoining beat—he'll be along now, soon. He'll use my drive for turning. There's his horn and here he is.

The night has stiffened, now it changes color suddenly. The phone again: the red's come through. Red is for roses and for human blood. The gate on which I sit out my patrol is wet with dew. I feel it through my pants. The stars are bright. This is my country and my night, this is the blacked-out ending to the day, the way they end a skit in a revue. Here, in the compulsory dark, I sit and feel again the matchless circle of the hours, the endless circle Porgy meant when he sang to Bess: "Mornin'-time and evenin'time . . ." It's almost midnight now. Nothing has meaning except the immediate moment, which is precious and indisputable. Morningtime and eveningtime . . . here on the gate, with my toes hooked under the second rail, I can smell the lost morning, which was memorable and good, hear the lost voices of the crows in sprucewoods calling, which were haunting and loud, feel with the flat of my hand the water being swished in the watering pails in the field, my first job on arising. The pullets come to drink, forming the circle around the pans; the day begins. My hair hurts slightly because it is still uncombed. I find one tiny range egg, laid by a four-months novice—a morning jewel, a perfect little thing in my hand, something to take back to the house at shaving time. Breakfast is not for a while. I shave carelessly, without removing my shirt. I shave mournfully, with hardly a grimace.

(This gate is dewy on a man's behind . . .)

The day is young, the sun shines on the orange juice and on the coffee with the news. Coffee bringeth the dark tidings—coffee with cream and a little sugar, allotted; black news, straight, no sugar. The bend of the Don at breakfast. The Don bends around my cup, the great bend. The men fall back, the men I don't know but call by the name Russians. The Germans advance, not much, not without losses, but always advancing, always getting where they want to go. I don't know them, but they advance. Then there are the conferences. I am informed that the leaders are talking but am not told what they are saying. Breakfast is over, all but the cigarette, all but the last falling back of the Russians and the last putting out of the cigarette against the saucer.

(No cars must move during the red, but none will be along.)

In midmorning the sun has gained in the southern sector (you can rely on that) and the sheep, relying on it, knowing that the sun gains no matter who falls back, come up and lie in the thin shade that the fence rails make at the top of the lane. I catch the ewe whose lamb we butchered in warm blood day before yesterday—first the hammer blow on the head, then the knife jab in the throat—the same lamb I sat up late in March for, with such apparent tenderness, the kind of tenderness that refuses to look ahead because it knows that to look ahead is fatal. The tenderness of March, the brutality of August, one lamb serving both moods. I catch the ewe to milk her and relieve her bag. Midmorning now, and all the civilized world at war, in every continent warring. The clouds in the fine blue sky assemble, squad by squad, answering the bugle of the noon, and I go indoors to work.

Stonily I sit at the machine, refusing, as a jumping horse refuses the hurdle. All that comes forth I drop without regret into the wastebasket; nothing seems to make sense, no matter how you spell it or arrange the words. You write something that sounds informative, throwing the words around in the usual manner, then you put your head out the door, or somebody puts his head in, a knob is turned, somebody says something to you, or your eye is caught by something in the news, a dog barks, and no longer is what you have said informative, or even sensible. At the mere barking of a dog the thing explodes in your hands, and you look down at your hands. As though you had crushed a light bulb and were bleeding slightly. And after lunch the thunder in the north.

It's almost midnight now. No cars must pass. In the west, from the other side of town, the church bell rings, so far away that I can barely make it out, yet there it is. Give me to hold the beloved sound, the enormous sky, the church bell in the night beyond the fields and woods, the same white church near which I stood my watch this afternoon. That was before the sky had cleared. The sky is now intemperately clear. Ring, bell . . . forever ring!

GETTING READY FOR A COW

T HIS month an event is scheduled to take place here that is the culmination of four years of preparation. I am going to get a cow. Perhaps I should put it the other way round—a cow is going to get me. (I suspect I am regarded hereabouts as something of a catch.)

To establish a herd, even to establish a herd of one, is a responsibility I do not lightly assume. For me this is a solemn moment, tinged with pure eagerness. I have waited a long time for this cow, this fateful female whom I have yet to meet. Mine has been a novitiate in which I have groomed myself faithfully and well for the duties of a husbandryman; I feel that now, at the end of these years, I have something to offer a cow.

Of course I could have got a cow immediately on arriving here in the country. There is no law against a man getting a cow before he, or she, is ready. I see by *Life* magazine that Chic Johnson, the Hellzapoppin farmer of Putnam County, N. Y., established his herd by "buying the World's Fair Borden Exhibit." This struck me as a clearcut case of a man who was perhaps not ready for his cows. He probably had not even had himself tested for Bangs. "At the dairy," said the article, describing a party the actor was throwing, "cows were milked and ridden bareback." Mr. Johnson was photographed in the act of trying to strike up an acquaintance with one of his own cows, but I noticed she had averted her gaze. He was wearing shorts and a jockey cap. From the photograph I judged that the cows were in clean, modern quarters, and there seemed to be a great many of them (I counted forty cows and ten milkmaids—enough to keep an actor in cream); but I think probably it will suit me better to have one cow with whom I am well acquainted than a barnful of comparative strangers in all stages of lactation.

I knew from the very first that some day there would be a cow here. One of the first things that turned up when we bought the place was a milking stool, an old one, handmade, smooth with the wax finish that only the seat of an honest man's breeches can give to wood. A piece of equipment like that kicking around the barn is impossible to put out of one's mind completely. I never mentioned the word "cow" in those early days, but I knew that the ownership of a milking stool was like any other infection—there would be the period of incubation and then the trouble itself. The stool made me feel almost wholly equipped—all I needed was the new plank floor under the cow, the new stanchion, the platform, the curb, the gutter, the toprail, the litter alley, the sawdust, the manger, the barn broom, the halter, the watering pail, the milk pail, the milk cans, the brushes, the separator, the churn, the cow, and the ability to milk the cow.

And there was the barn itself, egging me on. There it stood, with the old tie-ups intact. Every morning the sun rose, climbed, and shone through the south windows into the deserted stalls, scarred and pitted from bygone hooves. I tried not to look. But every time I walked past I admired the ingenious construction of the homemade stanchions, set in a solid wooden curb and locked with pegs and tumblers, everything handhewn by a man who had fashioned, with ax and chisel, whatever he had needed for himself and his creatures. Men familiar with the habits and desires of cows have advised me to take those old stanchions out because of their rigidity, which is too confining for a cow, and I have already begun the work, but not without many misgivings and a feeling of guilt. The urge to remodel, the spirit of demolition, are in the blood of all city people who move to the country, and they must be constantly guarded against. I have seen too many cases of farmhouses being torn limb from limb by a newly arrived owner, as though in fright or in anger.

There is something patronizing in the common assumption that an old house or an old barn must be hacked to pieces before it is a fit place in which to settle. The city man coming suddenly to the country customarily begins his new life by insulting someone else's old one; he knocks blazes out of his dwelling house, despite its having served former owners well for a hundred years or more. My own house is about a hundred and forty years old—three times my age—yet I, a mere upstart, approached it as though it didn't know its business and weren't quite fit for me the way it was, when the truth, as I now see it, was that I was not quite fit for *it*. Quite aside from the expense and inconvenience of razing one's newly acquired home, there is a subtle insult in the maneuver, the unmistakable implication that the former inhabitants lived either in squalor or in innocence, and that one's neighbors, in houses of similar design and appointments, are also living in squalor or innocence. Neither is true. But the demolition goes right ahead. The place of a newly arriving city man always looks more like a battleground than a home: earthworks are thrown up around the foundation wall, chimneys are reduced to rubble, and on the front lawn a cement mixer appears, with its little wheels and big round abdomen. It would be a comical sight if it were not so dispiriting.

I don't know why people act in this panicky way. I do know for a fact that a man can't know the quality of his home until he has lived in it a year or two; and until he knows its good and bad qualities how can he presume to go about remodeling it? In the frenzy of resettlement one often does queer things and lives to regret his mistakes. When I go into my neighbors' "unimproved" houses in the dead of winter and feel how comfortable they are and cheerful, the sills banked with spruce brush, the little heating stoves standing in candid warmth in the middle of the room, the geraniums and flowering maples blazing away in tin cans on the sunny shelf above the sink, with no pipes to freeze under the floors and no furnace around which huddle full ash cans like gloomy children, I always chuckle over the commotion city people make in their determination that their farmhouse shall be "livable." They have no idea how livable a farmhouse can be if you let it alone. We have too many preconceptions, anyway, about life and living. There is nothing so expensive, really, as a big, well-developed, full-bodied preconception.

But as far as my cow was concerned, it was not so much any hesitancy at ripping things up and changing things around, not so much a matter of equipment and housing; it was simply that I felt the need of a personal probationary period. If a man expects his cow to have freshened before he gets her, she has a right to expect that some important change will have been worked in him too. I didn't want a cow until I could meet her on her own ground, until I was ready, until I knew almost as much about the country as she did—otherwise it would embarrass me to be in her presence. I began this probation in 1938. For more than a year I kept my cow in the hindmost region of my thoughts. It was almost two years before I even allowed myself to dwell on her form and face. Then I began to lay the groundwork of my herd.

My first move was to purchase fifteen sheep and a case of dynamite. The sheep, I figured, would improve my pasture, and the dynamite would keep me out of mischief in the meantime. Before they were done, the sheep managed to serve another useful purpose: I had no desire to have a cow on the place until I had learned how an udder worked, and my first lambing time taught me a lot about that. The way to learn to sail a big boat is first to sail a little one, because the little one is so much harder to manage. The same is true of udders. I can milk a sheep now, with her small, cleverly concealed udder, and so I have no hesitancy about going on to a larger and more forthright bag. The dynamite also turned out to have a second purpose—it had the advantage of letting people know something was going on around here.

That fall when we dynamited for my cow was a great time. I set out to revive a run-out hayfield, and while I was at it I thought I would remove the rocks. I hadn't the slightest notion of what I was getting into, except that I knew I was establishing a cow, and, true to form, thought first of demolition. The rocks didn't look like much when I made my preliminary survey, but I discovered as time went on that a rock is much like an iceberg—most of it is down-under. A very great deal of spadework had to be done around the horse-size rocks before you could hook on to them with the team, and of course the others had to be drilled before they could be exploded. Hand drilling is tedious business, but I didn't have sense enough to charter an air-drill, which I learned later I could have done. The cow receded. There were days when I almost forgot her, so engrossed did I become in the amazing turn my probation had taken. It was the end of summer; the days were hot and bright. Across the broad field, newly plowed, would come the exultant warning cry of "Fie-ah!" Then the breathless pause, then the blast, and the dunnage and rock fragments flying into the sun, then another pause and the sound of falling wreckage.

Although the field had been turned over by the plow, the fragmentation from the blasting left it looking more like a gravel pit than a seedbed. There was a tremendous lot of work to be done just hauling away the debris after the bombing was over. The plowman hooked his team to the drag and I borrowed a tractor and another drag from a neighbor, and together we went at it. Day after day we loaded the drags, hauled them to the edge of the woods, and tossed the rocks off, creating a kind of hit and miss stone wall. I learned to throw the chain over a big rock with a "rolling holt," back the tractor up to it, and ease the rock on to the drag by giving it a nudge of power. The cow seemed a long way off, but I held her firmly in my thoughts, as a soldier holds the vision of home and peace through a long campaign in a foreign land. Rivers of sweat flowed into the dry, chewed-up soil, mountains of granite slogged along the drag-ways, all to achieve, in some remote time, the blade of new grass, the tiny jet of yellow milk. The whole thing seemed like a strangely tangential episode, as if I had wandered off on an idiot's holiday.

And after the rocks had been torn from the earth and removed, then there was the matter of dressing the field. Having no cow, I had no dressing, except a small amount of sheep manure and hen manure that would be needed for the gardens. The field would need thirty or forty spreader loads. After much exploring, some dressing was located in a barn cellar within reasonable trucking distance, and for some days I lived close to a dung fork. This phase of the work had a cow smell and seemed somehow closer to the main issue.

All winter the land and I lay waiting. In spring the frost opened cracks and seams in the field to receive the seed. I marked out courses with guide stakes and sowed the long lanes, working on a windless morning. The rains of spring never descended that year, and summer ushered in one of the most blistering droughts on record. The new grass drooped, the weeds jumped up and sang. The result of a year's labor seemed meager, doubtful. But it turned out that there was established in spite of the dry season what a farmer calls a good bottom. As soon as it got half a chance the field picked up miraculously. This summer, under benign rains, it has become a sweetly rolling green, like something Grant Wood might have sent me.

Meantime the sheep had been at work in the pasture, quietly, with no dynamite. Their golden hooves had channeled among the rocks and ferns, and they had fertilized easily as they went. The time was approaching when I might take unto myself a cow. I began to see her as a living being who was growing closer to me, whose path and mine were soon to cross. I began having the sort of daydreams I used to have at fifteen: somewhere in the world (I would think) is the girl who is some day to be my wife. What is she doing? Where is she? What is she like?

Of course there was still the matter of the barn—a fit place for this dream creature to spend her winter nights. The thought of a concrete floor flashed through my mind and was quickly gone. I had invested in one concrete floor when I built my henhouse, and one concrete floor is enough for any man's lifetime. The sensible thing would be to lay a good smooth plank floor, with a six-inch platform, and perhaps a gutter. I turned, as one always does turn in any critical time, to the mail order catalogue and began a study of floor plans—stalls and gutters and curbs and stanchions and rails and partitions. I learned about stanchions, stanchion anchors, alignment devices; I began to pit the high curb against the low curb, the single post stall against the double. One evening after dark I went to the barn with a two-foot rule and a flashlight and measured up the job, working carefully and late, in pitch black except for the concentrated beam of the flash—an odd tryst, as I think back on it, but part of my beautiful romance. When I returned to the house I made a plan, drawn to scale, showing a maternity pen, three stalls, a raised platform, an eleven-inch curb hollowed out to six inches at the anchor point, and a gate, everything worked out to the inch. The platform is to be cut on the bias—a long stall (4 foot 10) at one end, in case my lovely girl turns out to be an Amazon, a medium-size stall (4 foot 4) for a medium-size bride, and a short stall (3 foot 8) for the heifer that will inevitably bless this marriage.

There have been setbacks and reverses. Priorities worked against me, and I soon found out that barn furnishings were almost unobtainable. I sent to Sears for their Russet Cow Halter, 32D449, the one with the adjustable crown and the brown hardware to match her eyes and hair, but they returned the money, with a grim note, Form Number 7, rubber stamped. Where they got the rubber for the stamp I have no idea.

Tomorrow the carpenter arrives to start tearing out the old floor. When the last stanchion is anchored and the last brushful of whitewash has been applied to wall and rafter, I shall anoint myself and go forth to seek my love. This much I know, when the great day comes and she and I come marching home and pause for a moment in the barnyard before the freshly whitened door, *she's* got to carry *me* across the threshold. I'm tired.

BOND RALLY

Dorothy Lamour left Portland, Maine, at 7:20 on the morning of September 17th, passed through Woodfords at 7:25, Cumberland Center 7:39, Yarmouth Junction 7:49, and two hours later arrived in Augusta, where she parted with one of her handkerchiefs to a gentleman who bought an unusually large war bond. She left Augusta at 1:38 P.M., passed through Waterville at 2:04, Burnham Junction 2:35, Pittsfield 2:49, Newport Junction 3:01, and arrived in Bangor at 3:40, at the top of the afternoon.

Like most river towns, Bangor is a metropolis loved by the heat, and it was hot there under the train shed that afternoon, where a few dozen rubbernecks like myself were waiting to see a screen star in the flesh. The Penobscot flowed white and glassy, past the wharves and warehouses. On a siding a locomotive sighed its great sultry sighs. The reception committee wiped its forehead nervously with its handkerchief and paced up and down at the side of the waiting Buick roadster—which the daily *News,* in an excess of emotion, described as "blood-red." The guard of honor—a handful of soldiers from the air field—lounged informally, and a sergeant with a flash camera arranged himself on top of a baggage truck. In the waiting room a family of three sat in some embarrassment on a bench.

"I feel so silly," said the woman.

"What d'you care?" replied her husband, obviously the ringleader in this strange daylight debauchery. "Wh ' d'you care? I like to come down here to the station and see how things act once in a while." The teen-age daughter agreed with her father and backed him to the hilt, against her mother's deep-seated suspicion of the male errant.

Miss Lamour's train pulled in cautiously, stopped, and she stepped out. There was no pool, no waterfall, no long dark hair falling across the incomparable shoulders, no shadow cast by the moon. Dorothy the saleswoman strode forward in red duvetyn, with a brown fuzzy bow in her upswept hair. She shook hands, posed for a picture, and drove off through the cheering crowd in the blood-red car, up Exchange Street, where that morning I had seen a motley little contingent of inductees shuffling off, almost unnoticed, to the blood-red war.

While Miss Lamour was receiving the press in her rooms at the Penobscot Exchange Hotel I went down to the men's room to get a shine.

"See her?" I asked the porter.

"Yeah, I was standing right next to her at the curb." Then he added, studiously: "I'd say she was about thirty. A nice-looking woman."

"I suppose they're giving her the works here at the hotel," I said.

"I'll say they are. Took the furniture right out of Cratty's room. Hell, she's got chairs in there that wide."

Having assured myself that Dorothy was being properly cared for, and having brightened my own appearance to some extent, I went out to the Fair Grounds at the other end of town, where a stamp rally was scheduled to take place. The grandstand alongside the race track was already bulging with children, each of whom had bought a dollar's worth of stamps for the privilege of seeing Lamour. The sale of stamps had been brisk during the week. A booth had been maintained in the square, and Madame Zelaine, the local seeress, had personally handed out stamps and taken in the money for the Treasury. And now the grandstand was a lively place, with much yelling and chewing and anticipation. The Boys' Band of the American Legion, on the platform in the infield, was flashy in blue and yellow silks. In the still air, under the hard sun, gleamed the flags and the banners and the drum majorette's knees. When the car bearing the beloved actress appeared at the infield gate and swept to the bandstand the children hollered and whooped in their delight and little boys threw things at one another in the pure pleasure of a bought-and-paid-for outing.

The meeting got down to business with an abruptness that almost caused it to founder. Miss Lamour was introduced, stepped up, shaded her eyes with an orchid, made a short appeal, and before the little girls in the audience had figured out whether her hair was brown or green, she asked everyone to step along to the booth and buy some stamps. This was an unlooked-for development. Presumably most pockets were empty. Nobody made a move and the silence was oppressive. I have an idea that Miss Lamour herself didn't know quite what she was getting into and perhaps hadn't been told, or hadn't taken it in, that the children were already paid-up supporters of the war and that their presence there, inside the gates, was evidence that they had shelled out. It was simply one of those situations—a situation in the hard, uncompromising sunlight.

Miss Lamour, obviously a sincere and diligent patriot, saw that she was in a spot, and the chairman was visibly embarrassed. He and she hurriedly went into a huddle, shameless in the glaring sun. Then she grasped the mike. "Don't tell me business is *this* slow," she said, rather desperately.

Two or three little millionaires, in sheer anguish at seeing a dream person in distress, got up and moved toward the booth. Miss Lamour seized the moment. "Listen," she said, "I've come a long way to see you—don't let me down." (The bothersome question arose in all minds, the question who had come to see whom in this show.)

"Sing something!" hollered a youngster.

But there was undoubtedly something in her contract that prevented that. After another hurried conference the bandleader handed over his baton.

"I've never done this before," said Dorothy, "but I'm willing to try anything." She stepped up in front of the band, the leader got them started, and then gave over. Miss Lamour beat her way doggedly through a rather heavy number. In a long grueling bond-selling tour this was obviously one of the low moments for her. Low for the children too, some of whom, I am sure, had gone into hock up to their ears. It was just poor showmanship. Disillusion in the afternoon. The music ended and the star took a bow.

A couple of Fortresses flew overhead. This was a break. Miss Lamour pointed up excitedly. "If you think it doesn't cost money to build those things, look at them. That's what you're buying!"

"Sing something!" shouted the tiny heckler.

Some more customers filed awkwardly down to the booth and in a few minutes the meeting was adjourned.

"I figured her hair was going to be down," said a little girl next to me, coming out of a trance. Miss Lamour left in the Buick, respectfully encircled by the Army and the Navy, one man from each.

The big meeting was in the evening, after supper, in the Auditorium; and if Bangor had muffed its afternoon show it made up for it by a curiously happy night performance. It is no secret that enormous sums of money have been raised in America through the generous efforts of motion picture stars, and I was eager to be present at such an occasion. This particular brand of rally is a rather odd American phenomenon—that is, the spectacle of a people with homes and future at stake, their own lives threatened and the lives of their sons hanging by a thread, having to goad themselves to meet the challenge by indulging in a fit of actor worship and the veneration of the Hollywood gods. Everywhere in the country people have shown a peculiar willingness to buy bonds under the aegis of a star of the silver screen. Every race of people has of course its national and religious forms and ecstasies, its own way of doing business, its own system of getting results. The Japanese have their Emperor, an idol who is the same as God; the Germans have the State, closely identified with the Führer. Americans warm to a more diffuse allegiance —they have their Abe Lincoln and their Concord Bridge and their Bill of Rights, but these are somewhat intellectual appurtenances. For pure idolatry and the necessary hysteria that must accompany the separation of the individual from his money, they turn to Dorothy Lamour, or Beauty-at-a-Distance. At first glance this might appear to be a rather shabby sort of patriotic expression, but when you think about it, it improves. It may easily be a high form of national ardor after all, since the Hollywood glamour ideal is an ideal that each individual constructs for himself in the darkness and privacy of a motion picture house, after toil. The spell of Lamour, the sarong, the jungle code, the water lily in the pool—these tell the frustration of the civilized male, who yearns in the midst of the vast turmoil and complexities of his amazing little life, with its details and its fussiness, to chuck his desperate ways for a girl and an island moon—a dream of amorous felicity and carelessness. To bring this dream into line, for a national emergency, and adapt it to the exigencies of federal finance is an American miracle of imposing and quite jovial proportions. Miss Lamour was introduced as the "Bond Bombshell"; the water lily had become an orchid from a florist's shop, symbol of wealth and extravagance.

The Bangor people, about twenty-five hundred of them, assembled in the hall, which was a sort of overgrown grange hall. Admission was by bond only, plus the Annie Oakleys. The big buyers were in the front seats, the small fellows in the balcony. The notables and the Bombshell and the Dow Field military band and WLBZ assembled on the platform, a mixed group of civil and military servants, variously arrayed. Almost the first thing that happened was the arrival of a contingent of Navy recruits (about fifty of them) who were to submit to a public induction under the combined sponsorship of Uncle Sam and the motion picture industry. They filed down the center aisle and climbed sheepishly to the platform, a rag-tag-and-bobtail company in their ready-to-shed citizens' clothes, sober as bridegrooms and terribly real. This was it, and the people cheered. Miss Lamour, sensing the arrival of actors who could not fail to give an authentic performance and who would never get a retake, stepped deferentially into the wings. A Navy lieutenant lined up his charges and prepared to give the oath. On their faces, bothered by the sudden confusion of lights and the convergence of their personal fates, was a hangdog look, a little tearful, a little frightened, a little resolved. They were just a bunch of gangling boys in a moderately uncomfortable public position, but they seemed like precious stones. The dust of glamour had shifted imperceptibly from Miss Lamour and settled on their heads. After they were sworn in she glided back onto the stage, shook hands, and gave each her blessing as he shuffled out to gather up his cap and his change of underwear and disappear into the theater of war.

The program continued. A Negro quartet sang. Two heroes were produced—a pint-sized radioman who had been wounded in the Coral Sea, a big lumbering Tiger who had flown for Chennault. They were the "had been" contingent. The radioman told, in masterly understatements, about Pearl Harbor on that Sunday morning. The Tiger, a laconic man in shirtsleeves, was interviewed by a small dapper announcer for WLBZ, and when he was asked how it felt to be an American on foreign shores, he choked up, the strength went out of him, and he couldn't answer. He just walked away. After the band had performed, a young Jewish soldier stepped forward and played a violin solo. For him there could be nothing obscure about war aims. It was a war for the right to continue living and the privilege of choosing his own composer when he played his fiddle. He played solidly and well, with a strength that the Army had given his hands and his spirit. The music seemed to advance boldly toward the enemy's lines.

Here, for a Nazi, was assembled in one hall all that was contemptible and stupid—a patriotic gathering without strict control from a central leader, a formless group negligently dressed (even Dottie had neglected to change into evening dress, thereby breaking the hearts of the women in the audience), a group shamelessly lured there by a pretty girl for bait, a Jew in an honored position as artist, Negroes singing through their rich non-Aryan throats, and the whole affair lacking the official seal of the Ministry of Propaganda—a sprawling, goofy American occasion, shapeless as an old hat.

It made me feel very glad to be there. And somewhere during the evening I picked up a strong conviction that our side was going to win. Anyway, the quota was heavily oversubscribed in this vicinity. I would have bargained for a handkerchief if Miss Lamour had had one to spare. It's the ape-man in me probably.

A WEEK IN NOVEMBER

Sᴜɴᴅᴀʏ. Arose at six, twenty-seven hours ahead of the arrival of the Sunday paper, which gets here at nine o'clock Monday morning—a very great advantage, to my way of thinking. Sunday is my busiest day, since I am without help, and I should not be able to get through it at all if there were any newspapers that had to be read.

The wind blew from the SE and brought rain and the dreariest landscape of the fall. For several hours after arising everything went wrong; it was one of those days when inanimate objects deliberately plot to destroy a man, lying in wait for him cleverly ambushed, and when dumb animals form a clique to disturb the existing order. This is the real farm bloc, this occasional conspiracy—a cow with a bruised teat, a weanling lamb lamenting her separation from the flock, a chain-stitch on a grain sack that refuses to start in the darkness, an absentee cook, a child with a fever, a fire that fails to pick up, a separator in need of a new ring, a lantern dry of kerosene, all conniving under gray skies and with the wind and rain drawing in through the windows on the south side, wetting the litter in the hen pens and causing the flame of life to sputter on the wick. I used to find my spirits sagging during intervals of this sort, but now I have learned about them and know them for what they are—a minority report. I'm not fooled any more by an ill wind and a light that fails. My memory is too good.

More and more people and families are leaving here and going up to the cities, to go into factories or into the Services. It is sad to see so many shut houses along the road. One of our former neighbors, now working in a shipyard, turned up after dinner to call for the five bushels of potatoes he had spoken for earlier in the season. He had driven here on his Sunday off to look after his affairs, including the potatoes, and he told me about the pleasures of building destroyers. We went down cellar and I got some bags and a bushel basket and we measured out the spuds while he held forth about his job. Afterward he said he had something to show me, so we went out to where his car stood and he pointed to the four brand-new tires—a man apart, not like ordinary mortals.

Tomorrow the hunting season opens and the men in these parts will put aside whatever they are doing and go into the woods after some wild meat.

Monday. Noticed this morning how gray Fred is becoming, our elderly dachshund. His trunk and legs are still red but his muzzle, after dozens of major operations for the removal of porcupine quills, is now a sort of strawberry roan, with many white hairs, the result of worry. Next to myself he is the greatest worrier and schemer on the premises and always has too many things on his mind. He not only handles all his own matters but he has a follow-up system by which he checks on all of mine to see that everything is taken care of. His interest in every phase of farming remains undiminished, as does mine, but his passion for details is a kind of obsession and seems to me unhealthy. He wants to be present in a managerial capacity at every event, no matter how trifling or routine; it makes no difference whether I am dipping a sheep or simply taking a bath myself. He is a fire buff whose blaze is anything at all. In damp weather his arthritis makes stair-climbing a tortuous and painful accomplishment, yet he groans his way down cellar with me to pack eggs and to investigate for the thousandth time the changeless crypt where the egg crates live. Here he awaits the fall of an egg to the floor and the sensual delight of licking it up—which he does with lips drawn slightly back as though in distaste at the strange consistency of the white. His hopes run always to accidents and misfortunes: the broken egg, the spilt milk, the wounded goose, the fallen lamb, the fallen cake. He also has an insane passion for a kicked football and a Roman candle, either of which can throw him into a running fit from which he emerges exhausted and frothing at the mouth. He can block a kick, or he can drop back and receive one full on the nose and run it back ten or twelve yards. His activities and his character constitute an almost uninterrupted annoyance to me, yet he is such an engaging old fool that I am quite attached to him, in a half-regretful way. Life without him would be heaven, but I am afraid it is not what I want.

This morning early, after I had milked and separated, I managed to lose my grip on the bowl of new cream as I was removing it from under the spout and lost the whole mess on the floor where it spread like lava to the corners of the room. For a moment my grief at this enormous mishap suffused my whole body, but the familiar assistance of Fred, who had supervised the separation and taken charge of the emergency, came to my relief. He cleaned up a pint and a half of cream so that you would not have known anything had happened. As charboy and scavenger he is the best dog I ever was associated with; nothing even faintly edible ever has to be cleaned up from the floor. He handles it. I allow him to eat any substance he chooses, in order to keep him in fighting trim, and I must say he has never failed me. He hasn't had a sick day either since the afternoon I salvaged him from a show window on Madison Avenue, suffering from intestinal disorders of a spectacular sort. I have since that time put out a lot of money on him, but it has all been for anaesthetics to keep him quiet during the extraction of quills. Not one cent for panaceas.

The production records being made and broken all the time by war industries have set me to work figuring out how things are going in my own plant. Tonight, after a short struggle, I computed that an egg is laid on this place every 4.2 minutes during the day. This is a great gain over three years ago when sometimes a whole hour would go by on this farm without anything of any consequence happening. I am devoting practically half my time now to producing food, food being something I can contribute to the general cause. My production goals for 1942–1943 are 100 pounds of wool, 14 lambs, 4,000 dozen eggs, 10 spring pigs, 150 pounds of broilers and roasters, 9,000 pounds of milk, and all the vegetables, berries, and fruit needed for home consumption and canning. This is not much for a full-scale farmer, but it is about right for a half-time worker when labor is precarious and implements and materials are hard to get.

Tuesday. There are two distinct wars being fought in the world. One is the actual war, bloody and terrible and cruel, a war of ups and downs. The other is the imaginary war that is the personal responsibility of the advertising men of America—the war you see pictures of in the full-page ads in the magazines. This second war is a lovely thing. We are always winning it, and the paint job stays bright on the bombers that gleam in the strong clean light of a copywriter's superlative adventure. It is a war in which only the brave and true take part, in which the great heart of America beats in clipped sentences. Every morning the ad men strap on their armor and gird for the fray, usually in four colors. We leap rivers with Goodyear and the Engineers, span oceans with Kelvinator and the Air Force, peel off from a fighter formation with the manufacturer of a snap fastener, blow the daylights out of a Jap cruiser with a lens company located in the Squibb Building. The truth is of course that these manufacturers are indeed participating in mighty events because of the conversion in their plants, and every ad writer becomes a combatant by extension. Almost all of them call Hitler by his first name and taunt him openly. They identify themselves with the physical struggle and the heroic life, so that when the bomb bay door opens and the hand presses the lever you are never quite certain what is coming out—a bomb or a bottle of cleaning fluid. This vicarious ecstasy of the ad men always makes me think of the hero of James Thurber's story called "The Secret Life of Walter Mitty."

Wednesday. My cow turned out to be a very large one. The first time I led her out I felt the way I did the first time I ever took a girl to the theater—embarrassed but elated. In both instances the female walked with a firmer step than mine, seemed rather in charge of the affair, and excited me with her sweet scent.

We are having a mild fall. Still no furnace fire, except an occasional slabwood blaze in the morning to take the chill off. Broccoli and chard in the garden, and of course kale, which the frost improves. I like kale: it is the nearest I come to eating grass. Even after the snow comes we still eat kale, pawing for it like a deer looking for frozen apples.

Thursday. In time, ownership of property will probably carry with it certain obligations, over and above the obligation to pay the tax and keep the mortgage going. There are signs that this is coming, and I think it should come. Today, if a landowner feels the urge, he can put a back hoe into his hillside pasture and disembowel it. He can set his plow against the contours and let his wealth run down into the brook and into the sea. He can sell his topsoil off by the load and make a gravel pit of a hayfield. For all the interference he will get from the community, he can dig through to China, exploiting as he goes. With an ax in his hand he can annihilate the woods, leaving brush piles and stumps. He can build any sort of building he chooses on his land in the shape of a square or an octagon or a milk bottle. Except in zoned areas he can erect any sort of sign. Nobody can tell him where to head in—it is his land and this is a free country. Yet people are beginning to suspect that the greatest freedom is not achieved by sheer irresponsibility. The earth is common ground and we are all overlords, whether we hold title or not; gradually the idea is taking form that the land must be held in safekeeping, that one generation is to some extent responsible to the next, and that it is contrary to the public good to allow an individual, merely because of his whims or his ambitions, to destroy almost beyond repair any part of the soil or the water or even the view.

After some years in the country, during which time I have experienced the satisfactions of working the land, building the soil, and making brown into green, I am beginning to believe that our new world that will open up after the war should be constructed round a repopulated rural America, so that a reasonably large proportion of the population shall participate in the culture of the earth. The trend is often in the opposite direction, even in peace. As things are now in America, country living is possible only for those who have either the talents and instincts of a true farmer or the means to live wherever they choose. I think there are large numbers of people who have not quite got either but who would like to (and probably should) dwell in the open and participate to some degree in the agricultural life. Good roads and electric power make the farm a likely unit for a better world, and the country should be inhabited very largely and broadly by all the people who feel at home there, because of its gift of light and air and food and security, and because it supplies a man directly, instead of indirectly. The trend toward the ownership of land by fewer and fewer individuals is, it seems to me, a disastrous thing. For when too large a proportion of the populace is supporting itself by the indirections of trade and business and commerce and art and the million schemes of men in cities, then the complexity of society is likely to become so great as to destroy its equilibrium, and it will always be out of balance in some way. But if a considerable portion of the people are occupied wholly or partially in labors that directly supply them with many things that they want, or think they want, whether it be a sweet pea or a sour pickle, then the public poise will be a good deal harder to upset.

Friday. Four hours at the spotting post today in company with my wife, who hears four-motored bombers in running brooks; but the weather was bad and we saw no planes, friendly or hostile. The post has been moved from behind the postmistress's barn to the abandoned schoolhouse across the road—not such a good view as the old post but a fine place to get work done between watches, excellent desk facilities (a choice of thirteen little desks), also a Seth Thomas clock, a good stove, an American flag, a picture of Lincoln, a backhouse, and an ancient love message carved in the entry, celebrating MYRTLE.

Saturday. Sent my trousers off for their quarterly pressing yesterday. They travel forty-nine miles to the ironing board, a round trip for them of ninety-eight miles. My pants are without question the best traveled part of me nowadays, and I sometimes envy them their excursions to town. Quite a lark, these days, to go all that distance on rubber. I noticed that the truck that called for them was driven by a girl, taking the place of the young fellow who has gone off to war. She told us that she loved the work—made her feel that she was having her part in the war effort; which surprised me, that anybody should derive that feeling from carting my pants around the country. But I feel exactly the same way about the eggs I produce, even though I know well enough that most of them are being gobbled by voracious people in the environs of Boston.

Found my wife and son and dachshund, all three, sitting under a lap robe on the back porch in the beautiful sunlight this afternoon listening to the Cornell-Yale game on a portable radio, this being the first time in two weeks my boy had been out of bed and the first time the dog had attended a Cornell game. (He was shaking like a leaf with pent-up emotion, and Cornell was behind.) But the three of them looked very wonderful and comical sitting there in their private bowl, and I laughed out loud. My wife, who is just getting through reading the autumn crop of children's books, informed me that we have a new ritual to look forward to on Christmas eve. (This was from a book called *Happy Times in Norway.*) We are to go to the barn and give an extra feeding to the animals, saying: "Eat and drink, my good cow, our Lord is born tonight." I intend to do it, and luckily I have the hay to spare this year. To make it a truly American ritual, however, I suspect we should have to wear smocks and dirndls and perhaps invite a photographer or two from *Vogue.*

CONTROL

Mʀ. Kɪᴘʟɪɴɢᴇʀ warned me in the mail this morning that I could expect more controls, and he was right. Twenty minutes later I went out to the barn and there they were—two of them. They were from the State. One of them had put a hook in my cow's nose and was pulling hard, the other was poised with a needle, about to draw a sample of blood from her neck. She was still my cow, as I recalled it, and it was still my barn, but you wouldn't have known it from their manner, which was one of complete authority. When I expressed a mild interest in the proceedings they explained that it was the Bang's test and that the State was putting on a campaign or something.

It happens that I thoroughly approve of the Bang's test. I like it so well I had made certain before buying the cow that she had recently been tested by a veterinary. (The men in my barn didn't ask about that.) I also thoroughly approve of the old idea that a man's home is his castle and that anyone who arrives with a needle is expected to knock before entering. Seeing the hook in Sukey's nose and the look of pain in her eyes gave me the same sort of start a person might get from suddenly entering his own home and finding his wife trussed up with sash-cord. I think it was probably a very lucky thing indeed that I thoroughly approved of the Bang's test, otherwise the State might have found itself with one less control.

The incident sticks in the mind. The dismal thing about controls—which Mr. Kiplinger failed to put in his letter—is that they seem unable to make our lives more agreeable in some particulars without making them insupportable in others. In its zeal to wipe out undulant fever in my neighborhood, the State had caused me to run quite a temperature in my own barn. I was patient and helped the State restore my health, but it will never be the same again, and I can imagine the effect the incident might have had on a cow owner who was unsympathetic toward the whole idea of cow testing.

I suppose the tightening of the controls round our lives is punishment for our early waywardness, but it does not make us feel any better about the matter. The reason there were a couple of men in my barn this morning, annoying my cow, is that some farmers had been dilatory about testing cows even after science had made such tests easy and practical and doctors and undertakers had made the alternative plain. And the reason there will be a couple of strangers in all your barns and offices from now on, poking through your piles of accumulated trouble, is that somewhere in the past there were those vast untested herds spreading their fevers through the world. This is a sad outlook but one we shall have to face with what cheer is left in us.

On the whole the most alarming thing about control is the time it takes. Here, in war, with our emergency measures and our ration books, we are beginning to learn something about that. In peace it will be a proliferation and an extension of the same. Life will be paper work; death will be a questionnaire.

I have a little half-ton truck that I wanted to keep rolling, to carry dressing to the fields and to run the interminable errand that is farming; but when I came to apply for the certificate that would permit me to use this vehicle I found a government instruction book as long as a modern novel and ever so much more plotty. It took me two solid days of study and inquiry before I was ready to fill in the blanks, and I am a man with one of those college educations that you hear about. And it will take me much more than two days additional if I am to write the long journal of my trucking life now required of me as a holder of the certificate. My truck has come to be like the State in my life—it is no longer my assistant, it is my boss. Under the circumstances, my tendency is never to go near the thing, which is unenterprising in me and full of serious consequences, eventually, for the State.

The most challenging control that occupies the attention of our social architects and designers is of course the control of wealth. Observe the manly attempt that is being made, here and abroad, to keep the profit system alive by artificial respiration. In England, Sir William Beveridge has completed a magnificent edifice of general insurance in which everyone will contribute toward a common fund designed to minimize the hard luck of everyone else. Here is the actuary's dream. England becomes a nation of bookkeepers, and a man walks from the cradle to the grave hand in hand with the claims adjuster and the notary public. Even the author of this notable plan by which the ultimate risk is calculated admits that the whole business will collapse unless the policy-holders, in their myriad enterprises, prosper.

This is super-control. It is the end of forests and the beginning of files. In America we shall presumably devise a similar system, as well as other comical expedients such as placing a $67,200 limit on income.

I sometimes think that the profit system, which today is undergoing such extensive alterations that it will emerge unrecognizable, might easily have been made to serve everyone rather well if it had been given a fair trial. The trouble with the profit system has always been that it was highly unprofitable to most people. The profits went to the few, the work went to the many. I think our phrase "common man" came to mean the man who never managed to get his hands on anything but a pay envelope, and sometimes not on that. You became uncommon when you had capital to invest or an idea to develop. Usually you had neither, and were common as dirt. Profits flowed into closely guarded channels that led into a mysterious sea.

The system of private enterprise, our scapegrace yet beloved system of profit and spoils, might have been made to fit the common man like a glove if the designers had taken a good look at their man. I believe what he wanted really was a sense of participation. This he never had. This he will not have in the new revised system of mutual benefit. He will become a policy-holder in the most intricate firm on earth, but even a policy-holder feels no sense of participation in anything much but death. What he wanted, back there in the days of free enterprise, was a share in the profits. He wanted the excitement of fluctuation, the agony of risk, the rewards of black ink. But nobody ever cut him in. Well, hardly anybody. He worked for a flat fee. It was flat when he started as a boy, it was flat when he ended as an old man. He worked and toiled, he sickened and died, but he never participated. He had no capital and he had no ideas; he was just a man with time on his hands.

Today this common man is said to be on the threshold of a century designed specially for him, like a custom-built suit. I hope he is not going to have the same trouble with fitters that I do. Fitters always assume that I wear suspenders to hold my pants up, and although I tell them plainly that I do not and show them how I allow my pants to hang from my hipbones like an old dead vine from a wall, they shake their heads and cut the trousers to suit their idea of a man, instead of the man himself. As for the common man and his century, I am not sure the fitters have got him either. Right now the common man is probably as uncomfortable and suspicious as is any man who is standing while the fitter runs the tape up into his crotch to get the inseam measure. I notice by reading my newspaper that the designers of the new century are allowing for a bigger stomach, but I think their man is going to bulge in other places too. And I am worried about the sleeve length: the common man has been reaching for something for many, many years and has exceptionally long arms. It will be a tragedy if this new century skimps him in vital spots.

So far, the persons who are constructing the century have agreed on certain fundamental points. They have agreed that their man must be secure. He must hold insurance. He is not to be permitted to starve to death, or run up hospital bills, or dodge a midwife, or be buried without proper rites. They have agreed that he is to be allowed to compete freely with other common men who hope to become president of the company. And finally they stipulate that if he *does* get to be president (and here they sigh a tiny regretful sigh) he is not to make a yearly sum of more than $67,200, or $25,000 after taxes are paid. The century has gone to the cutter. It may come out all right, but I am uneasy.

The true shape of man is an elusive thing. One thing I am sure of— he is a natural-born gambler whose normal instincts in this regard have long been frustrated. He has commonly been interested less in security than in gain, less in safety than in risk, and he has always been a fool for anything that gave him a chance at the jackpot. (He forms public safety societies in order to keep up his interest in safety, but he never has to whip himself in the direction of danger.) Wages bore him. Low wages infuriate him, but all wages bore him. The trouble with the profit system, as far as this man was concerned, was that he seemed to bear no relation to the result. It could prosper without his prospering too. He felt lonely and out of things. It could fail and he still felt lonely and in need of another job. No one thought it worth while, or sensible, to try to express, by mathematical means, the true relationship between the common man and the unusual returns. After all, he was only contributing his time— plus what little skill he possessed. Why should his fortunes improve merely because the enterprise succeeded? This was always the answer to a question that was seldom asked.

In many ways the system of free enterprise, the spoils system of yesterday, uncontrolled and predatory and unfair, was a peculiarly hopeful and desirable affair. Its tyrannies and abuses became so great we are likely to forget this—that in essence it was a good thing that might have fitted people like a glove. It quickened them, it kept them on their toes, it had the curious elasticity which made it compensate quickly in a society in which every individual was up to a different trick. It recognized private property, thus endearing itself to all; since to own something is an abiding satisfaction of our most primitive desires. But it was a chancy system of life, and because man is not a generous animal but has to arrive at generosity the hard way, it failed to include the majority of people in the winnings. You can see the effect of this today. The terrible urge of the multitudes to participate in the chancy side of life, to recover the gift they were cheated out of by their lack of capital and their lack of initiative, is everywhere discernible. It accounts for the enormous preoccupation with pinball games, number games, bingo, race horses, stock markets, pools, lotteries—millions of people called "common" trying to make up for the fact that their normal activities still bring them only a flat and unchangeable payment in a world that is neither flat nor unchangeable. Even in a last extremity, with neither money nor hope, a man seizes a deck of cards and tries to win at solitaire, to restore himself and taste the wine of luck.

Luck, I think, is a distributable commodity. We have never tried it because we have never tried profit sharing—except of course at Christmas, season of generosity and remorse. Luck is not something that you can talk to economists about, because it does not fit into the hard-earned grooves of social thought. (Actually it is at the bottom of the actuary's mind; only he thinks in terms of hard luck instead of good luck—which is a negative and roundabout attitude to take.) Luck is not something you can mention in the presence of self-made men. The Society of Movers and Doers is a very pompous society indeed, whose members solemnly accept all the responsibility for their own eminence and success. Nothing could be more ridiculous really. In every tablet there are as many grains of luck as of any other drug. Even intelligence is an accident of Nature, and to say that an intelligent man deserves his rewards in life is to say that he alone is entitled to be lucky. Maybe he is, but I sometimes wonder.

It would be a very fine thing for the world if everyone were entitled, in some slight degree, to be lucky. In free enterprises profit is a way of stating luck in easy terms. There should be a glass through which we could see, to show us what would have happened to the common man (how he would be feeling today) if all persons employed in bold and profitable enterprises had been included in the luck—that is, if they had been paid, in addition to their simple fee, a royalty based on results. I once mentioned this heretical nonsense to a business man at luncheon and he crinkled up like a strip of bacon. Obviously the idea was one of unparalleled odiousness. I felt as though I had deliberately proposed that he take the eighty-five cent lunch instead of the breast of guinea fowl. (Perhaps I had, without knowing it.) It was around Christmas time and I was dreamily trying to translate the bonus into pure economics, to establish an honest ratio between pluck and luck. Here in the bonus was good luck arrived at by toil and yet expressed so whimsically that it seemed almost indecent.

The bonus is really one of the great give-aways in business enterprise. It is the annual salve applied to the conscience of the rich and the wounds of the poor. If there is any justification for it at all mathematically, then it should be given a ring and a name and made into an honest woman. Meanwhile the stockroom clerk haunts the pinball parlor, the churchman worships the gods of chance at the bingo board, and the common man turns to the dog tracks and chancy places of the earth, driven there because he has never been admitted to the large council chambers of Chance and to the spoils system in his own office and factory. He has never known what it feels like to bet two dollars on his own horse.

I am not pretending that a general profit-sharing system would work but am merely pointing out that it has never been tried. In isolated cases it has been flirted with, but it is obviously not one of those journeys where you can go alone. It has to be everybody or nobody, all or nothing. I tried it once myself, on the only occasion when I have found myself the agitator of a business venture. The venture was a book that involved the already published works of other writers. I was editor and boss. Much to my surprise I discovered that there were really no ground rules for this sort of thing: I could take all the profits and merely buy the material, or I could get material for nothing and share the profits, and in that case I could take ninety per cent and share ten, or take ten and share ninety. This was most revealing. But although I elected to share the rewards with the other persons according to a ratio that I arrived at mysteriously, it wasn't really profit sharing, I realized, because it didn't include the publisher's telephone operator and my own cook. In short, the common man, as usual, didn't make the cut. Of those who did, almost all were delighted to be included in the risks and the rewards. The case convinced me, though, that profit sharing was an innocent and simple affair, easily arranged provided you wanted to arrange it.

However, the day of minimums and other dreary controls is here, for better or for worse. Probably we have lost our chance of making an honest woman out of a Christmas bonus. We shall instead receive the benefits of a kindly state, and we shall receive them the hard way—luck through hard luck, prosperity through adversity, profits through taxation, and paper work for all.

COLD WEATHER

There is always the miracle of the by-products. Plane a board, the shavings accumulate around your toes ready to be chucked into the stove to kindle your fires (to warm your toes so that you can plane a board). Draw some milk from a creature to relieve her fullness, the milk goes to the little pig to relieve his emptiness. Drain some oil from a crankcase, and you smear it on the roosts to control the mites. The worm fattens on the apple, the young goose fattens on the wormy fruit, the man fattens on the young goose, the worm awaits the man. Clean up the barnyard, the pulverized dung from the sheep goes to improve the lawn (before a rain in autumn); mow the lawn next spring, the clippings go to the compost pile, with a few thrown to the baby chickens on the way; spread the compost on the garden and in the fall the original dung, after many vicissitudes, returns to the sheep in the form of an old squash. From the fireplace, at the end of a November afternoon, the ashes are carried to the feet of the lilac bush, guaranteeing the excellence of a June morning.

᠅

Even the small tufts of wool that the sheep leave around on the fence rails where they have rubbed find their way back into circulation. I save them for surgical dressings. At docking time when I chop off a lamb's tail I put a little wool on the stub to start the clotting of the blood.

᠅

There has been more talk about the weather around here this year than common, but there has been more weather to talk about. For about a month now we have had solid cold—firm, business-like cold that stalked in and took charge of the countryside as a brisk housewife might take charge of someone else's kitchen in an emergency. Clean, hard, purposeful cold, unyielding and unremitting. Some days have been clear and cold, others have been stormy and cold. We have had cold with snow and cold without snow, windy cold and quiet cold, rough cold and indulgent peace-loving cold. But always cold. The kitchen dooryard is littered with the cylinders of ice from frozen water buckets that have been thawed out in the morning with hot water. Storm windows weren't enough this winter—we resorted to the simplest and best insulating material available, the daily newspaper applied to north windows with thumbtacks. Mornings the thermometer would register ten or twelve below. By noon it would have zoomed up to zero. As the night shut in, along about four-thirty, it would start dropping again. Even in the tight barn, insulated with tons of hay, the slobber from the cow's nose stiffened in small icicles, and the vapor rose from the warm milk into the milker's face. If you took hold of a latch with ungloved hands, the iron seized you by the skin and held on.

There is a fraternity of the cold, to which I am glad I belong. Nobody is kept from joining. Even old people sitting by the fire belong, as the floor draft closes in around their ankles. The members get along well together: extreme cold when it first arrives seems to generate cheerfulness and sociability. For a few hours all life's dubious problems are dropped in favor of the clear and congenial task of keeping alive. It is rather soothing when existence is reduced to the level of a woodbox that needs filling, a chink that needs plugging, a rug that needs pushing against a door.

I remember that first morning. It was twelve below just before daylight. Most of us had realized the previous afternoon that we were in for a cold night. There is something about the way things look that tells you of approaching cold—a tightening, a drawing in. Acting on this tip, I had laid a fire in the old drum stove in the garage, a few feet from the car's radiator. Before I went to bed I lit it and threw in another stick of wood. Then I went down to the sheep shed, whose door ordinarily stands open night and day, winter and summer, and kicked the snow away with my boot and closed the door. Then I handed the cow a forkful of straw instead of her usual teaspoonful of sawdust, and also threw some straw down through the hatch to the hog. We didn't open our windows much when we went to bed. (The windows in this house have to be propped up with a window stick, and on nights like this we don't use the window stick; we just take a piece of stove wood and lay it flat on the sill and let the window down on that.)

Morning comes and bed is a vise from which it is almost impossible to get free. Once up, things seem very fine and there are fires to be made all over the house, and the old dog has to be wrapped in a wool throw because of his rheumatism. (He and I have about the same amount of this trouble, but he makes more fuss about it than I do and is always thinking about wool throws.) Then everybody compares notes, each reads the thermometer for himself, and wonders whether the car will start. From the gray waters of the bay the vapor rises. In the old days when the vapor used to rise from the sea people would wink and say: "Farmer Jones is scalding his hog."

The phone jingles. It's the mailman. He can't start his car. I'm to pick him up if my car will start and carry him to the town line. The phone rings again (cold weather stirs up the telephone). It's Mrs. Dow. I am to pick her up on my way back from the store because it's most too cold to walk it this morning. Thanks to my all-night fire in the drum stove my car starts easily, third time over. The garage is still comfortably warm from the night before and there are embers in the stove.

The question of clothes becomes a topic for everybody. The small boy, who has relied thus far on a hunting cap with flaps down, digs up an old stocking cap as midwinter gear. I exhume my Army underdrawers, saved from the little war of 1918. The snow squeaks under the rubber tread of the boot, and the windows of the car frost up immediately. The geese, emerging from their hole in the barn, trample a yard for themselves in the deep drift. They complain loudly about a frozen water pan, and their cornmeal mash is golden-yellow against the blue snow.

The mailman is full of charitable explanations about his car—he thinks it was sediment in the carburetor. The general cheerfulness is in part surprise at discovering that it is entirely possible to exist in conditions that would appear, offhand, to be fatal. The cold hasn't a chance really against our club, against our walls, our wool, the blaze in the stove, the clever mitten, the harsh sock, the sound of kindling, the hot drink, the bright shirt that matches the bright cap. A truck driver, through the slit in his frosted windshield, grins at me and I grin back through the slit in mine. This interchange, translated, means: "Some cold, Bud, but nothing but what your buggy and my buggy can handle." Word gets round that the school bus won't start. Children wait, chilly but busy, along the route, testing surfaces for skis and runners, some of them waiting indoors and peering out the windows. A truckman has to go down and tow the bus to get it started. Scholars will be tardy today. This makes *them* cheerful. It is a fine thing to be late for school all together in one vast company of mass delinquency, with plenty of support and a cold bus for alibi.

If a man were in any doubt as to whether it is a cold day or not there is one way he can always tell. On a really cold day the wooden handle of a pitchfork is as cold as a pinchbar. And when he picks up a scrubbing brush to clean out a water pail the brush has turned to stone. I don't know any object much colder than a frozen brush.

ૐ

After a long spell of cold, with little sun and little relief, sometimes a man's thoughts turn to warmer climates with longing. I have been reading, with considerable pleasure, some essays of James Norman Hall's on the warmth and indolence of Tahiti. It is alluring, but I doubt that I could last long away from the New England seasons. Under my thatched roof I should remember the days in fall when the wind blows half a gale and the bell on the barn rings without any other compulsion, keeping up a lonely warning like a channel buoy. I should, I am sure, remember the clear sparkling days, bright and cool, that come toward the end of summer, the sort of day my neighbor Mr. Dameron can't endure. He calls them "suicide days." Since I too have sometimes been saddened by the last days of August, I have tried to find out what it is about them that clutches at Mr. Dameron's vitals; but he can only say that he feels depressed, as though something were hanging over him. They provide perfect weather for hauling his traps, but that doesn't seem in any way to compensate for the melancholy messages he receives, collect, from the white clouds in the perfect sky. In darkness and cold Mr. Dameron is always cheerful; in the difficult, tempestuous periods of the year he is at his best. I have often come upon him in the brutal rain of a bleak November, his big hands swollen from the spines of sea urchins, no jacket over his cotton shirt, erect and at peace with the elements and himself. Evidently it is not bleak times but the intimation of bleak times ahead that makes a man's spirits sag. There is no word in the language for end-of-summer sadness, but the human spirit has a word for it and picks up the first sound of its approach.

ૐ

One of my geese left the flock for a while and lived wild, in the coldest part of winter. She is back in the barnyard again, but it seems to me the other geese have not received her back into their curious society. She stays a little bit apart. I imagine something of this sort would happen if I were to return to the city. . . . I'm not sure you can ever go back even if you should want to.

Ik Marvel, who took to the farm almost a century ago, set down some cautionary words on this subject. "On your visits to the city," he wrote, "friends will remark your seediness, not unkindly, but with an oblique eye-cast up and down your figure—as a jockey measures a stiff-limbed horse, long out to pasture. You may wear what toggery you will—keeping by the old tailors, and showing yourself *bien ganté,* and carefully read up on the latest dates; still you shall betray yourself in some old dinner joke—dead long ago. And the friends will say kindly, after you are gone, 'How confoundedly seedy Rus has grown!' Were this all, it were little. But the clash and alarum of cities have stirred things to their marrow, which you know only outsidedly. The great nervous sensorium of a continent ... is packed with subtle and various meanings, which you, living on an outer strand of the web, can neither understand nor interpret. Mere accidental contact will not establish affinity. In a dozen quarters a boy puts you right; and some girl tells you newnesses you never suspected. The rust is on your sword; thwack as hard as you may, you cannot flesh it, as when it had every day scouring into brightness."

There is truth in his words. The last time I went to town I had a dozen small reminders that my membership had lapsed. The rust is on my sword. It is a gloomy thought, somewhat mitigated by the realization that my hands are harder than they used to be—I can seize a club and lay about me with that.